A
MORE PERFECT
UNION

A
MORE PERFECT
UNION
Documents in U.S. History

SECOND EDITION

VOLUME I: TO 1877

Paul F. Boller, Jr.

Ronald Story
University of Massachusetts, Amherst

HOUGHTON MIFFLIN COMPANY • BOSTON

Dallas   Geneva, Illinois   Palo Alto   Princeton, New Jersey

Cover: Impression of the Great Seal of the United States, 1782 design. The National Archives.

Printed in the U.S.A.

Library of Congress Catalog Card Number: 87-81489

ISBN: 0-395-35920-1

ABCDEFGHIJ-B-9543210-8987

To Martin and Eliza

CONTENTS

CHAPTER ONE
Planters and Puritans

――――――

CHAPTER TWO
Strides Toward Freedom

――――――

CHAPTER THREE
Nationalists and Partisans

CHAPTER FOUR

The Age of Reform

CHAPTER FIVE

Rebels, Yankees, and Freedmen

A STATISTICAL APPENDIX
(after page 252)

PREFACE

Our two-volume reader, **A More Perfect Union: Documents in U.S. History,** presents key documents chosen to provide students with the original words of speeches, political and legal writings, and literature that reflected, precipitated, and implemented developments and events during America's past four centuries. The readings in Volume I cover the era from the founding of the Virginia and Massachusetts Bay colonies to Reconstruction; Volume II begins with the post–Civil War period, repeating some of the first volume's final readings, and concludes with selections that concern contemporary issues. We are pleased with the reception that **A More Perfect Union** has received, and we have worked toward refining the contents in this second edition.

About a third of the material is new to this second edition, which contains more documents and Counterpoint source data than the first edition. New selections include such readings as Samuel Parris's "Christ Knows How Many Devils There Are" (from the Salem witch-trial period), Meriwether Lewis's "Report on the Missouri and Columbia Rivers," and Margaret Fuller's "Woman in the Nineteenth Century," all in Volume I, and "Report of the Joint Committee on Reconstruction" (in both volumes, on Klansmen of the Carolinas), Knute Rockne's "A Sales Promotion Address," and Ronald Reagan's "Address on Lebanon and Grenada." The Counterpoints have been closely integrated with the documents' subject matter. The introductions to the Counterpoints have been completely revised; they explain what facts and trends can be gleaned from the data presented in the tables and figures drawn from historians' original research. These tables and figures are, for the most part, new to this edition.

The readings in these volumes represent what we believe to be an attractive blend of social and political history, together with cultural and economic trends, suitable for introductory courses in American history. Three considerations guided our selection of items. First, we looked for famous documents with a lustrous place in the American tradition. These—the Mayflower Compact, for example, or the Gettysburg Address, or Franklin Roosevelt's first inaugural address—we chose for their great mythic quality, as expressions of fundamental ideals with which students should be familiar. Second, we searched out writings that had immediate impact and caused something to happen. Examples from this very large group include the Virginia slave statutes, Thomas Paine's

The Crisis, the Emancipation Proclamation, and Earl Warren's decision in **Brown** v. **The Board of Education of Topeka**—all famous pieces and influential as well. Finally, we included documents that seemed to reflect important attitudes or developments. Into this group fall Thomas Hart Benton's racial views as well as the writings of Upton Sinclair on industrial Chicago and Martin Luther King, Jr., on Vietnam. In this category, where the need for careful selection from a wide field was most apparent, we looked especially for thoughtful pieces with a measure of fame and influence. Horace Mann's statement on schools reflected common attitudes; it also caused something to happen and is a well-known statement of reformist concern. We have also intermixed familiar documents with unexpected ones (Andrew Jackson, say, and T. S. Arthur, or Woodrow Wilson and Margaret Sanger).

Once a document was chosen, we did not hesitate to edit it severely when the selection seemed too long. This consideration obviously affected book-length works but also was applicable to such pieces as John Peter Zenger's account of his trial for libel or Joseph McCarthy's speech on Communist subversion. In some cases, particularly with writings from the colonial era, we have modernized spelling and punctuation.

With the documents are pedagogical features to aid students in comprehending the role and significance of these readings. Each document has a lengthy headnote that summarizes the relevant trends of the era, provides a specific setting for the document, and sketches the life of the author. The headnotes are followed by study questions to guide students through the prose and suggest ways of thinking about the selections. The headnotes, and especially the study questions, contain many cross-references to other documents in the collection to provide perspective and encourage comparative analysis.

Each chapter concludes with a Counterpoint, a group of tables and sometimes charts and figures that deal with some aspect of American society relevant to the era and theme of that chapter's documents. Generally the work of distinguished modern historians, often "classic" studies in their own right, the Counterpoints touch on issues raised in different ways by the documents—such as the Jacksonian assault on privilege, or difficulties faced by blacks and immigrants in industrial America. The Counterpoints expose students to historical statistical evidence, which provides a contrast to the historical record of documents and speeches; they also add a further flavor of social history to what, given our concern with the famous and influential, is still a predominantly political, constitutional, and diplomatic collection. All Counterpoints have introductions and cross-references, similar to those for the documents.

The Statistical Appendix, comprising statistics on population, government, and the economy spanning the life of the nation, is offered in the same spirit as the Counterpoints are—as an alternative way, or in some instances perhaps the only way, of seeing important long-term historical trends. The documents are creations of particular moments; the Counterpoints provide close-ups of particular eras; the Appendix offers, in its fashion, the whole sweep of American history. The Statistical Appendix thus supplies a background for both the documents and the Counterpoints.

We would like to thank the following people who reviewed the manuscript for one or both volumes:

William Breitenbach, University of Puget Sound
Terry A. Cooney, University of Puget Sound
Anne Day, Clarion University of Pennsylvania
Joseph Ellis, Trenton State College
Ronald Lora, University of Toledo
Roderick Nimtz, Miami University
Margaret Patoski, Texas Wesleyan College
Eldon R. Turner, University of Florida

We also wish to thank the staff of Houghton Mifflin Company for their encouragement and assistance in the preparation of this work.

P. F. B.
R. S.

A
MORE PERFECT
UNION

INTRODUCTION

The two volumes of **A More Perfect Union: Documents in U.S. History** bring together a wide variety of documents illustrating political, social, economic, cultural, constitutional, and intellectual history for use in college courses in American history and culture. Volume I begins with the Virginia Ordinance of 1621 and ends with a post-Reconstruction speech by Frederick Douglass (1883). Volume II starts with the Reconstruction period and Abraham Lincoln's second inaugural address (1865) and continues to the present time, concluding with a speech by Ronald Reagan (1983).

The documentary readings cover the major themes in American history. In Volume I these include: the strides toward freedom and independence during the colonial period; the growth of nationalism during the early nineteenth century; the reform movements during the first half of that century; the sectional conflict at mid-century; and the perennial American racial dilemma. Volume II repeats the last theme and adds these three: the responses to the periodic crises faced by the American economy since the late nineteenth century; the impetus toward humanitarian reform at every period of our national history; and the development of the United States into a superpower in the twentieth century. Both volumes also portray the perpetual tension throughout our history between freedom and security, individual enterprise and social justice, popular democracy and responsible leadership. The documents encompass a great deal of political history, but also contain social and economic developments. In the charters, laws, treaties, speeches, announcements, and reports—together with the end-of-chapter Counterpoint sections, which present statistics covering trends in American life—it is possible to observe American history in the making.

History, a multifaceted enterprise, at its most basic level is a collection of facts. Historians keep records of treaties, elections, legislative acts, conferences, battles, legal decisions, and other significant happenings so that these are available to lawyers, diplomats, public officials, journalists, and other interested parties to consult. Some collections of documents are little more than reference books. Our volumes are not intended to be used in this way, but they do contain many fundamental records of American history for ready reference: the Declaration of Independence, the Monroe Doctrine, the **Dred Scott** decision, the Emancipation Proclamation, Franklin Roosevelt's first inaugural address, the Supreme Court

1

decision in **Brown** v. **Board of Education**, and Dwight D. Eisenhower's warning about the military-industrial complex.

But history is more than encyclopedia; history is also story. American history is filled with dramatic events: America's Declaration of Independence in 1776; Mississippi's secession cry in 1860; Lincoln's signing of the Emancipation Proclamation in 1863; Franklin Roosevelt's call for war on Japan after the attack on Pearl Harbor; the Woodstock Festival in 1969; the Watergate crisis in 1972–1974. **A More Perfect Union** is an anthology, not narrative history, so it does not recount any of these stories. Nevertheless, the basic materials from which narrative historians do reconstruct such stories are contained in these volumes: John Peter Zenger's trial in 1735; David Walker's appeal for justice for American blacks in 1829; Woodrow Wilson's impassioned call for war on Germany in 1917; and Richard Nixon's surprise visit to the People's Republic of China in 1972 after years of U.S. hostility toward the Chinese Communists.

Original records often make more fascinating reading than mere summaries of events written by persons who were not on the scene. Who can read David Walker's appeal today and not be deeply moved by what he said about the plight of blacks in the United States in 1829? Or read the description of the treatment of the Cheyenne and not be filled with indignation? Or read Jefferson's first inaugural address and not be filled with hope? Written records form the very substance of narrative history.

History is not, however, merely story, not merely a collection of facts. It is more than a series of dramatic moments. Life for most people of every era consists largely of habit, ritual, convention, schedule, and routine. One of the historian's primary tasks is to reconstruct life as it was lived at times and in places enormously different from our own: colonial Massachusetts, antebellum Philadelphia, Chicago at the turn of the century, American society at the time of the Great Depression. **A More Perfect Union** supplies ample materials—statistics as well as documents—for recapturing life in both the near and distant past in this country.

The how and the why behind historical developments are more fascinating than the dates when events occurred. To encourage you to think about the how and the why, the authors have provided questions throughout **A More Perfect Union**. In the introduction to each document, after a general commentary and biographical information where it is appropriate, the last paragraph contains questions to consider. The end-of-chapter Counterpoint sections also have questions pertaining to the tables, and some queries appear in the Statistical Appendix.

We are all culture-bound. We tend to judge other peoples, places, and periods by our own standards, and it is hard for us to comprehend other cultures in their deepest reaches. But if, after mastering the records of a past culture, we succeed in overcoming the parochialism of the present and in penetrating the central vision of societies quite different from our own, we can become wiser about what human beings have accomplished in other times and places and can be more realistic about our own achievements. The documents in these volumes will enable readers to enter the lives of Americans whose experiences were totally different from their own: people in Pennsylvania in the middle of the eighteenth century, Cherokee Indians in Georgia in the 1830s, chattel slaves in colonial Virginia, emancipated blacks after the Civil War, Chicago stockyard workers in the early twentieth century, and young people at the Woodstock Festival in 1969 at the height of the counterculture movement. Variety, not uniformity, has been the spice of life in America since the very first settlements after Columbus.

But history is more than the study of past cultures. Students who want to understand the American past cannot stop with descriptions of what people did in earlier times; they will want to know why Americans acted as they did, and why, at critical junctures in our history, they took actions laden with momentous consequences for the future. A historian's most challenging task is to find out why social change occurred. Why did colonial Americans decide to strike for independence in 1776? What brought on the Civil War? Why did the United States decide to go to war in 1898, 1917, 1941, and 1950? What caused the Great Depression of the 1930s? What brought about the Great Inflation of the 1970s and 1980s?

Students of history search for factors that cause change. Are technological innovations at the root of historical change, or are new ways of producing and distributing material goods the basic developers? Or is it novelty of outlook—the appearance of new ideas—that transforms society? Undoubtedly, ideas and economic interests are both at work. At the same time there is much that is accidental and unexpected in human affairs.

One purpose of **A More Perfect Union** is to stimulate you to think about the tremendous changes that have taken place on the American scene and to try to account for these changes. Original documents form a good basis for such an inquiry. They supply information about why Americans thought and acted as they did at particular points in time. In addition, many records in this anthology explain why Americans behaved as they did at decisive moments. The Declaration of Independence gives reasons why the American people decided on revolution in 1776. **The Federalist,** Number Ten, contains a theory of how societies in general, and American society in particular, operate. Woodrow Wilson's address to Congress on the eve of war with Germany in 1917 contains a theory about the relation of nations to each other.

Past, present, and future are co-implicated in the documents in **A More Perfect Union.** Historical records contain factual data, material for dramatic stories, descriptions of bygone cultures, and suggestions for understanding social change. But the records also contain guidelines for action. The Declaration of Independence sets forth ideals, goals, and aspirations for the American people to act upon, as well as explanations of actions taken. Thomas Jefferson's first inaugural address and Andrew Jackson's Bank Veto Message do the same. Franklin Roosevelt's first inaugural address in the midst of the Great Depression and his war message to Congress after the attack on Pearl Harbor also combine ideals and actions. The basic documents in these volumes contain prescriptions as well as descriptions: manifestoes, appeals, recommendations, suggestions, and calls to action.

The written word continues, of course, to be the major source for those seeking to understand the American past. But a striking development in historical scholarship during the past twenty years is the extensive use of nonverbal evidence, such as art work and statistical data, to illuminate the past. These sources can enhance, modify, or explain the written record. Cartoons of Andrew Jackson, for example, tell us something about his popular reputation; photographs from the Great Depression reveal the forces behind the birth of Social Security. In other cases, nonverbal sources, particularly statistical ones, have a story of their own to tell.

The Counterpoints and Statistical Appendix offer samples of the kind of statistical data that historians are relying on increasingly. The Counterpoint section at the end of each chapter is based upon a series of statistics. These concern mainly the American population, economy, and government—obviously important areas in which statistics are abundantly available. The purpose of these Counterpoints is to give you an opportunity to discover how historians draw conclusions from raw data. An introduction alerts you to the principal issues to think about and gives some guidance in reading the tables and charts and extracting their information. You are encouraged to study them carefully, and to consider the implications of the data. The effort will be repaid by an insight into the nature of the historical enterprise, by a sense of how history is extracted out of the documents of the past.

At the conclusion of each volume is a Statistical Appendix (the same Statistical Appendix appears in both volumes). The information in this Appendix, which spans periods up to the current decade, reveals a great deal about the America of earlier times, just as the Counterpoint tables do. Statistics on population, on changes in wages and consumer prices for different economic sectors, on religious affiliations, and on federal expenditures for defense, debt service, the postal service, and veterans' benefits, all have much to tell about the ways Americans have led their lives. As in the Counterpoints, an introduction to each table explains its relevance and guides the reader toward an understanding of the table's data.

We do not believe numbers will ever supplant words as the basic stuff of historical study. Nevertheless, with the aid of literary records, such figures, stark and ambiguous though they may seem, reveal trends in industry and labor, social and economic problems, and patterns of mobility, to mention only a few possibilities. Quantitative material has become indispensable to fully comprehending the past, and it will become even more significant in the future. Thus, in the two volumes of **A More Perfect Union,** a combination of numbers and original words is presented to give depth to the images of America's past and to shed light on its future.

Plymouth Plantation.   Houses as they appeared in the early 1620s are huddled closely together in the village style favored by the early New Englanders. (Plimoth Plantation)

CHAPTER ONE

Planters and Puritans

1.

FIRST RIGHTS AND PRIVILEGES

The first representative body in the New World was the Virginia Assembly—or House of Burgesses. This development came about when the directors of the Virginia Company, a joint-stock corporation of British investors, decided to allow more freedom in order to attract more colonists. The directors scrapped the colony's military and communal organization when the little settlement at Jamestown, established in 1607, failed to produce a profit and came close to collapsing due to disease and starvation. The company directors distributed land to the settlers, arranged to transport craftsmen and servants, as well as women, to the colony, and authorized the election of a general assembly to help govern the colony. On July 30, 1619, twenty-two burgesses, chosen by the settlers, met for the first time with the governor and the council, appointed by the company.

The document authorizing the House of Burgesses has been lost, but the "ordinance" of 1621 is believed to reproduce the provisions of 1619. Largely the work of Sir Edwin Sandys, one of the leading directors of the Virginia Company, the ordinance provided for a Council of State, appointed by the company, as well as for an assembly elected by the people. The Virginia Assembly had the power to "make, ordain, and enact such general Laws and Orders, for the Behoof of the said Colony, and the good Government thereof, as shall, from time to time, appear necessary or requisite," subject to the company's approval. The new governmental arrangements, together with the discovery that tobacco could be a lucrative crop, soon made Virginia a thriving enterprise, and these arrangements were continued after Virginia became a royal colony in 1624.

Questions to consider. In examining the ordinance's description of the two councils for governing Virginia, it is helpful to consider the following questions: How large was the Council of State? How was it chosen? What responsibilities did it possess? How did the responsibilities of the General Assembly compare in importance with those of the Council of State? Who possessed the ultimate authority in Virginia?

The Virginia Ordinance of 1621

An ordinance and Constitution of the Treasurer, Council, and Company in England, for a Council of State and General Assembly. Dated July 24, 1621.

To all People, to whom these Presents shall come, be seen, or heard the Treasurer, Council, and Company of Adventurers and Planters for the city of *London* for the first colony of *Virginia,* send Greeting. . . .

We . . . the said Treasurer, Council, and Company, by Authority directed to us from his Majesty under the Great Seal, upon mature Deliberation, do hereby order and declare, that, from henceforward, there shall be TWO SUPREME COUNCILS in *Virginia,* for the better Government of the said Colony aforesaid.

The one of which Councils, to be called THE COUNCIL OF STATE (and whose Office shall chiefly be assisting, with their Care, Advise, and Circumspection, to the said Governor) shall be chosen, nominated, placed and displaced, from time to time, by Us, the said Treasurer, Council, and Company, and our Successors: Which Council of State shall consist, for the present, only of these Persons, as are here inserted, *viz.* Sir *Francis Wyat,* Governor of *Virginia,* Captain *Francis West,* Sir *George Yeardley,* Knight, Sir *William Neuce,* Knight Marshal of *Virginia,* Mr. *George Sandys,* Treasurer, Mr. *George Thorpe,* Deputy of the College, Captain *Thomas Neuce,* Deputy for the Company, Mr. *Pawlet,* Mr. *Leech,* Captain *Nathaniel Powel,* Mr. *Harwood,* Mr. *Samuel Macock,* Mr. *Christopher Davison,* Secretary, *Doctor Pots,* Physician to the Company, Mr. *Roger Smith,* Mr. *John Berkley,* Mr. *John Rolfe,* Mr. *Ralph Hamer,* Mr. *John Pountis,* Mr. *Michael Lapworth.* Which said Counsellors and Council we earnestly pray and desire, and in his Majesty's Name strictly charge and command, that (all Factions, Partialities, and sinister Respect laid aside) they bend their Care and Endeavors to assist the said Governor; first and principally in the Advancement of the Honour and Service of God, and the Enlargement of his Kingdom amongst the Heathen People; and next, in erecting of the said Colony in due obedience to his Majesty, and all lawful Authority from his Majesty's Directions; and lastly, in maintaining the said People in Justice and *Christian* Conversation amongst themselves, and in Strength and Ability to withstand their Enemies. And this Council, to be always, or for the most Part, residing about or near the Governor.

The other Council, more generally to be called by the Governor, once yearly, and no oftener, but for very extraordinary and important occasions, shall consist, for the present, of the said Council of State, and of two Burgesses out of every Town, Hundred, or other particular Plantation, to be respectively chosen by the Inhabitants; Which Council shall be called THE GENERAL ASSEMBLY, wherein (as also in the said Council of State) all Matter shall be

From F. N. Thorpe, ed., **The Federal and State Constitutions** (7 v., Government Printing Office, Washington, D.C., 1909), VII: 3810–3812.

First meeting of the Assembly in Virginia, August 1619.   During the early years in Jamestown, the laws governing the colonists were extremely harsh. But in 1618 the Virginia Company placed the colony under English common law. This meant that trial by jury, free speech, and freedom from imprisonment except for specified crimes were guaranteed to the Virginians. The company also provided for a representative assembly with power to make new laws, subject to the consent of the company directors. On July 30, 1619, twenty-two "burgesses," chosen by the settlers, met for the first time with the governor and council, appointed by the company. (Library of Congress)

decided, determined, and ordered, by the greater Part of the Voices then present; reserving to the Governor always a Negative Voice. And this General Assembly shall have free Power to treat, consult, and conclude, as well of all emergent Occasions concerning the Public Weal of the said Colony and every Part thereof, as also to make, ordain, and enact such general Laws and Orders, for the Behoof of the said Colony, and the good Government thereof, as shall, from time to time, appear necessary or requisite. . . .

Whereas in all other Things, we require the said General Assembly, as also the said Council of State, to imitate and follow the Policy of the Form of Government—Laws, Customs, and Manner of Trial, and other administration of Justice, used in the Realm of *England,* as near as may be, even as ourselves, by his Majesty's Letters Patent, are required.

Provided, that no Law or Ordinance, made in the said General Assembly, shall be or continue in Force or Validity, unless the same shall be solemnly ratified and confirmed, in a General Quarter Court of the said Company here in England and so ratified, be returned to them under our Seal; It being our Intent to afford the like Measure also unto the said Colony, that after the Government of the said Colony shall once have been well framed, and settled accordingly, which is to be done by Us, as by Authority derived from his Majesty, and the same shall have been so by Us declared, no Orders of Court afterwards shall bind the said Colony, unless they be ratified in like Manner in the General Assemblies. IN WITNESS whereof we have here unto set our Common Seal, the 24th of *July* 1621, and in the Year of the Reign of our Sovereign Lord, JAMES, King of *England,* &c.

2.

THE UNDERSIDE OF PRIVILEGE

In 1619 a Dutch trader brought twenty "Negars" from Africa and sold them in Jamestown. For a long time, however, black slavery, though common in Spanish and Portuguese colonies in the New World, was not important in Virginia. For many years white indentured servants from England performed most of the labor in the colony; after three decades there were still only about three hundred blacks in the English colonies. By the end of the seventeenth century, however, transporting Africans to America had become a profitable business for English and American merchants, and the slave trade had grown to enormous proportions.

In Virginia the planters used blacks as cheap labor on their plantations and also employed them as household servants, coachmen, porters, and skilled workers. Their status was indeterminate at first, and they may have been treated somewhat like indentured servants for some time. As tobacco became important, however, and the number of blacks working on plantations soared, the position of blacks declined rapidly. The Virginia Assembly began enacting laws governing their behavior and regulating their relations with whites. The statutes, some of which are reproduced here, do not show whether racial prejudice and discrimination preceded slavery, followed it, or, more likely, accompanied it. But they do dramatize the fact that in Virginia, as elsewhere, the expansion of freedom and self-government for whites could go hand in hand with the exploitation and oppression of blacks.

Questions to consider. How strictly did the Virginia lawmakers attempt to control the behavior of blacks in the colony? How severe were the punishments provided for offenders against the law? What penalties were provided for the "casual killing" of slaves? What appeared to be the greatest fear of the Virginia lawmakers?

Virginia Slavery Legislation (1630–1691)

[1630]   September 17th, 1630. Hugh David to be soundly whipped, before an assembly of Negroes and others for abusing himself to the dishonor of God and shame of Christians, by defiling his body in lying with a negro; which fault he is to acknowledge next Sabbath day.

[1640]   Robert Sweet to do penance in church according to laws of England, for getting a negro woman with child and the woman whipt.

[1661]   *Be it enacted* That in case any English servant shall run away in company with any negroes who are incapable of making satisfaction by addition of time, *Be it enacted* that the English so running away in company with them shall serve for the time of the said negroes absence as they are to do for their own by a former act.

[1668]   Whereas some doubts, have arisen whether negro women set free were still to be accompted tithable according to a former act, *It is declared by this grand assembly* that negro women, though permitted to enjoy their Freedom yet ought not in all respects to be admitted to a full fruition of the exemptions and impunities of the England, and are still liable to payment of taxes.

[1669]   Whereas the only law in force for the punishment of refractory servants resisting their master, mistress or overseer cannot be inflicted upon negroes, nor the obstinancy of many of them by other than violent means supprest, *Be it enacted and declared by this grand assembly,* if any slave resist his master (or other by his master's order correcting him) and by the extremity of the correction should chance to die, that his death shall not be accompted Felony, but the master (or that other person appointed by the master to punish him) be acquit from molestation, since it cannot be presumed that prepensed malice (which alone makes murder Felony) should induce any man to destroy his own estate.

[1680]   *It is hereby enacted by the authority aforesaid,* that from and after the publication of this law, it shall not be lawful for any negro or other slave to carry or arm himself with any club, staff, gun, sword, or any other weapon of defence or offence, nor to go to depart from his master's ground without a certificate from his master, mistress or overseer, and such permission not to be granted but upon particular and necessary occasions; and every negro or slave so offending not having a certificate as aforesaid shall be sent to the next

From William Hening, ed., **The Laws of Virginia, 1619–1792** (13 v., Samuel Pleasants, Richmond, 1809–1823).

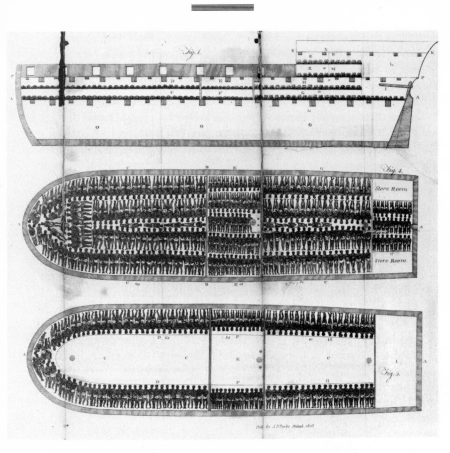

Cutaway sectional view of a slave ship. During the seventeenth and eighteenth centuries thousands of slaves were brought to the colonies from Africa. The voyage across the Atlantic was horrendous. Some slave-traders tried to avoid overcrowding, but most of them packed as many slaves as they could into the hold of their ships to maximize profits. In most ships there was a "slave deck," or shelf, in the middle of the hold, to carry additional slaves. Some ships even had two slave decks. Every so often small groups of slaves were taken on deck and forced to dance to restore their blood circulation. Nets along the sides of the ships kept them from jumping overboard. When they refused to eat, funnels were forced down their throats and "slabber juice," a mixture of palm oil, horse beans, and flour, was poured down the funnel. (Library of Congress)

constable, who is hereby enjoined and required to give the said negro twenty lashes on his bare back well laid on, and so sent home to his said master, mistress or overseer. *And it is further enacted by the authority aforesaid* that if any negro or other slave shall presume to lift up his hand in opposition against any christian, shall for every such offense, upon due proof made thereof by the oath of the party before a magistrate, have and receive thirty lashes on his bare back well laid on.

[1691]   *It is hereby enacted,* that in all such cases upon intelligence of any such negroes, mulattoes, or other slaves lying out, two of their majesties' justices of the peace of that county, whereof one to be of the quorum, where such negroes, mulattoes or other slave shall be, shall be impowered and commanded, and are hereby impowered and commanded, to issue out their warrants directed to the sheriff of the same county to apprehend such negroes, mulattoes, and other slaves, which said sheriff is hereby likewise required upon all such occasions to raise such and so many forces from time to time as he shall think convenient and necessary for the effectual apprehending such negroes, mulattoes and other slaves, and in case any negroes, mulattoes or other slave or slaves lying out as aforesaid shall resist, run away, or refuse to deliver and surrender him or themselves to any person or persons that shall be by lawful authority employed to apprehend and take such negroes, mulattoes or other slaves that in such cases it shall and may be lawful for such person and persons to kill and destroy such negroes, mulattoes, and other slave or slaves by gun or any other ways whatsoever.

3.

SEPARATIST BEGINNINGS

The Mayflower Compact was a covenant or agreement drawn up by a group of Separatists, a small group of religious extremists who had separated from the Church of England because they did not think it was "pure" enough in its religious observances. Like all Puritans, the Separatists disliked the elaborate ceremonies of the Church of England; they favored plain and simple church services centered on the Bible. They also rejected the hierarchical structure of the Anglican church, with its archbishops and bishops. For them the congregation, organized by devout people who had experienced conversion, was the center of religious authority. The congregation had the power to choose its own ministers and deacons and to adopt rules and regulations for governing the church. Regarded with hostility by the government and with suspicion by their neighbors, the Separatists left England in 1608 and the following year formed a "community of saints" in Holland. But they did not feel at home among the Dutch, and they decided to move to the American wilderness, where they could organize their own Congregational churches and worship God as they pleased.

In September 1620, thirty-five "Pilgrims" (called that because of their many wanderings in search of a place to live) sailed for the New World on the **Mayflower.** They had received a grant from the Virginia Company to establish a settlement in "northern Virginia" and financial aid from some London merchants. Sixty-seven additional emigrants, not all of whom were Puritans, were aboard the **Mayflower**—they were along to help make the colony profitable for the London investors. Arriving off Cape Cod in November, before landing, the Pilgrim leaders sought to retain their authority over the settlers and unify them for the difficult tasks lying ahead by drawing up the Mayflower Compact.

Although the Compact professed allegiance to the king of England, it was actually an extension of the Separatists' church covenant to matters of civil government. Since the Pilgrims who settled at Plymouth never managed to obtain a royal charter for their colony, the Mayflower Compact itself served as their constitution until Plymouth was absorbed by Massachusetts Bay Colony in 1691. It thus became a precedent for the formation of new governments in America.

Questions to consider. What objectives other than religious ones did the Pilgrims set forth in the compact? Examine the list of people who signed it. What does this list reveal about the representation of the

102 settlers, their status, and their view of women? Of what significance is the use of the title **Mr.** before some of the names? What does the compact tell you about the Pilgrims' belief in self-government? Why did the Pilgrims draft the compact at this particular moment? Why might it have suddenly been necessary to have a government?

The Mayflower Compact (1620)

In the Name of God, Amen. We, whose names are underwritten, the Loyal Subjects of our dread Sovereign Lord King *James,* by the Grace of God, of *Great Britain, France,* and *Ireland,* King, *Defender of the Faith,* &c. Having undertaken for the Glory of God, and Advancement of the Christian Faith, and the Honour of our King and Country, a Voyage to plant the first colony in the northern Parts of Virginia; Do by these Presents, solemnly and mutually in the Presence of God and one another, covenant and combine ourselves together into a civil Body Politick, for our better Ordering and Preservation, and Furtherance of the Ends aforesaid; and by Virtue hereof do enact, constitute, and frame, such just and equal Laws, Ordinances, Acts, Constitutions, and Offices, from time to time, as shall be thought most meet and convenient for the general Good of the Colony; unto which we promise all due Submission and Obedience. In WITNESS whereof we have hereunto subscribed our names at *Cape Cod* the eleventh of *November,* in the Reign of our Sovereign Lord King *James of England, France,* and *Ireland,* the eighteenth and of *Scotland,* the fifty-fourth. *Anno Domini,* 1620.

Mr. John Carver	Mr. Stephen Hopkins
Mr. William Bradford	Digery Priest
Mr. Edward Winslow	Thomas Williams
Mr. William Brewster	Gilbert Winslow
Isaac Allerton	Edmund Margesson
Miles Standish	Peter Brown
John Alden	Richard Bitteridge
John Turner	George Soule
Francis Eaton	Edward Tilly
James Chilton	John Tilly
John Craxton	Francis Cooke

[names continued]

From Benjamin Perley Poore, ed., **The Federal and State Constitutions, Colonial Charters, and Other Organic Laws of the United States** (2 v., Government Printing Office, Washington, D.C., 1878), I: 931.

John Billington
Joses Fletcher
John Goodman
Mr. Samuel Fuller
Mr. Christopher Martin
Mr. William Mullins
Mr. William White
Mr. Richard Warren
John Howland

Thomas Rogers
Thomas Tinker
John Ridgate
Edward Fuller
Richard Clark
Richard Gardiner
Mr. John Allerton
Thomas English
Edward Doten
Edward Liester

Signing of the Compact. This c. 1900 painting by Edward Percy Moran shows the artist's portrayal of the Pilgrims signing the agreement they had drawn up in the dark Great Cabin of the **Mayflower.** The Pilgrims had obtained a grant from the Virginia Company to settle in Virginia. The voyage, though, was rough, and when the ship reached the harbor of Cape Cod in New England, the Pilgrims decided to land there instead of going on to Virginia. Since Cape Cod was not within the area controlled by the Virginia Company, they were able to devise a government of their own for Plimouth Plantation. (Pilgrim Society)

4.

THE PURITAN VISION

In 1630 began the Great Migration of Puritans to America. That summer, under the direction of John Winthrop, a fleet of seventeen ships carrying about one thousand men and women crossed the Atlantic to Massachusetts Bay. A few months later, the settlers founded a colony on the site of the present city of Boston. Within a few years Massachusetts Bay Colony was the largest of all the English colonies on the American mainland.

John Winthrop, a college-educated squire from Groton Manor, Suffolk, had been elected governor of the new colony even before the settlers left England. Though not a clergyman, he was a devout Puritan. During the passage he delivered a lecture called "A Model of Christian Charity" to his coreligionists on the flagship **Arbella**. In it he reminded them of their Puritan ideals and outlined the religious and social purposes by which he expected them to organize their settlement in the New World. He wanted Massachusetts Bay Colony to be a model "Christian commonwealth," that is, a kind of "city upon a hill" for the rest of the world to admire and perhaps imitate. The settlers, he said, had a special commission from God to establish such a community in the New World. The new colony was to be dedicated to the glory of God rather than to worldly success. The "care of the public," he declared, "must oversway all private respects," and the settlers must strive at all times "to do justly, to love mercy, to walk humbly with our God."

For almost two decades Winthrop dominated Massachusetts Bay Colony. John Cotton, Boston's leading clergyman, called him "a brother . . . who has been to us a mother," but he was a father as well. He was convinced he was destined to rule and was an exacting parent. Born to wealth in Suffolk in 1588, he was educated at Trinity College, Cambridge, became prominent in the legal profession, and served as justice of the peace and lord of Groton Manor before heading the expedition to America. A strong leader who opposed both religious dissent and popular rule in Massachusetts, Winthrop served as governor for twelve years; when not governor he served as deputy governor and member of the governing council. He regarded democracy as "the meanest and worst form of government," and most people agreed with him in those days. When criticized for highhandedness, he managed to convince his critics that "liberty" meant not the right to do as one pleased but, rather, emancipation from selfish desires and obedience to the moral law. A journal he kept from the inception of the colony until his death in 1649 is a rich source for the early history of Massachusetts Bay Colony.

Questions to consider. In his lecture to the settlers, Winthrop spoke of the "law of the Gospel." In what ways did he make the Bible the basis of his plans for Massachusetts Bay Colony? How close were relations between church and state to be in the new settlement? Which was to come first: the individual or the community? What principles of behavior did he consider essential to the success of the enterprise? What did he mean by his statement that the Puritans were operating under a "special overruling providence"? What did he think would be the fate of the colonists if they failed to carry out the high purposes he had outlined for them?

———

A Model of Christian Charity (1630)
John Winthrop

This law of the Gospel propounds likewise a difference of seasons and occasions. There is a time when a Christian must sell all and give to the poor as they did in the apostles' times; there is a time also when a Christian, though they give not all yet, must give beyond their ability, as they of Macedonia (II Cor. 8). Likewise, community of perils calls for extraordinary liberality, and so doth community in some special service for the church. Lastly, when there is no other means whereby our Christian brother may be relieved in this distress, we must help him beyond our ability, rather than tempt God in putting him upon help by miraculous or extraordinary means.

1. For the persons, we are a company professing ourselves fellow members of Christ, in which respect only, though we were absent from each other many miles, and had our employments as far distant, yet we ought to account ourselves knit together by this bond of love, and live in the exercise of it, if we would have comfort of our being in Christ.

2. For the work we have in hand, it is by mutual consent, through a special overruling providence and a more than an ordinary approbation of the churches of Christ, to seek out a place of cohabitation and consortship, under a due form of government both civil and ecclesiastical. In such cases as this, the care of the public must oversway all private respects by which not only

From **The Winthrop Papers** (5 v., Massachusetts Historical Society, Boston, 1931), II: 282–295. Reprinted by permission.

John Winthrop, second governor of Massachusetts. This engraving (undated) shows Winthrop in the prime of life. He was forty-two when he succeeded Matthew Cradock as governor of Massachusetts in 1629. The next year he came to America on the **Arbella** with a fleet of seventeen ships carrying close to one thousand men and women. He settled at Charlestown first and began building a house there, but soon changed his mind and moved to Boston, where he spent the rest of his life. Winthrop's term as governor was one year, and he was re-elected three times. But when John Cotton, prominent Boston clergyman, announced that competent magistrates ought to be re-elected continually, the freemen showed their independence by choosing someone else in 1634. They turned to Winthrop again, however, in 1642, and from 1645 to 1649, the year of his death, he was re-elected annually. (American Antiquarian Society)

conscience but mere civil policy doth bind us; for it is a true rule that particular estates cannot subsist in the ruin of the public.

3. The end is to improve our lives to do more service to the Lord, the comfort and increase of the body of Christ whereof we are members, that ourselves and posterity may be the better preserved from the common corruptions of this evil world, to serve the Lord and work out our salvation under the power and purity of His holy ordinances.

4. For the means whereby this must be effected, they are twofold: a conformity with the work and the end we aim at; these we seek are extraordinary, therefore we must not content ourselves with usual ordinary means. Whatsoever we did or ought to have done when we lived in England, the same must we do, and more also where we go. That which the most in their churches maintain as a truth in profession only, we must bring into familiar and constant practice: as in this duty of love we must love brotherly without dissimulation; we must love one another with a pure heart fervently, we must bear one another's burdens, we must not look only on our own things but also on the things of our brethren. Neither must we think that the Lord will bear with such failings at our hands as He doth from those among whom we have lived. . . .

Thus stands the cause between God and us; we are entered into covenant with Him for this work; we have taken out a commission, the Lord hath given us leave to draw our own articles. We have professed to enterprise these actions upon these and these ends; we have hereupon besought Him of favor and blessing. Now if the Lord shall please to hear us and bring us in peace to the place we desire, then hath He ratified this covenant and sealed our Commission, [and] will expect a strict performance of the articles contained in it. But if we shall neglect the observation of these articles which are the ends we have propounded, and dissembling with our God, shall fall to embrace this present world and prosecute our carnal intentions, seeking great things for ourselves and our posterity, the Lord will surely break out in wrath against us, be revenged of such a perjured people, and make us know the price of the breach of such a covenant.

Now the only way to avoid this shipwreck and to provide for our posterity is to follow the counsel of Micah: to do justly, to love mercy, to walk humbly with our God. For this end, we must be knit together in this work as one man. We must entertain each other in brotherly affection; we must be willing to abridge ourselves of our superfluities for the supply of others' necessities; we must uphold a familiar commerce together in all meekness, gentleness, patience and liberality. We must delight in each other, make others' condition our own, rejoice together, mourn together, labor and suffer together: always having before our eyes our commission and community in the work, our community as members of the same body. So shall we keep the unity of the spirit in the bond of peace, the Lord will be our God and delight to dwell among us, as His own people, and will command a blessing upon us in all our ways, so that we shall see much more of His wisdom, power, goodness, and truth than formerly we have been acquainted with. We shall find that the God of Israel is among us, when ten of us shall be able to resist a thousand of our enemies, when He shall make us a praise and glory, that men shall say of succeeding plantations: "The Lord make it like that of New England." For we must consider that we shall be as a city upon a hill, the eyes of all people are upon us. So that if we shall deal falsely with our God in this work we have undertaken, and so cause Him to withdraw His present help from us, we shall be made a story and a by-word through the world: we shall open the mouths of enemies to speak evil of the ways of God and all professors for God's sake; we shall shame the faces of many of God's worthy servants, and cause their prayers to be turned into curses upon us, till we be consumed out of the good land whither we are going.

And to shut up this discourse with that exhortation of Moses, that faithful servant of the Lord, in his last farewell to Israel (Deut. 30): Beloved, there is now set before us life and good, death and evil, in that we are commanded this day to love the Lord our God, and to love one another, to walk in His ways and to keep His commandments and His ordinance and His laws and the articles of our covenant with Him, that we may live and be multiplied, and that the Lord our God may bless us in the land whither we go to possess it: but if our hearts shall turn away so that we will not obey, but shall be seduced and worship . . . other gods, our pleasures and profits, and serve them, it is propounded unto us this day, we shall surely perish out of the good land whither we pass over this vast sea to possess it.

> Therefore, let us choose life,
> that we, and our seed,
> may live; by obeying His
> voice and cleaving to Him,
> for He is our life and
> our prosperity.

5.

A GATHERING OF INDIVIDUALS

Massachusetts Bay Colony was not a theocracy; ministers, though important there, could not serve as magistrates, nor could magistrates be ministers. Yet in Massachusetts the Puritans made the Congregational church the official state church, supported it by taxation, and prohibited people who did not share their views from worshipping as they pleased in the colony. In 1631, a devout young Puritan preacher named Roger Williams arrived in Boston and almost immediately began challenging the Puritan establishment. Williams favored separation of church and state; he thought religion was corrupted when it got involved in politics. He also championed religious liberty; authentic religion, he insisted, flourishes only when people can practice it freely without government coercion.

To the consternation of John Winthrop and other Massachusetts leaders, Williams began attracting support for his views among some of the people in the colony. In 1635 they put him on trial, convicted him of spreading "dangerous opinions," and banished him from the colony. In January 1636 Williams and some of his followers fled into the wilderness. They made their way southward and finally reached the shores of Narragansett Bay, where they founded Providence Plantation. In 1640 the inhabitants of Providence drew up a "Plantation Agreement" for governing their town, emphasizing "liberty of conscience" and the settlement of disputes by peaceful arbitration. Eventually Providence joined with other settlements in the area to form the colony of Rhode Island, for which Williams secured a charter in 1644. Williams wrote many eloquent tracts setting forth his views on religious liberty and freedom of conscience; and in Rhode Island, where he held office for many years, there was religious freedom for Catholics and Jews as well as for Protestants of all denominations. In 1644 he published a book presenting his opinions entitled **The Bloody Tenent (Tenet) of Persecution for the Cause of Conscience,** the conclusion of which appears below.

Williams, the son of a tailor, was born in London around 1603. He studied theology at Cambridge University and served as chaplain to a Puritan nobleman before coming to America. In Massachusetts he angered the authorities by both his political and his religious heresies. Not only did he espouse a democratic form of government ("The sovereign, original, and foundation of civil powers lies in the people"), but he also insisted that the colonists were not entitled to the land on which they settled until they bought it from the Indians. In Rhode Island

Williams purchased land from the Indians; he also made a study of their language and published a book about it. And he engaged Massachusetts's John Cotton in a lively controversy about religious liberty. When Cotton blasted Williams's **Bloody Tenent of Persecution for the Cause of Conscience** with a book entitled **The Bloody Tenent Washed and Made White in the Blood of the Lamb** (1647), Williams responded with **The Bloody Tenent Yet More Bloody by Mr. Cotton's Endeavor to Wash it White in the Blood of the Lamb** (1652). Williams's fight against religious repression continued until his death in 1683.

Questions to consider. Two questions come at once to mind in reading the following summary of the major points made in Williams's book. What were his main arguments against religious uniformity? How far did his toleration of religious diversity extend? Toleration today rests largely in indifference. Can it be said that Williams's toleration of differing religious beliefs and practices grew out of a lukewarm faith?

━━━━━

The Bloody Tenent of Persecution (1644)

Roger Williams

(Twelve Conclusions)

First, that the blood of so many hundred thousand souls of Protestants and Papists, spilt in the wars of present and former ages, for their respective consciences, is not required nor accepted by Jesus Christ the Prince of Peace.

Secondly, pregnant scriptures and arguments are throughout the work proposed against the doctrine of persecution for cause of conscience.

Thirdly, satisfactory answers are given to scriptures, and objections produced by Mr. Calvin, Beza [French theologian, 1519–1605], Mr. Cotton, and the ministers of the New English churches and others former and later, tending to prove the doctrine of persecution for cause of conscience.

Fourthly, the doctrine of persecution for cause of conscience is proved guilty of all the blood of the souls crying for vengeance under the altar.

Fifthly, all civil states with their officers of justice in their respective constitutions and administrations are proved essentially civil, and therefore not judges, governors or defenders of the spiritual or Christian state and worship.

From Roger Williams, **The Bloody Tenent of Persecution** (London?, 1644), 3–4.

Sixthly, it is the will and command of God that (since the coming of his Son the Lord Jesus) a permission of the most paganish, Jewish, Turkish, or anti-christian consciences and worships, be granted to all men in all nations and countries: and they are only to be fought against with that sword which is only (in soul matters) able to conquer, to wit, the sword of God's spirit, the Word of God.

Seventhly, the state of the land of Israel, the kings and people thereof in peace and war, is proved figurative and ceremonial, and no pattern nor precedent for any kingdom or civil state in the world to follow.

Eighthly, God requireth not an uniformity of religion to be enacted and enforced in any civil state; which enforced uniformity (sooner or later) is the greatest occasion of civil war, ravishing of conscience, persecution of Christ Jesus in his servants, and of the hypocrisy and destruction of millions of souls.

Ninthly, in holding an enforced uniformity of religion in a civil state, we must necessarily disclaim our desires and hopes of the Jews' conversion to Christ.

Tenthly, an enforced uniformity of religion throughout a nation or civil state confounds the civil and religious, denies the principles of Christianity and civility, and that Jesus Christ is come in the flesh.

Eleventhly, the permission of other consciences and worships than a state professeth only can (according to God) procure a firm and lasting peace (good assurance being taken according to the wisdom of the civil state for uniformity of civil obedience from all sorts).

Twelfthly, lastly, true civility and Christianity may both flourish in a state or kingdom, notwithstanding the permission of divers and contrary consciences, either of Jew or Gentile.

6.

PURITAN TWILIGHT

Men and women of the seventeenth century believed in the invisible spirit world far more than most people today can comprehend, and the New England Puritans were no different. Most of the Puritans were farmers whose livelihoods depended on the inexplicable ebbs and flows of disease and weather. Like all farmers and peasants of their time, they looked for signs of divine will to explain why rain did or did not fall or why calves were born healthy or dead. And in Massachusetts Bay, as Saints, or members of the true Church, they sought constantly for hopeful signs—shooting stars, a bird killing and devouring a snake or rodent—of God's continuing favor for their Holy enterprise.

But spiritual belief had a dark side. If the invisible spirit of God was everywhere, so, too, was the invisible spirit of Satan. For the Puritans, Satan was a constant presence, a powerful, evil, menacing force constantly seeking to undo the work of Christ and the lives of Christians. Sometimes the Devil himself was present, employing his own "evil hand" to kill farm animals, cause haystacks to burn, sicken children. More commonly, Satan employed followers: witches or, occasionally, their male counterparts, wizards. In Europe in the 1500s and 1600s, tens of thousands perished at the burning stake for witchcraft, and a few were hanged in early New England.

Thus it was not in itself startling when accusations of witchcraft surfaced in early 1692 in Salem Village, a little rural community just west of the bustling port of Salem Town. But things soon became startling. Most outbreaks of witchcraft in New England were minor affairs that flared briefly and then subsided. In Salem Village, however, the outbreak did not subside. It spread wider and wider, eventually encompassing hundreds of people in the local area and numerous figures from the commercial and political elites of nearby Salem Town and even of the provincial capital, Boston. And not only were hundreds accused. Dozens of them stood trial for the crime of witchcraft, and of these a full score or more went to their deaths on the sinister gallows atop Witch's Hill. Only the belated intervention of the colony's most powerful ministers and officeholders finally brought the killing to a halt late in 1692.

The ghastly business had begun when a group of adolescent girls started telling fortunes with a West Indian slave, then went into bizzare hysterical seizures, and finally turned to accusations of witchcraft to relieve their torment. When adult relatives and friends of the girls joined the cry, the village found itself awash in mystery, terror, and recrimination. Soon standing in the center of the fray was the local minister,

Samuel Parris. His involvement was not surprising. Several of the afflicted girls were living in Parris's house when the outbreak began, and members of his congregation—actual Saints able to partake of Sabbath communion!—had fallen under suspicion. So it was fitting for Parris to warn his parishioners of Satan's legions and to offer guidance as to the character of the witches lurking not just around them but also in their very midst.

Parris preached, as he always did, in the plain, direct, unadorned style that was the hallmark of Puritan preaching, the form used repeatedly since the 1630s to bring parishioners close to God's Word and purposes. In 1692 Parris scarcely needed adornment to make his point. His sermon "Christ Knows How Many Devils There Are," an outline of which is excerpted below, in fact resembled the woeful "jeremiads," the dire warnings that ministers had used for years to assail the corruption of faith by worldliness and lust. In style and content, if not in its obsession with witches, Parris's sermon was thoroughly familiar, although it was probably more important than most since it helped get a lot of people killed. But just as the Salem affair was New England's last significant witchhunt, so Parris's sermon was one of its last jeremiads. Neither witchcraft nor jeremiad, it seems, could withstand the materialism of the eighteenth century.

Samuel Parris was born in 1653 in London, the younger son of a speculator in West Indian goods. Seeing little future for himself in England, Parris sailed in about 1680 for Boston, where he tried trading with the Indies himself before turning to the ministry as a calling. He arrived in Salem Village in late 1689—just in time to play his fateful role in the accusations and executions of the purported witches. Parris's overzealousness in what amounted to a local civil war made it impossible for him to play a healing role once the trials stopped, and although he received the support of a majority of villagers during various campaigns to remove him, he finally resigned in 1696. He tried briefly to continue his ministry elsewhere, but fighting witches and corruption was out of fashion. He wound up a schoolmaster and petty tradesman in Sudbury, Massachusetts, where he died in 1720.

Questions to consider. What was Samuel Parris's motive in preaching this particular sermon? Why might he have felt obligated to preach it at this particular time? Did he really believe in witchcraft? What, according to Parris, were the chief evils of witches and wizards? If you had been sitting in the meetinghouse that Sunday, what kind of person would you have suspected of witchcraft? Was it significant that Salem Village lay very near the commercial port of Salem Town? What would John Winthrop (Document 4) and Roger Williams (Document 5) have thought about Parris's sermon?

Christ Knows How Many Devils There Are (1692)

Samuel Parris

27 March 1691/92, Sacrament day.

Occasioned by dreadful Witchcraft broke out here a few weeks past, and one Member of this Church, and another of Salem, upon public examination by Civil Authority vehemently suspected for she-witches, and upon it committed.

John 6: 70. "Have not I chosen you twelve, and one of you is a Devil." . . .

Doctrine: *Our Lord Jesus Christ knows how many Devils there are in his Church, and who they are.*

1. There are devils as well as saints in Christ's Church.
2. Christ knows how many of these devils there are.
3. Christ knows who these devils are.

Proposition 1: There are devils as well as saints in Christ's church. Here three things may be spoken to: (1) Show you what is meant here by *devils;* (2) That there are such devils in the church; (3) That there are also true saints in such churches.

(1). What is meant here by *devils*? "One of you is a devil." Answer: By *devil* is ordinarily meant any wicked angel or spirit. Sometimes it is put for the prince or head of the evil spirits, or fallen angels. Sometimes it is used for vile and wicked persons—the worst of such, who for their villainy and impiety do most resemble devils and wicked spirits. Thus Christ in our text calls Judas a devil: for his great likeness to the devil. "One of you is a devil": i.e., a devil for quality and disposition, not a devil for nature—for he was a man, etc.—but a devil for likeness and operation (John 8: 38, 41, 44—"Ye are of your father the devil.")

(2). There are such devils in the church. Not only sinners, but notorious sinners; sinners more like to the devil than others. So here in Christ's little Church. (Text.) This also Christ teacheth us in the parable of the tares (Matth. 13: 38), where Christ tells us that such are the children of the wicked one—i.e., of the devil. Reason: Because hypocrites are the very worst of men— *corruptio optimi est pessimi.* Hypocrites are the sons and heirs of the devil, the free-holders of hell—whereas other sinners are but tenants. When Satan repossesseth a soul, he becomes more vile and sinful (Luke 11: 24–26). As the jailer lays loads of iron on him that hath escaped. None are worse than those who have been good, and are naught; and might be good, but will be naught. . . .

From Paul S. Boyer and Stephen Nissenbaum: **Salem Village Witchcraft: A Documentary Record of Local Conflict in Colonial New England,** Belmont, Calif., Wadsworth Publishing, 1972, pp. 129–130. Reprinted by permission of the authors.

Accusation of a witch. This twentieth-century rendering captures the tensions and terror that pervaded the Salem Village Meetinghouse during the witchcraft trials of 1692. A minimum of 234 people were accused of being witches in seventeenth-century New England. Of these, authorities executed 36. Salem Village, with its 19 executions, thus accounted for over half of all New England's executions, obviously a horrendous outbreak of fear and death for so small a place. About three-quarters of those accused were women, and two-thirds of these women were over forty years old—sinister reinforcement of the stereotype identifying the witch as an aged crone. (Courtesy, Essex Institute, Salem, Mass.)

Proposition 2: Christ knows how many of these devils there are in his churches. As in our text there was one among the twelve. And so in our churches God knows how many devils there are: whether one, two, three, or four in twelve—how many devils, how many saints. He that knows whom he has chosen (John 13: 18), he also knows who they are that have not chosen him, but prefer farms and merchandise above him and above his ordinances (2 Tim. 4: 10). . . .

Use 1. Let none then build their hopes of salvation merely upon this: that they are church members. This you and I may be, and yet devils for all that (Matth. 8: 11–12—"Many shall come from the east and west, and shall sit down, etc. And however we may pass here, a true difference shall be made shortly, etc.").

Use 2. Let none then be stumbled at religion, because too often there are devils found among the saints. You see, here was a true church, sincere converts and sound believers; and yet here was a devil among them.

Use 3. Terror to hypocrites who profess much love to Christ but indeed are in league with their lusts, which they prefer above Christ. Oh! remember that you are devils in Christ's account. Christ is lightly esteemed of you, and you are vilely accounted for by Christ. Oh! if there be any such among us, forbear to come this day to the Lord's table, lest Satan enter more powerfully into you—lest while the bread be between your teeth, the wrath of the Lord come pouring down upon you (Psalm 78: 30–31). . . .

Use 5. Examine we ourselves well, what we are—what we church members are. We are either saints or devils: the Scripture gives us no medium. The Apostle tells us we are to examine ourselves (2 Cor. 13: 5). Oh! it is a dreadful thing to be a devil, and yet to sit down at the Lord's table (1 Cor. 10: 21). Such incur the hottest of God's wrath (as follows—v. 22). Now, if we would not be devils, we must give ourselves wholly up to Christ, and not suffer the predominancy of one lust—and particularly that of covetousness, which is made so light of, and which so sorely prevails in these perilous times. Why, this one lust made Judas a devil (John 12: 6, Matth. 26: 15). And no doubt it has made more devils than one. For a little pelf [money], men sell Christ to his enemies, and their souls to the devil. But there are certain sins that make us devils; see that we be not such:

1. A liar or murderer (John 8: 44)
2. A slanderer or an accuser of the godly
3. A tempter to sin
4. An opposer of godliness, as Elymos (Acts 13: 8 etc.)
5. Envious persons as witches
6. A drunkard (I Sam. 1: 15–16)
7. A proud person

Finis textus

7.

AN IMPERIAL PRESENCE

The Navigation Act of 1696 systematized various regulatory laws passed by Parliament during the preceding half-century. The act made clearer than ever the aim of British mercantilist policy: to advance the interests of English merchants, shippers, shipbuilders, and producers and to make England, not other parts of the Empire, wealthy. There were, to be sure, some benefits for Americans. The English government paid bounties to producers of naval stores and indigo in America and saw to it that American tobacco had a preferential position in England. The British navy, moreover, protected the colonies as well as the mother country. But there were disadvantages as well as advantages. Mercantilism hurt the northern colonies, which concentrated on shipping and trade, more than it did the southern colonies, which engaged primarily in agriculture, and American enterprisers, eager to forge ahead on their own, found British policies increasingly irksome.

Since earlier laws had been only loosely enforced, the Navigation Act of 1696 tried to address the enforcement problem directly by providing for a variety of inspection and customs officials and making clear which ports were legal for Imperial shippers and which were not. But in the first half of the eighteenth century Britain was engaged in wars with France and again failed to crack down on Americans who ignored the laws. After winning the French and Indian War in 1760 and taking over Canada from France by treaty in 1763, however, Britain turned its fullest attention to American economic activities. When Britain began to enact legislation (such as the Sugar Act of 1764 and the Stamp Act of 1765) that seemed designed to raise money as well as control trade, the reaction was violent. Americans denied that Britain had the right to regulate their economy and began calling for economic autonomy. American merchants moved increasingly to protest, evasion of the law, resistance, and, in the end, outright rebellion.

Questions to consider. Some parts of the Navigation Act excerpted here deal mainly with trade routes and shipping. What specific English economic interests were addressed? If the Act had been passed seventy-five years earlier or seventy-five years later, do you think it would have contained the same provisions? Did these provisions reflect mainly the way the Empire was put together as of 1696 or mainly economic developments within England? The act contains several enforcement provisions. Of these, which ones were most likely to cause political trouble eventually? Might this act have been enforced without causing political trouble? Does this act, as some have argued, appear to contain the seeds of the American Revolution?

═══════

The Navigation Act of 1696

II. Be it enacted . . . That after the five and twentieth day of March, 1698, no goods or merchandizes whatsoever shall be imported into, or exported out of, any colony or plantation to his Majesty, in Asia, Africa, or America, belonging, or in his possession, . . . or shall be laden in, or carried from any one port or place in the said colonies or plantations to any other port or place in the same [or] the kingdom of England . . . in any ship or bottom, but what is or shall be of the built of England, [or] Ireland, or the said colonies or plantations, and wholly owned by the people thereof, or any of them, and navigated with the masters and three fourths of the mariners of the said places only . . . under pain of forfeiture of ship and goods. . . .

VI. [And] be it further enacted . . . That the officers for the collecting and managing his Majesty's revenue, and inspecting the plantation trade, in any of the said plantations, shall have the same powers and authorities, for visiting and searching of ships, and taking their entries, and for seizing and securing or bringing on shore any of the goods prohibited to be imported or exported . . . or for which any duties are payable or ought to have been paid. . . . as are provided for the officers of the customs in England [and also] to enter houses or warehouses, to search for and seize any such goods. . . .

IX. And it is further enacted . . . That all laws, by-laws, usages or customs, at this time, or which hereafter shall be in practice . . . in any of the said plantations, which are in any wise repugnant to the before mentioned laws, or any of them, so far as they do relate to the said plantations, or any of them, or which are any ways repugnant to this present act, or to any other law hereafter to be made in this kingdom, so far as such law shall relate to and mention the said plantations, are illegal, null and void. . . .

XIV. And whereas several ships and vessels laden with tobacco, sugars, and other goods of the growth and product of his Majesty's plantations in America, have been discharged in . . . Scotland and Ireland, contrary to the laws and statutes now in being, under pretence that the said ships and vessels were driven thither by stress of weather or for want of provisions . . . be it enacted . . . That from and after the first day of December, 1696, it shall not

From Danby Pickering, **The Statutes at Large from the Magna Charta to the End of the Eleventh Parliament of Great Britain, anno 1761** (46 v., J. Bentham, Cambridge, 1806), 9: 428–430.

be lawful, on any pretence whatsoever, to put on shore in . . . Scotland or Ireland, any goods or merchandize of the growth or product of any of his Majesty's plantations aforesaid, unless the same shall have been first landed in the kingdom of England . . . and paid the rates and duties wherewith they are chargeable by law. . . .

XVI. And be it further enacted . . . That all persons and their assignees, claiming any right or propriety in any islands or tracts of land upon the continent of America, by charter or letters patents, shall not at any time hereafter aliene [transfer], sell or dispose of any of the said islands, tracts of lands or proprieties, other than to the natural-born subjects of England [and] Ireland . . . without the licence and consent of his Majesty . . . ; and all governors nominated and appointed by any such persons or proprietors, who shall be entitled to make such nomination, shall be allowed and approved of by his Majesty . . . and shall take the oaths enjoined by this or any other act to be taken by the governors or commanders in chief in other of his Majesty's colonies and plantations, before their entering upon their respective governments, under the like penalty, as his Majesty's governors and commanders in chief are by the said acts liable to.

COUNTERPOINT I

Slavery and Society

The statutes of early Virginia and Maryland show the gradual development of a codified body of law concerning forced labor generally, including indentured servants, and African and Afro-American slaves in particular. But the statutes themselves reveal only a part of the overall picture of slavery in the southern colonies. Historians have therefore ransacked other sources, including court records, plantation papers, letters, and wills, to help fill the blank spaces. Those with a statistical bent have tried their hand, too, unearthing in the process information that would be difficult to attain through literary sources.

In an attempt to discover information about the composition and characteristics of the newly arrived slave population and how the importing of slaves affected the white population, Russell Menard examined estate inventories and lists of early officeholders in Virginia's Chesapeake neighbor, Maryland. His work on surviving estate inventories in four Maryland counties (table A) indicates that in the mid-1600s most slaves were between 16 and 50 years old and that, although there were a few more females than males in the total slave population, the dominant age group had more men than women. These patterns, argues Menard, reflect recent arrival—thus few young slaves—and the desire for tobacco labor—thus more males in the dominant age group. The patterns, moreover, persisted late into the 1600s because as area planters put more land under cultivation, they continued to import most of their forced labor; in the process they retained the age and gender ratios that seemed most logical to them. The numbers for the 1720s are different, however, in two respects. First, the proportion of young slaves (ages 0–15) had increased to 40 percent, indicating that natural increase had begun to contribute significantly to the growth of the slave population. Second, the dominant labor age group had a higher ratio of males to females, about 3 to 2, than ever before, indicating that the direct purchase of imported field workers was still a major growth factor for the slave population.

Menard also found that once in the New World, at least in the early years, the slaves were fairly widely dispersed (see table B.1). Half the planters owned only 1 or 2, and less than a third of the slaves lived on an estate with 20 or more other slaves. But by the eighteenth century and possibly before, this was no longer the case (see table B.2). At this time only a third of the planters each owned one or two slaves, and almost half of the slaves lived on estates with at least 20 others. Since farmers bought slaves as field workers, those with more fields and money necessarily became larger slaveholders, thus adding an inequality of labor ownership to the existing inequality of land ownership. Therefore, although the increase in slave labor may have increased colonial wealth by increasing the total acreage cultivated, it also apparently made the unequal distribution of this wealth even more unequal.

Menard suggests further that just as slavery made the distribution of plantation wealth more uneven, it may also have changed the nature of colonial officeholding and politics. Thus the proportion of local officeholders who had been indentured servants ranged from one-fifth to one-third in the 26 years before 1660 (see table C.1). But this proportion dropped to only one-seventh in the 1660s, and after 1670 to only a tenth. The figures for officeholders who were illiterate and presumably began poor are even more striking (table C.2). Before 1670 the proportion of illiterate officeholders was a fourth; thereafter, it was less than a tenth. Slavery increased colonial wealth at the same time that it transformed colonial law. It seems to have increased economic and political inequality as well.

A. Profile of Slaves Listed in Estate Inventories in Calvert, Charles, Prince George's, and St. Mary's Counties, Maryland, 1658–1730

	1658–1670	1681–1690	1721–1730
Males 0–15	3	21	185
Females 0–15	5	11	164
Sex unknown 0–15	6	25	34
Total 0–15	14 (27%)	57 (28%)	383 (40%)
Males 16–50	17	74	287
Females 16–50	13	54	188
Total 16–50	30 (59%)	128 (61%)	475 (49%)
Old males	1	7	53
Old females	6	15	47
Old sex unknown	0	0	2
Total old	7 (14%)	22 (11%)	102 (11%)
Slaves, age, sex unknown	3	31	14
Total slaves	54	238	974

SOURCE: From Russell R. Menard, "The Maryland Slave Population, 1658 to 1730," as published in *William and Mary Quarterly* (1975). Reprinted by permission.

B. Distribution of Slaves in Maryland, 1658–1730

1. Distribution of Slaves on Maryland's Lower Western Shore, 1658–1710

No. of Slaves per Estate	No. of Estates	Percentage of Estates	No. of Slaves	Percentage of Slaves
1–2	145	48.3	198	12.2
3–5	70	23.3	273	16.9
6–10	47	15.7	356	22.0
11–20	23	7.7	340	21.0
21 +	15	5.0	451	27.9
	300	100.0	1,618	100.0

2. Distribution of Slaves in Charles and Prince George's Counties, Maryland, 1721–1730

No. of Slaves per Estate	No. of Estates	Percentage of Estates	No. of Slaves	Percentage of Slaves
1–2	40	34.2	57	5.9
3–5	26	22.2	105	10.8
6–10	26	22.2	188	19.3
11–20	14	12.0	198	20.3
21 +	11	9.4	426	43.7
	117	100.0	974	100.0

SOURCE: From Russell R. Menard, "The Maryland Slave Population, 1658 to 1730," as published in *William and Mary Quarterly* (1975). Reprinted by permission.

C. Colonial Officeholders, 1634–1689, According to Former Servitude and Illiteracy

1. Servant Officeholders, 1634–1689

(Former servants serving as burgess, justice of the peace, and sheriff in Charles, Kent, and St. Mary's counties, Maryland, 1634–1689, by date of first appointment.)

	New Officials	Servants	
		Number	*Percentage*
1634–1649	57	11–12	19.3–22.8
1650–1659	39	12	30.8
1660–1669	64	9	14.1
1670–1679	44	4–5	9.1–11.4
1680–1689	46	4	8.7

2. Illiterate Officeholders, 1634–1689

(Illiterates serving as burgess, justice of the peace, and sheriff in Charles, Kent, and St. Mary's counties, Maryland, 1634–1689, by date of first appointment.)

	New Officials	Illiterates	
		Number	*Percentage*
1634–1649	57	16	28.1
1650–1659	39	9	23.1
1660–1669	64	17	26.6
1670–1679	44	1	2.3
1680–1689	46	4	8.7

SOURCE: From Russell R. Menard, "From Servant to Freeholder," as published in *William and Mary Quarterly* (1973). Reprinted by permission.

George Washington at Princeton.   A study by Revolutionary portraitist Charles Willson Peale of the Commander-in-Chief at the scene of his victory over British regulars in early 1777. (The Pennsylvania Academy of the Fine Arts)

CHAPTER TWO

Strides Toward Freedom

8.

A RIGHT TO CRITICIZE

In 1735 came the first great battle over freedom of the press in America. Two years earlier, John Peter Zenger, publisher of the outspoken **New-York Weekly Journal,** began printing articles satirizing corruption and highhandedness in the administration of William Cosby, the new royal governor of New York, and he also distributed song sheets praising those who would "boldly despise the haughty knaves who keep us in awe." In 1734 Cosby arranged for Zenger to be arrested, charged with seditious libel, and thrown in prison. He also ordered copies of the **New-York Weekly Journal** burned in public. When Zenger's case came before the court in 1735, Andrew Hamilton, a prominent Philadelphian who was the most skillful lawyer in America, agreed to defend him. According to English law, a printed attack on a public official, even if true, was considered libelous; and the judge ruled that the fact that Zenger had criticized the New York governor was enough to convict him. But Hamilton argued that no one should be punished for telling the truth; Zenger, he pointed out, had told the truth and should not be convicted of libel. In "a free government," he insisted, the rulers should "not be able to stop the people's mouths when they feel themselves oppressed." Liberty, he added, is the "only bulwark against lawless power." Hamilton was so eloquent in his plea that in the end the jury voted "not guilty" and spectators in the courtroom cheered the verdict.

After his release, Zenger printed a complete account of the trial in his paper (some of which appears below) and also arranged to have it printed separately as a pamphlet. The report of the trial aroused great interest in Britain as well as in America and went through many editions. Hamilton's plea to the jury on behalf of "speaking and writing the truth" was one of the landmarks in the struggle for a free press in America. Though other royal judges did not accept the principle enunciated by Hamilton, the decision in the Zenger case did set an important precedent against judicial tyranny in libel suits. Gouverneur Morris, a statesman and diplomat from New York, called it "the morning star of that liberty which subsequently revolutionized America."

Zenger did not speak on his own behalf during the trial. But he had planned, if found guilty, to make a speech reminding the jurors that he and his parents had "fled from a country where oppression, tyranny, and arbitrary power had ruined almost all the people." Zenger, who was born in Germany in 1697, came to America, along with many other German immigrants, when he was twelve years old and was indentured to William Bradford, "the pioneer printer of the middle colonies." In 1726 he set up a printing shop of his own, publishing tracts and pamphlets mainly of a religious nature, and in 1730 he published the first arithmetic text in New York. A few years after his famous trial he became public printer for the colony of New York and a little later for New Jersey as well. He died in 1746.

Questions to consider. In the following exchange between the prosecuting attorney and Hamilton, Zenger's lawyer, why did Hamilton place such emphasis on the word **false**? What complaint did he make about his effort to present evidence to the court on behalf of his client? What did he mean by saying that "the suppression of evidence ought always to be taken for the strongest evidence"? Why did he think Zenger's case was so important? Do you consider his final appeal to the jury a convincing one?

John Peter Zenger's Libel Trial (1735)

MR. ATTORNEY. . . . The case before the court is whether Mr. Zenger is guilty of libeling His Excellency the Governor of New York, and indeed the whole administration of the government. Mr. Hamilton has confessed the printing and publishing, and I think nothing is plainer than that the words in the information [indictment] are scandalous, and tend to sedition, and to disquiet the minds of the people of this province. And if such papers are not libels, I think it may be said there can be no such thing as a libel.

MR. HAMILTON. May it please Your Honor, I cannot agree with Mr. Attorney. For though I freely acknowledge that there are such things as libels, yet I must insist, at the same time, that what my client is charged with is not a libel. And I observed just now that Mr. Attorney, in defining a libel, made use of the words "scandalous, seditious, and tend to disquiet the people." But (whether with design or not I will not say) he omitted the word "false."

MR. ATTORNEY. I think I did not omit the word "false." But it has been said already that it may be a libel, notwithstanding it may be true.

MR. HAMILTON. In this I must still differ with Mr. Attorney; for I depend upon it, we are to be tried upon this information now before the court and jury, and to which we have pleaded not guilty, and by it we are charged with printing and publishing a certain false, malicious, seditious, and scandalous libel. This word "false" must have some meaning, or else how came it there? . . .

From J. P. Zenger, **The Tryal of J. P. Z. of New York** (London, 1738), 10–17.

MR. CHIEF JUSTICE. You cannot be admitted, Mr. Hamilton, to give the truth of a libel in evidence. A libel is not to be justified; for it is nevertheless a libel that it is true. . . .

MR. HAMILTON. I thank Your Honor. Then, gentlemen of the jury, it is to you we must now appeal, for witnesses, to the truth of the facts we have offered, and are denied the liberty to prove. And let it not seem strange that I apply myself to you in this manner. I am warranted so to do both by law and reason.

The law supposes you to be summoned out of the neighborhood where the fact [crime] is alleged to be committed; and the reason of your being taken out of the neighborhood is because you are supposed to have the best knowledge of the fact that is to be tried. And were you to find a verdict against my client, you must take upon you to say the papers referred to in the information, and which we acknowledge we printed and published, are false, scandalous, and seditious. But of this I can have no apprehension. You are citizens of New York; you are really what the law supposes you to be, honest and lawful men. And, according to my brief, the facts which we offer to prove were not committed in a corner; they are notoriously known to be true; and therefore in your justice lies our safety. And as we are denied the liberty of giving evidence to prove the truth of what we have published, I will beg leave to lay it down, as a standing rule in such cases, that the suppressing of evidence ought always to be taken for the strongest evidence; and I hope it will have weight with you. . . .

I hope to be pardoned, sir, for my zeal upon this occasion. It is an old and wise caution that when our neighbor's house is on fire, we ought to take care of our own. For though, blessed be God, I live in a government [Pennsylvania] where liberty is well understood, and freely enjoyed, yet experience has shown us all (I'm sure it has to me) that a bad precedent in one government is soon set up for an authority in another. And therefore I cannot but think it mine, and every honest man's duty, that (while we pay all due obedience to men in authority) we ought at the same time to be upon our guard against power, wherever we apprehend that it may affect ourselves or our fellow subjects.

I am truly very unequal to such an undertaking on many accounts. And you see I labor under the weight of many years, and am borne down with great infirmities of body. Yet old and weak as I am, I should think it my duty, if required, to go to the utmost part of the land, where my service could be of any use, in assist—to quench the flame of prosecutions upon informations, set on foot by the government, to deprive a people of the right of remonstrating (and complaining too) of the arbitrary attempts of men in power. Men who injure and oppress the people under their administration provoke them to cry out and complain; and then make that very complaint the foundation for new oppressions and prosecutions. I wish I could say there were no instances of this kind.

THE·TRIAL·OF·JOHN·PETER·ZENGER·FOR·LIBEL
RESULTING·IN·THE·VICTORY·FOR·FREE·PRESS·AUG·4·1735

The trial of John Peter Zenger.   This tapestry depicts the New York courtroom in August 1735, when a jury acquitted the printer of a charge of libel. Crown officers and attorneys wore white-powdered wigs, as officials did in England, to emphasize their authority. Since imperial bureaucrats such as these not only were distant geographically from the real center of British power in London but also had to deal with obstreperous colonials such as Zenger, they may have taken even more care than their counterparts at home to keep their wigs white and imposing as symbols of British authority. (The Metropolitan Museum of Art)

But to conclude. The question before the court and you, gentlemen of the jury, is not of small nor private concern. It is not the cause of a poor printer, nor of New York alone, which you are now trying. No! It may, in its consequence, affect every freeman that lives under a British government on the main[land] of America. It is the best cause. It is the cause of liberty. And I make no doubt but your upright conduct, this day, will not only entitle you to the love and esteem of your fellow citizens; but every man who prefers freedom to a life of slavery will bless and honor you, as men who have baffled the attempt of tyranny, and, by an impartial and uncorrupt verdict, have laid a noble foundation for securing to ourselves, our posterity, and our neighbors, that to which nature and the laws of our country have given us a right—the liberty both of exposing and opposing arbitrary power (in these parts of the world, at least) by speaking and writing truth. . . .

9.

THE GREAT AWAKENING

Jonathan Edwards was upset by the "extraordinary dullness in religion" he observed around him. During the first part of the eighteenth century, as the population of the colonies increased and Americans developed a thriving trade with other parts of the world, they became increasingly worldly in their outlook. It wasn't that they abandoned religion; what they abandoned was the stern, harsh religion that Edwards considered essential to salvation. Edwards, like John Winthrop, was a devout Puritan. He believed human beings were incorrigible sinners, filled with greed, pride, and lust, and that a just God had condemned them to eternal damnation for their transgressions. But God was merciful as well as just. Because Jesus had atoned for man's sins by dying on the cross, God agreed to shed his grace on some men and women and elect them for salvation. The individual who was chosen for salvation experienced God's grace while being converted. For Edwards the conversion experience was the greatest event in a person's life. After conversion, the individual dedicated himself to the glory of God and possessed a new strength to resist temptation.

In his sermons, Edwards, pastor of the Congregational church in Northampton, Massachusetts, tried to impress on people the awful fate that awaited them unless they acknowledged their sinfulness and threw themselves upon the mercy of God. During the last part of 1734 Edwards delivered a series of sermons that moved his congregation deeply. In them he gave such vivid descriptions of human depravity and the torments awaiting the unredeemed in the next world that people in the congregation wept, groaned, and begged for mercy. Edwards's sermons produced scores of conversions. During the winter and spring over three hundred people were converted and admitted to full membership in the church. "This town," wrote Edwards joyfully, "never was so full of Love, nor so full of Joy, nor so full of distress as it has lately been." The religious revival that Edwards led in Northampton was only one of many revivals sweeping America at this time—in New England, in the Middle Colonies, and in the South. The Great Awakening, as the revivalist movement was called, affected the Presbyterians as well as the Congregationalists, and also swept through other denominations, keeping the churches in turmoil from about 1734 to 1756. The Great Awakening did produce a renewed interest in religion, but not always in Edwards's austere Puritanism. Edwards led revivals only in New England. George Whitefield, an English associate of John Wesley, the founder of

Methodism, came to America, toured the colonies, and led revivals wherever he went. He helped make the Great Awakening an intercolonial movement. It was the first movement in which all the colonies participated before the American Revolution.

Edwards, who was born in East Windsor, Connecticut, in 1703, was a precocious lad. He wrote a treatise on spiders at age twelve and entered Yale College at age thirteen. The son of a Congregational minister, he experienced conversion as a young man, dedicated his life to the church, and pursued theological studies at Yale after graduation. In 1726 he became associate pastor of the Congregational church in Northampton, and in 1729 he was appointed pastor. For twenty-one years he labored hard in Northampton, studying, writing, and preaching; he also launched his ambitious plan for publishing treatises on all of the great Puritan doctrines. He wrote, too, a psychological analysis of the conversion experience, based on his study of the revivals that took place in Northampton and elsewhere. He delivered his famous sermon, "Sinners in the Hands of an Angry God" in Enfield, Connecticut, in 1741. In 1750 he took his family to Stockbridge, Massachusetts. There he spent the rest of his life, preaching and serving as missionary to the Indians. In 1758 he was appointed president of the College of New Jersey (Princeton), but he died of smallpox before beginning his duties there.

Questions to consider. Edwards was not a spellbinder like Whitefield. He delivered his sermons in a quiet, though impassioned, tone of voice and looked at the back wall of the church, not the congregation, while preaching. How, then, was he able, in a sermon like "Sinners in the Hands of an Angry God," to arouse the rapt attention of the people? In what ways did he set forth the sovereignty of God, a prime doctrine of the Puritans? Do you think there is any inconsistency in his belief that only a few people (the elect) are saved and his insistence that everybody strive for salvation? Can you think of any contemporary examples of people who share Edwards's outlook? In what ways might the Great Awakening have fostered anti-establishment, anti-imperial attitudes among the American colonists?

Sinners in the Hands of an Angry God (1741)

Jonathan Edwards

. . . This that you have heard is the case of every one of you that are out of Christ. That world of misery, that lake of burning brimstone, is extended abroad under you. There is the dreadful pit of the glowing flames of the wrath of God; there is hell's wide gaping mouth open; and you have nothing to stand upon, nor any thing to take hold of; there is nothing between you and hell but the air; 'tis only the power and mere pleasure of God that holds you up.

You probably are not sensible of this; you find you are kept out of hell, but don't see the hand of God in it, but look at other things, as the good state of your bodily constitution, your care of your own life, and the means you use for your own preservation. But indeed these things are nothing; if God should withdraw his hand, they would avail no more to keep you from falling, than the thin air to hold up a person that is suspended in it.

Your wickedness makes you as it were heavy as lead, and to tend downwards with great weight and pressure towards hell; and, if God should let you go, you would immediately sink, and swiftly descend and plunge into the bottomless gulf; and your healthy constitution, and your own care and prudence, and best contrivance, and all your righteousness, would have no more influence to uphold you and keep you out of hell, than a spider's web would have to stop a falling rock. Were it not that so is the sovereign pleasure of God, the earth would not bear you one moment; for you are a burden to it; the creation groans with you; the creature is made subject to the bondage of your corruption, not willingly; the sun don't willingly shine upon you, to give you light to serve sin and Satan; the earth don't willingly yield her increase to satisfy your lusts, nor is it willingly a stage for your wickedness to be acted upon; the air don't willingly serve you for breath to maintain the flame of life in your vitals, while you spend your life in the service of God's enemies. God's creatures are good, and were made for men to serve God with, and don't willingly subserve to any other purpose, and groan when they are abused to purposes so directly contrary to their nature and end. And the world would spue you out, were it not for the sovereign hand of him who hath subjected it in hope. There are the black clouds of God's wrath now hanging directly over your heads, full of the dreadful storm, and big with thunder; and, were it not for the restraining hand of God, it would immediately burst forth upon you. The sovereign pleasure of God for the present stays his rough wind; otherwise it would come with fury, and your destruction would come like a whirlwind, and you would be like the chaff of the summer threshing-floor.

From Samuel Austin, ed., **The Works of President Edwards** (6 v., Isaiah Thomas, Worcester, 1808), II, 72–79.

The wrath of God is like great waters that are dammed for the present; they increase more and more, and rise higher and higher, till an outlet is given; and the longer the stream is stopt, the more rapid and mighty is its course when once it is let loose. 'Tis true, that judgment against your evil works has not been executed hitherto; the floods of God's vengeance have been withheld; but your guilt in the mean time is constantly increasing, and you are every day treasuring up more wrath; the waters are continually rising, and waxing more and more mighty; and there is nothing but the mere pleasure of God that holds the waters back that are unwilling to be stopt, and press hard to go forward. If God should only withdraw his hand from the floodgate, it would immediately fly open, and the fiery floods of the fierceness and wrath of God would rush forth with inconceivable fury, and would come upon you with omnipotent power; and if your strength were ten thousand times greater than it is, yea ten thousand times greater than the strength of the stoutest, sturdiest, devil in hell, it would be nothing to withstand or endure it.

The bow of God's wrath is bent, and the arrow made ready on the string; and justice bends the arrow at your heart, and strains the bow; and it is nothing but the mere pleasure of God, and that of an angry God, without any promise or obligation at all, that keeps the arrow one moment from being made drunk with your blood.

Thus are all you that never passed under a great change of heart, by the mighty power of the spirit of God upon your souls; all that were never born again, and made new creatures, and raised from being dead in sin, to a state of new, and before altogether unexperienced light and life. However you may have reformed your life in many things, and may have had religious affections, and may keep up a form of religion in your families and closets, and in the house of God, and may be strict in it, you are thus in the hands of an angry God; 'tis nothing but his mere pleasure that keeps you from being this moment swallowed up in everlasting destruction.

However unconvinced you may now be of the truth of what you hear, by and by you will be fully convinced of it. Those that are gone from being in the like circumstances with you, see that it was so with them; for destruction came suddenly upon most of them, when they expected nothing of it, and while they were saying, peace and safety. Now they see, that those things that they depended on for peace and safety, were nothing but thin air and empty shadows.

The God that holds you over the pit of hell, much as one holds a spider or some lothsom insect over the fire, abhors you, and is dreadfully provoked; his wrath towards you burns like fire; he looks upon you as worthy of nothing else but to be cast into the fire; he is of purer eyes than to bear to have you in his sight; you are ten thousand times so abominable in his eyes as the most hateful venomous serpent is in ours. You have offended him infinitely more than ever a stubborn rebel did his prince; and yet 'tis nothing but his hand that holds you from falling into the fire every moment. 'Tis to be ascribed to nothing else, that you did not go to hell the last night; that you was suffered to awake again in this world, after you closed your eyes to sleep. And there is no other reason to be given why you have not dropt into hell since you arose in the morning, but that God's hand has held you up. There is no other reason to be given why you haven't gone to hell since you have sat here in the House of God, provoking his pure eyes by your sinful wicked manner of attending his solemn worship; yea, there is nothing else that is to be given as a reason why you don't this very moment drop down into hell.

O Sinner! Consider the fearful danger you are in. 'Tis a great furnace of wrath, a wide and bottomless pit, full of the fire of wrath, that you are held over in the hand of that God, whose wrath is provoked and incensed as much against you as against many of the damned in hell. You hang by a slender thread, with the flames of divine wrath flashing about it, and ready every moment to singe it, and burn it asunder; and you have no interest in any mediator, and nothing to lay hold of to save yourself, nothing to keep off the flames of wrath, nothing of your own, nothing that you ever have done, nothing that you can do, to induce God to spare you one moment. . . .

How dreadful is the state of those that are daily and hourly in danger of this great wrath, and infinite misery! But this is the dismal case of every soul in this congregation that has not been born again, however moral and strict, sober and religious they may otherwise be. Oh that you would consider it, whether you be young or old! There is reason to think, that there are many in this congregation, now hearing this discourse, that will actually be the subjects of this very misery to all eternity. We know not who they are, or in what seats they sit, or what thoughts they now have. It may be they are now at ease, and hear all these things without much disturbance, and are now flattering themselves that they shall escape. If we knew that there was one person, and but one, in the whole congregation, that was to be the subject of this misery, what an awful thing would it be to think of! If we knew who it was, what an awful sight would it be to see such a person! How might all the rest of the congregation lift up a lamentable and bitter cry over him! But alas! instead of one, how many is it likely will remember this discourse in hell? And it would be a wonder if some that are now present should not be in hell in a very short time, before this year is out; and it would be no wonder if some person that now sits here in some seat of this meeting-house, in health, and quiet and secure, should be there before to-morrow morning. . . .

10.

MULTIPLICITY AND ABUNDANCE

Between 1749 and 1754 more than thirty thousand Germans came to Pennsylvania. Soon they came to constitute about one-third of the colony's population. Most Germans coming to America at this time were indentured servants (that is, they were contracted to work for a master for a certain period of time before striking off on their own). They were also known as "redemptioners." To pay for the trip across the Atlantic they sold their labor for a period of two to seven years. On reaching America they "redeemed" themselves by working for a farmer or merchant until they had paid off the debt they had contracted. Slaves were scarce in Pennsylvania, and there was a great demand for redemptioners to work as farm laborers, skilled craftsmen, and domestic servants. Unfortunately, there was much skullduggery in the redemption system. Although redemptioners from England received written contracts or indentures specifying the service they owed, German immigrants received only verbal assurances from shipmasters and merchants as to their future obligations. Once they reached America their labor was auctioned off to the highest bidder, they had nothing to say about their terms of service, and they were often cruelly exploited.

Gottlieb Mittelberger, a native of Württemberg, arrived in Philadelphia late in 1750. He was one of about five hundred passengers aboard the ship **Osgood.** Mittelberger settled in a German community not far from Philadelphia and became organist and schoolmaster there. But less than four years later he returned to Germany, where he spent the rest of his life. In 1756 he published a little volume entitled **Journey to Pennsylvania** describing life in the New World. He filled his book with statistics, geographical information, and anecdotes, but he also had much to say about conditions among German immigrants like himself in America.

Mittelberger was especially critical of "Newlanders" (agents of shipmasters charged with recruiting redemptioners) who traveled about Germany exaggerating the opportunities for immigrants in the "New Land." Not only was Mittelberger distressed by the exploitation of the redemptioners, he was also bothered by the disregard for rank in Pennsylvania, by the laxity in religion, and by the free and easy manners of the backcountry Pennsylvanians whom he encountered. Immigrants from Germany belonged to a variety of religious sects, and in Pennsylvania they were free to practice their religion as they pleased. Mittelberger was struck by the bounteous freedom which the colony offered its in-

habitants, but feared it might jeopardize social stability. Mittelberger's
book did not stop the flow of Germans to America. Though conditions
in America were not as glorious as the Newlanders portrayed them, life
was still considerably better there than in Germany, which was ravaged
by war, famine, and poverty.

Questions to consider. In the following extract from **Journey to
Pennsylvania** Mittelberger recorded his observations of religious and
economic life in Pennsylvania in the early 1750s. What impressed him
the most about religion in the colony? Did he entirely approve of it?
How much economic freedom did he find in the colony? How much
opportunity to get ahead did he think existed there? What comments
did he make on the size of America as compared with that of Europe?
Do you think his overall impression of America was a favorable one?

Journey to Pennsylvania (1756)
Gottlieb Mittelberger

In Pennsylvania there exist so many varieties of doctrines and sects that it is
impossible to name them all. Many people do not reveal their own particular
beliefs to anyone. Furthermore there are many hundreds of adults who not
only are unbaptized, but who do not even want baptism. Many others pay
no attention to the Sacraments and to the Holy Bible, or even to God and His
Word. Some do not even believe in the existence of a true God or Devil,
Heaven or Hell, Salvation or Damnation, the Resurrection of the Dead, the
Last Judgment and Eternal Life, but think that everything visible is of merely
natural origin. For in Pennsylvania not only is everyone allowed to believe
what he wishes; he is also at liberty to express these beliefs publicly and freely.

Thus when young people not raised in the fundamentals of religion must
go into service for many years with such freethinkers and unbelievers and are
not permitted by these people to attend any church or school, especially when
they live far away from them, then such innocent souls do not reach a true
knowledge of the Divine and are brought up like heathen or Indians. . . .

To come back to Pennsylvania again. It offers people more freedom than
the other English colonies, since all religious sects are tolerated there. One can
encounter Lutherans, members of the Reformed Church, Catholics, Quakers,

Reprinted by permission of the publishers from **Journey to Pennsylvania** by Gottlieb Mittelberger,
trans. & ed. by Oscar Handlin, Cambridge, Mass.: The Belknap Press of Harvard University Press,
Copyright © 1960 by the President and Fellows of Harvard College.

Mennonites or Anabaptists, Herrenhüter or Moravian Brothers, Pietists, Seventh-Day Adventists, Dunkers, Presbyterians, New-born, Freemasons, Separatists, Freethinkers, Jews, Mohammedans, Pagans, Negroes, and Indians. But the Evangelicals and the Reformed constitute the majority. There are several hundred unbaptized people who don't even wish to be baptized. Many pray neither in the morning nor in the evening, nor before or after meals. In the homes of such people are not to be found any devotional books, much less a Bible. It is possible to meet in one house, among one family, members of four or five or six different sects.

Freedom in Pennsylvania extends so far that everyone's property—commercial, real estate, and personal possessions—is exempt from any interference or taxation. For owning a hundred morgen [Dutch unit of land] one is assessed an annual tax of not more than one English shilling. This is called ground-rent or quit-rent. One shilling is worth approximately eighteen kreuzer in German money. What is peculiar is that single men and women must pay two to five shillings annually, in proportion to their earnings, the reason for this being that they have none but themselves to look after. In Philadelphia the money raised in this way is used to purchase lights by which the streets of the city are illuminated every night. . . .

In Pennsylvania no profession or craft needs to constitute itself into a guild. Everyone may engage in any commercial or speculative ventures, according to choice and ability. And if someone wishes or is able to carry on ten occupations at one and the same time, then nobody is allowed to prevent it. And if, for example, a lad learns his skill or craft as an apprentice or even on his own, he can then pass for a master and may marry whenever he chooses. It is an admirable thing that young people born in this new country are easily taught, clever, and skillful. For many of them have only to look at and examine a work of skill or art a few times before being able to imitate it perfectly. Whereas in Germany it would take most people several years of study to do the same. But in America many have the ability to produce even the most elaborate objects in a short span of time. When these young people have attended school for half a year, they are generally able to read anything.

The province of Pennsylvania is a healthy one; for the most part it has good soil, good air and water, lots of high mountains, and lots of flat land. There are many woods, and where these are not inhabited, there is natural forest through which flow many small and large rivers. The land is also very fertile, and all kinds of grain flourish.

The province is well populated, inhabited far and wide, and various new towns have been founded here and there, namely Philadelphia, Germantown, Lancaster, Reading, Bethlehem, and New Frankfort. Many churches have also been built in this region, but it takes a great many people two, three, four, five, and up to ten hours to get to church. But everyone, men and women, ride to church on horseback, even though they could walk the distance in half an hour. This is also customary at weddings and funerals. At times at such formal country weddings or funerals, it is possible to count up to four hundred or five hundred persons on horseback. One can easily imagine that on such occasions, just as at Holy Communion, nobody appears in black crepe or in a black cloak. . . .

Concerning the size of America, people in Pennsylvania say that this part of the world is supposed to be far larger than Europe, and that it would be impossible to explore it completely on account of the lack of roads, and because of the forests, and the rivers, great and small. Pennsylvania is not an island, as some simpletons in Germany believe it to be. I took the opportunity of talking about the size of this part of the world with an English traveler, who had been with the savages far inland. He told me that he had been with the Indians in the country, trading for skins and furs, more than 700 miles from Philadelphia, that is a journey of 233 Swabian [Swabia = German duchy] hours. He had spoken about this topic with a very aged Indian who gave him to understand in English that he and his brother had at one time traveled straight across the country and through the bush toward the setting sun, starting out from the very place where the meeting with the English traveler took place. And according to their calculations they had journeyed 1,600 English miles. But when they realized that they had no hope of reaching the end of the country they had turned back again. . . .

In the province of Pennsylvania three principal roads have been constructed, all of which lead from Philadelphia into the country as far as it is inhabited. The first runs from Philadelphia to the right hand by the Delaware to New Frankfort; the second or middle road runs toward Germantown, Reading, and Tulpehocken, extending across the Blue Mountains; the third road runs to the left toward Lancaster and Bethlehem, where there is a monastery and convent full of Dunker Brethren and Sisters. The men do not shave their beards; many among them have beards half an ell [an old English unit of length] in length. They wear cowls like the Capuchin monks, in winter of the same cloth or at least the same color, in summer, however, of fine white linen. The Sisters dress in the same manner. These people are not baptized until they are grown up and can testify to their faith, when it is done by dunking in deep water. They keep Saturdays instead of Sundays as holidays. Their convent Sisters, however, frequently bring forth living fruit with much patience.

11.

COLONIAL WISDOM

Benjamin Franklin was amazingly versatile: he was at various times printer, journalist, editor, educator, satirist, reformer, scientist, inventor, and public servant. He also knew how to make money. His printing business did so well that he was able to retire from active work while in his forties and devote the rest of his life to public service, humanitarian causes, and science and invention. In **Poor Richard's Almanac,** an annual journal containing weather and astronomical information that he published from 1733 to 1758, he scattered mottoes, epigrams, and proverbs throughout every issue making the point that diligence, temperance, moderation, and thrift were prime essentials to worldly success.

The **Way to Wealth,** which Franklin printed in 1758, is a compilation of the best of the sayings from **Poor Richard's Almanac.** All had a similar theme: if you want to succeed in life you must work hard, shun excess, and use your time carefully. Some of the mottoes were invented by Franklin himself, but most of them came from a wide variety of sources, ancient and modern, and were put by him into homespun language that he thought would appeal to his readers. Some of them are still familiar: "Early to bed, and early to rise, makes a man healthy, wealthy, and wise"; "God helps them that help themselves"; "One today is worth two tomorrows." Others are no longer popular, but the point they make is familiar enough: "Keep thy shop and thy shop will keep thee"; "Beware of little expenses; a small leak will sink a great ship"; "Dost thou love life, then do not squander time, for that's the stuff life is made of."

In The **Way to Wealth** Franklin puts all of these mottoes into the mouth of Father Abraham, who preaches the gospel of thrift and industry to a large crowd of people. The tone of the discourse appears to be deadly serious, even stuffy, throughout. But when Father Abraham finishes, Franklin tells us, tongue in cheek, the people "approved the Doctrine and immediately practiced the contrary, just as if it had been a common Sermon." Still, when he was a young man, Franklin lived very much by the rules he sets forth in his book, and he thought other people could get ahead in life the way he did if they also practiced these virtues.

Franklin surely knew something about rising in the world. Born in Boston in 1706, the son of a candlemaker, he was apprenticed to his brother, a printer, at the age of twelve. At seventeen, having mastered the trade, Franklin ran away to Philadelphia and soon established a thriving printing establishment of his own. Not only did he become famous as a writer and publisher, he also became active in civic affairs (he founded a fire department, a library, and a scientific society in Philadelphia) and in politics (he represented the colonies in England from 1757 to 1775 and served as minister to France during the war for independence). For his pioneering work in the field of electricity he was as famous in Europe as in America. In his **Autobiography,** which he wrote for his son in 1777, he dwelt on his early years, in order, he said, to make it "of more general use to young readers, as exemplifying strongly the effects of prudent and imprudent conduct in the commencement of a life of business." He continued active until his death in 1790, becoming president of the executive council of Pennsylvania at the age of seventy-nine and representing his state in the Constitutional Convention, which met in Philadelphia in 1787.

Questions to consider. What did Franklin say about his "Brother Authors" at the beginning of **The Way to Wealth**? What did he mean by "solid Pudding"? How does Father Abraham respond to the people's complaints about taxes? What does he consider the "greatest Prodigality?" How much truth is there in his contention that industrious people "shall never starve"? What is his attitude toward leisure? Why does he link frugality so closely with diligence? How do the goals presented by Franklin compare with those outlined by John Winthrop on the **Arbella** (Document 4)? How much validity do you think there is in Father Abraham's outlook on life? In what way is **The Way to Wealth** one of the first do-it-yourself books printed in America?

═══════

The Way to Wealth (1758)
Benjamin Franklin

I have heard that nothing gives an Author so great Pleasure, as to find his Works respectfully quoted by other learned Authors. This Pleasure I have seldom enjoyed; for tho' I have been, if I may say it without Vanity, an *eminent Author* of Almanacks annually now a full Quarter of a Century, my Brother Authors in the same Way, for what Reason I know not, have ever been very sparing in their Applauses, and no other Author has taken the least Notice of me, so that did not my Writings produce me some solid *Pudding,* the great Deficiency of *Praise* would have quite discouraged me. . . .

Judge, then, how much I must have been gratified by an Incident I am going to relate to you. I stopt my Horse lately where a great Number of

From Albert Henry Smyth, ed., **The Writings of Benjamin Franklin** (9 v., Haskell House, New York, 1907), III: 407–418.

People were collected at a Vendue of Merchant Goods. The House of Sale not being come, they were conversing on the Badness of the Times and one of the Company call'd to a plain clean old Man, with white Locks, "Pray, Father Abraham, what think you of the Times? Won't these heavy Taxes quite ruin the Country? How shall we be ever able to pay them? What would you advise us to?" Father *Abraham* stood up, and reply'd, "If you'd have my Advice, I'll give it to you in short, for *A Word to the Wise is enough, and many Words won't fill a Bushel,* as *Poor Richard* says." They join'd in desiring him to speak his Mind, and gathering round him he proceeded as follows:

"Friends," says he, "and Neighbours, the Taxes are indeed very heavy. *Poor Richard* says, *the greatest Prodigality;* since as he elsewhere tells us, and if those laid on by the Government were the only Ones we had to pay, we might more easily discharge them; but we have many others, and much more grievous to some of us. We are taxed twice as much by our Idleness, three times as much by our *Pride,* and four times as much by our *Folly;* and from these Taxes the Commissioners cannot ease or deliver us by allowing an Abatement. However let us hearken to good Advice, and something may be done for us; *God helps them that help themselves,* as *Poor Richard says,* in his Almanack of 1733.

It would be thought a hard Government that should tax its People one-tenth Part of their *Time,* to be employed in its Service, But *Idleness* taxes many of us much more, if we reckon all that is spent in absolute *Sloth,* or doing of nothing, with that which is spent in idle Employment or Amusements that amount to nothing. *Sloth,* by bringing on Diseases, absolutely shortens life. *Sloth, like Rust, consumes faster than Labour wears; while the used key is always bright,* as *Poor Richard* says. *But dost thou love Life, then do not squander Time, for that's the stuff Life is made of,* as *Poor Richard* says. How much more than is necessary do we spend in sleep, forgetting that *The sleeping Fox catches no Poultry,* and that *There will be sleeping enough in the Grave,* as *Poor Richard* says.

If Time be of all Things the most precious, wasting Time must be, as *Poor Richard* says, *the greatest Prodigality;* since, as he elsewhere tells us, *Lost Time is never found again; and what we call Time enough, always proves little enough:* Let us then up and be doing, and doing to the Purpose; so by Diligence shall we do more with less Perplexity. *Sloth makes all Things difficult, but Industry all easy,* as *Poor Richard* says; and *He that riseth late must trot all Day, and shall scarce overtake his Business at Night;* while *Laziness travels so slowly, that Poverty soon overtakes him,* as we read in *Poor Richard,* who adds, *Drive thy Business, let not that drive thee;* and *Early to Bed, and early to rise, makes a Man healthy, wealthy, and wise.*

So what signifies *wishing* and *hoping* for better Times. We may make these Times better, if we bestir ourselves. . . . If we are industrious, we shall never starve; for, as *Poor Richard* says, *At the working Man's House Hunger looks in, but dares not enter.* Nor will the Bailiff or the Constable enter, for *Industry pays Debts, while Despair encreaseth them,* says *Poor Richard.* What though you have found no Treasure, nor has any rich Relation left you a Legacy, *Diligence is the Mother of Good-luck* as *Poor Richard* says *and God gives all Things to Industry.*

Then plough deep, while sluggards sleep, and you shall have Corn to sell and to keep,
says *Poor Dick*. Work while it is called To-day, for you know not how much
you may be hindered To-morrow, which makes *Poor Richard* say, *One to-day
is worth two To-morrows,* and farther *Have you somewhat to do To-morrow, do it
To-day.* If you were a Servant, would you not be ashamed that a good Master
should catch you idle? Are you then your own Master, *be ashamed to catch
yourself idle,* as *Poor Dick* says. When there is so much to be done for yourself,
your Family, your Country, and your gracious King, be up by Peep of Day. . . .

So much for Industry, my Friends, and Attention to one's own Business;
but to these we must add *Frugality*, if we would make our *Industry* more
certainly successful. A Man may, if he knows not how to save as he gets, *keep
his Nose all his Life to the Grindstone,* and die not worth a *Groat* at last. *A fat
Kitchen makes a lean Will,* as *Poor Richard* says; and

> *Many Estates are spent in the Getting,*
> *Since Women for Tea forsook Spinning and Knitting,*
> *And Men for Punch forsook Hewing and Splitting.*

If you would be wealthy, says he, in another Almanack, *think of Saving as well
as of Getting: The Indies have not made Spain rich, because her Outgoes are greater
than her Incomes.*

Away then with your expensive Follies, and you will not then have so
much Cause to complain of hard Times, heavy Taxes, and chargeable
Families; for, as *Poor Dick* says,

> *Women and Wine, Game and Deceit,*
> *Make the Wealth small and the Wants great.*

And farther, *What maintains one Vice, would bring up two Children.* You may
think perhaps that a *little* Tea, or a *little* Punch now and then, Diet a *little* more
costly, Clothes a *little* finer, and a *little* Entertainment now and then, can be
no *great* Matter; but remember what *Poor Richard* says, *Many a Little makes a
Mickle;* and farther, *Beware of little Expences; A small Leak will sink a great Ship;*
and again, *Who Dainties love, shall Beggars prove;* and moreover, *Fools make
Feasts, and wise Men eat them.*

Here you are all got together at this Vendue of *Fineries* and *Knicknacks.*
You call them *Goods;* but if you do not take Care, they will prove *Evils* to
some of you. You expect they will be sold *cheap,* and perhaps they may for
less than they cost; but if you have no Occasion for them, they must be *dear*
to you. Remember what *Poor Richard* says; *Buy what thou hast no Need of, and
ere long thou shalt sell thy Necessaries.* . . . Many a one, for the Sake of Finery
on the Back, have gone with a hungry Belly, and half-starved their Families.
Silks and Satins, Scarlet and Velvets, as *Poor Richard* says, *put out the Kitchen Fire.*

These are not the *Necessaries* of Life; they can scarcely be called the *Con-
veniences;* and yet only because they look pretty, how many *want* to *have* them!

Poor Richard, **1733.**

A N

Almanack

For the Year of Chrift

1733,

Being the Firft after LEAP YEAR:

And makes fince the Creation	Years
By the Account of the Eastern _Greeks_	7241
By the Latin Church, when ☉ ent. ♈	6932
By the Computation of _W. W._	5742
By the _Roman_ Chronology	5682
By the _Jewish_ Rabbies	5494

Wherein is contained

The Lunations, Eclipfes, Judgment of the Weather, Spring Tides, Planets Motions & mutual Afpects, Sun and Moon's Rifing and Setting, Length of Days, Time of High Water, Fairs, Courts, and obfervable Days.

Fitted to the Latitude of Forty Degrees, and a Meridian of Five Hours Weft from _London,_ but may without fenfible Error, ferve all the adjacent Places, even from _Newfoundland_ to _South-Carolina._

By _RICHARD SAUNDERS_, Philom.

PHILADELPHIA:
Printed and fold by _B. FRANKLIN_, at the New Printing-Office near the Market.

Poor Richard, 1733. An Almanac.   Just about every colonial household acquired an almanac: a little paperbound book published at the end of each year containing weather forecasts, recipes, jokes, poems, and proverbs. Franklin entered the field in December 1732 with **Poor Richard, 1733,** which sold for five-pence a copy. **Poor Richard** was an immediate success; soon it was doing better than all the other almanacs being sold, in great measure because of the character, Richard Saunders, that Franklin created. Poor Richard entertained his readers with pithy maxims, homely little poems, and witty remarks. He also regaled them with stories about his quarrels with his wife Bridget. (Library of Congress)

The *artificial* Wants of Mankind thus become more numerous than the *Natural;* and, as *Poor Dick* says, *for one poor Person, there are an hundred indigent.* By these, and other Extravagancies, the Genteel are reduced to poverty, and forced to borrow of those whom they formerly despised, but who through Industry and Frugality have maintained their Standing; in which Case it appears plainly, that *A Ploughman on his Legs is higher than a Gentleman on his Knees,* as *Poor Richard* says. . . .

> *Fond Pride of Dress is sure a very Curse;*
> *E'er Fancy you consult, consult your Purse.*

And again, *Pride is as loud a Beggar as Want, and a great deal more saucy.* When you have bought one fine Thing, you must buy ten more, that your Appearance may be all of a Piece; but *Poor Dick* says, *'Tis easier to suppress the first Desire, than to satisfy all that follow it.* And 'tis as truly Folly for the Poor to ape the Rich, as for the Frog to swell in order to equal the ox.

> *Great Estates may venture more,*
> *But little Boats should keep near shore.*

'Tis, however, a Folly soon punished; for *Pride that dines on Vanity, sups on Contempt,* as *Poor Richard* says. And in another Place, *Pride breakfasted with Plenty, dined with Poverty, and supped with Infamy.* And after all, of what Use is this *Pride of Appearance,* for which so much is risked so much is suffered? It cannot promote Health, or ease Pain; it makes no Increase of Merit in the Person, it creates Envy, it hastens Misfortune.

> *What is a Butterfly? At best*
> *He's but a Caterpillar drest.*
> *The gaudy Fop's his Picture just.*

as *Poor Richard* says.

But what Madness must it be to *run in Debt* for these Super-Fluities! We are offered, by the Terms of this Vendue, *Six Months' Credit;* and that perhaps has induced some of us to attend it, because we cannot spare the ready Money, and hope now to be fine without it. But, ah, think what you do when you run in Debt; *you give to another Power over your Liberty.* If you cannot pay at the Time, you will be ashamed to see your Creditor; you will be in Fear when you speak to him; you will make poor pitiful sneaking Excuses, and by Degrees come to lose your Veracity, and sink into base downright lying; for, as *Poor Richard* says, *The second Vice is Lying, the first is running in Debt.* And again, to the same Purpose, *Lying rides upon Debt's Back.* Whereas a free-born *Englishman* ought not to be ashamed or afraid to see or speak to any Man living. But Poverty often deprives a Man of all Spirit and Virtue: *'Tis hard for an empty Bag to stand upright,* as *Poor Richard* truly says."

12.

A SHATTERED EMPIRE

On June 7, 1776, Richard Henry Lee, delegate from Virginia to the Second Continental Congress meeting in Philadelphia, proposed a resolution calling for independence from Great Britain. Three days later Congress appointed a committee of five to prepare a statement giving reasons for independence. The committee appointed a subcommittee, consisting of John Adams and Thomas Jefferson, to draft such a statement. The sub-committee met, according to Adams, and Jefferson suggested that Adams write up a statement. "I will not," said Adams emphatically. "You should do it," said Jefferson. "Oh, no," persisted Adams. "Why will you not?" asked Jefferson. "You ought to do it." "I will not," said Adams stubbornly. "Why?" cried Jefferson. "Reasons enough," said Adams. "What can be your reasons?" Jefferson wanted to know. Explained Adams: "Reason first—you are a Virginian, and a Virginian ought to appear at the head of this business. Reason second—I am obnoxious, suspected, and unpopular. You are very much otherwise. Reason third— you can write ten times better than I can." "Well," said Jefferson, "if you are decided, I will do as well as I can." In the end, Jefferson wrote the Great Declaration, minor changes being made by Adams and Franklin, and after the Continental Congress made some additional changes in it, the delegates voted to adopt it on July 4. Two days earlier Congress had accepted Lee's resolution for independence. But July 4, not July 2, soon became the great day for patriotic celebrations.

Jefferson's "peculiar felicity of expression," according to John Adams, made him the ideal choice for writing the Declaration. In simple, lucid, logical language, Jefferson explained to the world what he thought the American people were fighting for: to establish a government based, not on force and fraud, but on the freely given consent of the people and dedicated to safeguarding the basic rights of all citizens. Jefferson's Declaration made it clear that the American Revolution was more than a fight for independence. "Take away from the Declaration of Independence its self-evident truths," said Adams, "and you rob the North American Revolution of all its moral principles, and proclaim it a foul and unnatural rebellion." After the United States achieved its independence in 1783, the Declaration continued to inspire countless reformers seeking to make their country a better place in which to live: abolitionists, feminists, farmers, and working people. The Declaration also influenced reformers and revolutionaries in other parts of the world—Europe, Asia, and Africa—during the nineteenth and twentieth centuries.

Questions to consider. In 1858, when Massachusetts lawyer Rufus Choate contemptuously dismissed the Declaration as a collection of "glittering generalities," Ralph Waldo Emerson exclaimed indignantly: "Glittering generalities! Say, rather, blazing ubiquities!" Do you agree with Choate or with Emerson? What are the main generalities set forth in the first two paragraphs of the Declaration? How valid do you think Jefferson's assertions are about equality, "unalienable Rights," and the right of the people to "alter or abolish" their governments? How much prudence do you think the Founding Fathers exercised in their decision to fight for independence? What were Jefferson's major charges against King George III? Do you think he was successful in his attempt to make a long list of abuses and usurpations by the king? Was he fair in blaming the king for all of these abuses and usurpations? Why did he attack the king and avoid any mention of Parliament? What did he say about the English people and why? Do you find any inconsistencies or omissions in the Declaration? Would you sign the Declaration of Independence today?

The Declaration of Independence (1776)

When in the Course of human events, it becomes necessary for one people to dissolve the political bands which have connected them with another, and to assume among the Powers of the earth, the separate and equal station to which the Laws of Nature and of Nature's God entitle them, a decent respect to the opinions of mankind requires that they should declare the causes which impel them to the separation.

We hold these truths to be self-evident, that all men are created equal, that they are endowed by their Creator with certain unalienable Rights, that among these are Life, Liberty and the pursuit of Happiness. That to secure these rights, Governments are instituted among Men, deriving their just powers from the consent of the governed. That whenever any Form of Government becomes destructive of these ends, it is the Right of the People to alter or to abolish it, and to institute new Government, laying its foundation on such principles and organizing its powers in such form, as to them shall seem most likely to effect their Safety and Happiness. Prudence, indeed, will dictate that Governments long established should not be changed for light and transient causes; and accordingly all experience hath shown, that mankind are more disposed to suffer, while evils are sufferable, than to right themselves by abolishing the forms to which they are accustomed. But when a long train of abuses and usurpations, pursuing invariably the same Object evinces a

From F. N. Thorpe, ed., *The Federal and State Constitutions* (7 v., Government Printing Office, Washington, D.C., 1909), I: 3.

design to reduce them under absolute Despotism, it is their right, it is their duty, to throw off such Government, and to provide new Guards for their future security.—Such has been the patient sufferance of these Colonies; and such is now the necessity which constrains them to alter their former Systems of Government. The history of the present King of Great Britain is a history of repeated injuries and usurpations, all having in direct object the establishment of an absolute Tyranny over these States. To prove this, let Facts be submitted to a candid world.

He has refused his Assent to Laws, the most wholesome and necessary for the public good.

He has forbidden his Governors to pass Laws of immediate and pressing importance, unless suspended in their operation till his Assent should be obtained; and when so suspended, he has utterly neglected to attend to them.

He has refused to pass other Laws for the accommodation of large districts of people, unless those people would relinquish the rights of Representation in the Legislature, a right inestimable to them and formidable to tyrants only.

He has called together legislative bodies at places unusual, uncomfortable, and distant from the depository of their Public Records, for the sole purpose of fatiguing them into compliance with his measures.

He has dissolved Representative Houses repeatedly, for opposing with manly firmness his invasions on the rights of the people.

He has refused for a long time, after such dissolutions, to cause others to be elected; whereby the Legislative Powers, incapable of Annihilation, have returned to the People at large for their exercise; the State remaining in the mean time exposed to all the dangers of invasion from without, and convulsions within.

He has endeavored to prevent the population of these States; for that purpose obstructing the Laws of Naturalization of Foreigners; refusing to pass others to encourage their migration hither, and raising the conditions of new Appropriations of Lands.

He has obstructed the Administration of Justice, by refusing his Assent to Laws for establishing Judiciary Powers.

He has made Judges dependent on his Will alone, for the tenure of their offices, and the amount and payment of their salaries.

He has erected a multitude of New Offices, and sent hither swarms of Officers to harass our People, and eat out their substance.

He has kept among us, in times of peace, Standing Armies without the Consent of our legislature.

He has affected to render the Military independent of and superior to the Civil Power.

He has combined with others to subject us to a jurisdiction foreign to our constitution, and unacknowledged by our laws; giving his Assent to their acts of pretended legislation:

For quartering large bodies of armed troops among us:

For protecting them, by a mock Trial, from Punishment for any Murders which they should commit on the Inhabitants of these States:

The Second Continental Congress. In this unfinished engraving by Edward Savage, Thomas Jefferson places his draft of the Declaration of Independence on a table in Mechanics Hall, Philadelphia. Around "Long Tom" are the other members of the drafting committee: John Adams, Roger Sherman, Robert Livingston, and (seated) Benjamin Franklin. Undetectable amid the stiff postures and proper clothing of Savage's delegates was the sweltering heat of Philadelphia in mid-July, made even worse than usual because the doors and windows were often shut in the interests of confidentiality. (American Antiquarian Society)

For cutting off our Trade with all parts of the world:

For imposing taxes on us without our Consent:

For depriving us in many cases, of the benefits of Trial by Jury:

For transporting us beyond Seas to be tried for pretended offences:

For abolishing the free System of English Laws in a neighbouring Province, establishing therein an Arbitrary government, and enlarging its Boundaries so as to render it at once an example and fit instrument for introducing the same absolute rule into these Colonies:

For taking away our Charters, abolishing our most valuable Laws, and altering fundamentally the Forms of our Governments:

For suspending our own Legislature, and declaring themselves invested with Power to legislate for us in all cases whatsoever.

He has abdicated Government here, by declaring us out of his Protection and waging War against us.

He has plundered our seas, ravaged our Coasts, burnt our towns, and destroyed the lives of our people.

He is at this time transporting large armies of foreign mercenaries to compleat the works of death, desolation and tyranny, already begun with circumstances of Cruelty & perfidy scarcely paralleled in the most barbarous ages, and totally unworthy the Head of a civilized nation.

He has constrained our fellow Citizens taken Captive on the high Seas to bear Arms against their Country, to become the executioners of their friends and Brethren, or to fall themselves by their Hands.

He has excited domestic insurrections amongst us, and has endeavoured to bring on the inhabitants of our frontiers, the merciless Indian Savages, whose known rule of warfare, is an undistinguished destruction of all ages, sexes and conditions.

In every state of these Oppressions We have Petitioned for Redress in the most humble terms: Our repeated Petitions have been answered only by repeated injury. A Prince, whose character is thus marked by every act which may define a Tyrant, is unfit to be the ruler of a free People.

Nor have We been wanting in attention to our British brethren. We have warned them from time to time of attempts by their legislature to extend an unwarrantable jurisdiction over us. We have reminded them of the circumstances of our emigration and settlement here. We have appealed to their native justice and magnanimity, and we have conjured them by the ties of our common kindred to disavow these usurpations, which, would inevitably interrupt our connections and correspondence. They too have been deaf to the voice of justice and of consanguinity. We must, therefore, acquiesce in the necessity, which denounces our Separation, and hold them, as we hold the rest of mankind, Enemies in War, in Peace Friends.

We, therefore, the Representatives of the united States of America, in General Congress, Assembled, appealing to the Supreme Judge of the world for the rectitude of our intentions, do, in the Name, and by Authority of the good People of these Colonies, solemnly publish and declare, That these United Colonies are, and of Right ought to be Free and Independent States; that they are Absolved from all Allegiance to the British Crown, and that all political connection between them and the State of Great Britain, is and ought to be totally dissolved; and that as Free and Independent States, they have full Power to levy War, conclude Peace, contract Alliances, establish Commerce, and to do all other Acts and Things which Independent States may of right do. And for the support of this Declaration, with a firm reliance on the Protection of Divine Providence, we mutually pledge to each other our Lives, our Fortunes and our Sacred Honor.

13.

IDEOLOGY AND AGITATION

On December 18, 1776, George Washington wrote to his brother discouragedly: "Between you and me, I think our affairs are in a very bad situation. . . . If every nerve is not strained up to the utmost to recruit the new army with all possible expedition, I think the game is up." A few days later Thomas Paine published the first number of **The Crisis,** a pamphlet calling attention to the heartbreaking difficulties the Americans faced in their struggle with Britain and appealing for renewed dedication to the Revolutionary cause. Paine said he wrote in "a passion of patriotism." His essay quickly "rallied and reanimated" the people, according to one observer, and before long "hope succeeded to despair, cheerfulness to gloom, and firmness to irresolution." In twelve more issues of **The Crisis** Paine continued his impassioned fight against apathy, indifference, and defeatism in American ranks. He also wrote additional numbers about American problems after the Yorktown victory in 1781.

Paine, a British corset maker and excise officer, was an ardent supporter of the American cause from almost the beginning. Shortly after arriving in Philadelphia in November 1774, he became editor of the **Pennsylvania Magazine,** discovered he had great gifts as a journalist, and in January 1776 published a little pamphlet entitled **Common Sense** urging Americans to convert their resistance to British oppression into a fight for national independence. Before long thousands of copies of his pamphlet were circulating in the colonies, and Washington arranged to have passages from it read to his troops. The first best seller in history, **Common Sense** persuaded many Americans who were wavering that separation from Britain was both possible and desirable.

Paine pioneered in a new kind of journalism. He avoided the elegant and ornate writing fashionable in aristocratic circles and wrote simply, naturally, and forcefully. He used homely metaphors, introduced everyday words and phrases into his essays, translated foreign phrases for his readers, interspersed his logical arguments with lively anecdotes, and brought a sense of immediacy to his writings by including personal, on-the-spot reports. He was, in short, writing for the plain people from whom he himself had come. His influence on the thinking of countless people was enormous.

Paine, born in England of Quaker parents in 1737, lived in obscurity until he came to America in 1774. He became editor of the **Pennsylvania Magazine** and quickly identified himself with the American cause. After the American Revolution he went to France, supported the revolution that broke out there in 1789, and published **The Rights of Man** (1791–

1792), a work defending the principles of the French Revolution. He also wrote **The Age of Reason** (1793–1795), criticizing both atheism and orthodox Christianity and calling for a religion based on reason. Though sympathetic to the French Revolution, Paine opposed the execution of King Louis XVI and was appalled by the Reign of Terror that accompanied the Revolution. In the end he was thrown in prison and sentenced to the guillotine, but he was saved by the intervention of the American minister in France, James Monroe. In 1802 Paine returned to America; but his religious radicalism and attacks he had made on George Washington for not being revolutionary enough made him an outcast. He died in New York, lonely, poverty-stricken, and largely forgotten, in 1809.

Questions to consider. Paine is eminently quotable. Do you find any passages in the essay that seem especially eloquent? Do you think Paine's appeal rests on substance as well as style? How did he attempt to whip up enthusiasm for the American cause? Do you think his handling of "tories," that is, Americans who were sympathetic to Britain, was effective? Was he fair? In these excerpts, as in all the numbers of **The Crisis,** Paine seems to write about the Quakers with particular venom. Were there strategic reasons for his concerns? Does his language suggest other, perhaps personal, motives? What parts of this essay might George Washington have chosen to read to his troops?

━━━━━━

The Crisis, Number Three (1777)
Thomas Paine

The principal arguments in support of independence may be comprehended under the four following heads.

First,—the natural right of the continent to independence.

Secondly,—Her interest in being independent.

Thirdly,—The necessity,—and

Fourthly,—The moral advantages arising therefrom.

I. The natural right of the continent to independence, is a point which never yet was called in question. It will not even admit of a debate. To deny such a right, would be a kind of atheism against nature: And the best answer to such an objection would be, *"The fool hath said in his heart, there is no God."*

From Daniel E. Wheeler, ed., **Life and Writings of Thomas Paine** (10 v., V. Parke and Co., New York, 1915), III: 32–44.

II. The interest of the continent in being independent is a point as clearly right as the former. America, by her own internal industry, and unknown to all the powers of Europe, was at the beginning of the dispute, arrived at a pitch of greatness, trade and population, beyond which it was the interest of Britain not to suffer her to pass, lest she should grow too powerful to be kept subordinate. She began to view this country with the same uneasy malicious eye, with which a covetous guardian would view his ward whose estate he had been enriching himself by for twenty years, and saw him just arriving at manhood. And America owes no more to Britain for her present maturity, than the ward would to his guardian for being twenty-one years of age. That America hath flourished *at the time* she was under the government of Britain, is true; but there is every natural reason to believe, that had she been an independent country from the first settlement thereof, uncontrouled by any foreign power, free to make her own laws, regulate and encourage her own commerce, she had by this time been of much greater worth than now. The case is simply this, The first settlers in the different colonies were left to shift for themselves, unnoticed and unsupported by any European government; but as the tyranny and persecution of the old world daily drove numbers to the new, and, as by the favor of Heaven on their industry and perseverance, they grew into importance, so, in a like degree, they became an object of profit to the greedy eyes of Europe. It was impossible in this state of infancy, however thriving and promising, that they could resist the power of any armed invader that should seek to bring them under his authority. In this situation Britain thought it worth her while to claim them, and the continent received and acknowledged the claimer. It was, in reality, of no very great importance who was her master, seeing, that from the force and ambition of the different powers of Europe she must, till she acquired strength enough to assert her own right, acknowledge some one. As well, perhaps, Britain as another; and it might have been as well to have been under the states of Holland as any. The same hopes of engrossing and profiting by her trade, by not oppressing it too much, would have operated alike with any master, and produced to the colonies the same effects. The clamor of protection, likewise, was all a farce; because, in order to make *that* protection necessary, she must first, by her own quarrels create us enemies. Hard terms, indeed! . . .

III. The necessity, likewise, of being independent, even before it was declared, became so evident and important, that the continent ran the risk of being ruined every day she delayed it. There were reasons to believe that Britain would endeavor to make an European matter of it, and rather than lose the whole, would dismember it like Poland, and dispose of her several claims to the highest bidder. . . . We had no credit abroad, because of our rebellious dependency. Our ships could claim no protection in foreign ports, because we afforded them no justifiable reason for granting it to us. The calling ourselves subjects, and at the same time fighting against the power we acknowledged, was a dangerous precedent to all Europe. If the grievances justified taking up arms, they justified our separation; if they did not justify our separation, neither could they justify our taking up arms. All Europe was interested in reducing us as rebels, and all Europe (or the greatest part at least) is interested in supporting us as independent states. . . .

IV. But, what weigh most with all men of serious reflection are the MORAL ADVANTAGES arising from independence: War and desolation are become the trades of the old world; and America neither could, nor can be under the government of Britain without becoming a sharer of her guilt, and a partner in all the dismal commerce of death. The spirit of duelling, extended on a national scale, is a proper character for European wars. They have seldom any other motive than pride, or any other object than fame. The conquerors and the conquered are generally ruined alike, and the chief difference at last is, that the one marches home with his honors, and the other without them. 'Tis the natural temper of the English to fight for a feather, if they suppose *that feather* to be an affront; and America, without the right of asking why, must have abetted in every quarrel and abided by its fate. It is a shocking situation to live in, that one country must be brought into all the wars of another, whether the measure be right or wrong, or whether she will or not; yet this, in the fullest extent, was, and ever would be, the unavoidable consequence of the connection. Surely! the Quakers forgot their own principles, when in their late testimony they called *this connection* with these military and miserable appendages hanging to it, *"The happy constitution."* . . .

On the whole, if the future expulsion of arms from one quarter of the world be a desirable object to a peaceable man;—if the freedom of trade to every part of it can engage the attention of a man of business;—if the support or fall of millions of currency can affect our interest;—if the entire possession of estates, by cutting off the lordly claims of Britain over the soil, deserves the regard of landed property;—and if the right of making our own laws, uncontrouled by royal or ministerial spies or mandates, be worthy our care as freemen;—then are all men interested in the support of independence; and may he that supports it not, be driven from the blessing, and live unpitied beneath the servile sufferings of scandalous subjection! . . .

We may not, perhaps, be wise enough to make all the advantages we ought of our independence; but they are, nevertheless, marked and presented to us with every character of GREAT and GOOD, and worthy the hand of Him who sent them. I look through the present trouble to a time of tranquility, when we shall have it in our power to set an example of peace to all the world. Were the Quakers really impressed and influenced by the quiet principles they profess to hold, they would, however they might disapprove the means, be the first of all men to approve of INDEPENDENCE, because, by separating from the cities of Sodom and Gomorrah, it affords an opportunity, never given to man before, of carrying their favorite principle of peace into general practice, by establishing governments that shall hereafter exist without wars. Oh ye fallen cringing priest and Pemberton-ridden people! what more can we say of ye than that a religious Quaker is a valuable character, and a political Quaker a real Jesuit. . . .[1]

I find it impossible in the small compass I am limited to, to trace out the progress which independence has made on the minds of the different classes of men, and the several reasons by which they were moved. With some, it was a passionate abhorrence against the king of England and his ministry, as a set of savages and brutes; and these men, governed by the agony of a wounded mind, were for trusting every thing to hope and Heaven, and bidding defiance at once. With others, it was a growing conviction that the scheme of the British court was to create, ferment and drive on a quarrel for the sake of confiscated plunder: Men of this cast ripened into independence in proportion as the evidence increased. While a third class, conceived it was the true interest of America, internally and externally, to be her own master, gave their support to independence, step by step, as they saw her abilities to maintain it enlarge. With many, it was a compound of all these reasons; while those who were too callous to be reached by either, remained, and still remain tories. . . .

The principal causes why independence has not been so universally supported as it ought, are *fear* and *indolence,* and the causes why it has been opposed, are, *avarice, downright villainy,* and *lust of personal power.* There is not such a being in America, as a tory from conscience; some secret defect or other is interwoven in the character of all those, be they men or women, who can look with patience on the brutality, luxury and debauchery of the British court, and the violations of their army here. A woman's virtue must sit very lightly on her who can even hint a favorable sentiment in their behalf. It is remarkable that the whole race of prostitutes in New-York were tories; and the schemes for supporting the tory cause, in this city, for which several are now in gaol, and one hanged, were concerted and carried on in common baudy-houses, assisted by those who kept them. . . .

Our support and success depend on such a variety of men and circumstances, that every one, who does but wish well, is of some use: There are men who have a strange awkwardness to arms, yet have hearts to risk every shilling in the cause, or in support of those who have better talents for defending it. Nature, in the arrangement of mankind, has fitted some for every service in life: Were all soldiers, all would starve and go naked, and were none soldiers, all would be slaves. As *disaffection* to independence is the badge of a tory, so *affection* to it is the mark of a whig [one opposed to royal authority and English rule]; and the different services of the whigs down from those who nobly contribute every thing, to those who have nothing to render but their wishes, tend all to the same centre, though with different degrees of merit and ability. The larger we make the circle, the more we shall harmonize,

---

[1] Israel Pemberton was a Quaker merchant in Philadelphia who opposed the break with England. Among Protestants, Jesuits were considered devious schemers.—Eds.

and the stronger we shall be. All we want to shut out, is disaffection, and, *that excluded,* we must accept from each other such duties as we are best fitted to bestow. A narrow system of politics, like a narrow system of religion, is calculated only to sour the temper, and live at variance with mankind.

All we want to know in America is simply this, who is for independence, and who is not? Those who are for it, will support it, and the remainder will undoubtedly see the reasonableness of their paying the charges; while those who oppose or seek to betray it, must expect the more rigid fate of the gaol and the gibbit [gallows].

14.

SECURING LIBERTY

In May 1787 delegates from every state except Rhode Island met in Philadelphia to revise the Articles of Confederation. But they disregarded their instructions; by mid-September they had drawn up an entirely new frame of government for the nation that had achieved its independence in 1783. The Constitutional Convention was a distinguished gathering; the states sent their ablest men to Philadelphia. George Washington was there; so were Benjamin Franklin, Alexander Hamilton, and James Madison. For many weeks the delegates labored mightily to construct a constitution that would "form a more perfect union" without jeopardizing liberty. In September they completed their work and submitted the Constitution to the states for ratification. At once a great debate commenced. In countless essays, editorials, pamphlets, and handbills the American people discussed the merits and defects of the new instrument of government offered for their consideration. The most famous of all the commentaries on the Constitution appeared in **The Federalist.**

The Federalist Papers consist of eighty-five essays appearing in various New York newspapers between October 1787 and August 1788. Hamilton, who had taken part in the Constitutional Convention, wrote the major portion of them; but James Madison, whose diligence in Philadelphia won him the nickname "Father of the Constitution," wrote a sizable number as well. John Jay, author of the New York State Constitution of 1777, also wrote a few. The essays, which were soon published in book form, discussed the weakness of the Confederation, the powers assigned to the federal government in the new Constitution and the organization of these powers into legislative, executive, and judicial branches of government, and the safeguards that were built into the Constitution to prevent oppression. Thomas Jefferson, who was in Paris at the time as minister to France, wrote to say he read the **Papers** with "care, pleasure, and improvement" and called them the "best commentary on the principles of government which was ever written."

The immediate impact of **The Federalist Papers** was probably not great. Most of the states had completed ratification before many of the essays were published. But the essays may have helped persuade New York and Virginia to ratify the Constitution, and their long-range influence has been profound. Since their first appearance the **Papers** have become a classic of political science. Scholars, legislators, judges, and Supreme Court justices have looked to them time and again for clues to understanding the Constitution that was accepted by the states in 1788. After the Declaration of Independence and the Constitution they are the nation's most important political statement. **The Federalist, Number Ten,** written by Madison, is perhaps the most famous. In it, Madison points out the inevitability of conflicts of interest (particularly economic interest) in free societies and insists that representative government can keep these conflicts from getting out of hand and endangering both private rights and the public good.

James Madison, son of a Virginia planter, was born in Port Conway, Virginia, in 1751, and attended the College of New Jersey (now Princeton). In 1776 he helped frame Virginia's constitution and declaration of rights. Between 1780 and 1783 he was a member of the Continental Congress; after the Revolution he served in Virginia's House of Delegates, where he sponsored legislation to disestablish the Anglican church and provide for religious freedom. As a member of Virginia's delegation to the Philadelphia convention in 1787 he played a major role in shaping the Constitution that was finally adopted; his notes on the debates are our main source for information about what was discussed at the convention. As a member of the First Congress under Washington he sponsored legislation establishing the State, Treasury, and War Departments and also introduced the first ten amendments to the Constitution (the Bill of Rights) into the House of Representatives. For eight years he served as Thomas Jefferson's secretary of state and succeeded him as president in 1809. His own presidency was a stormy one. Though a man of peace he presided over the controversial War of 1812 with Britain ("Mr. Madison's War"), which ended with a treaty settling none of the outstanding disputes between the two countries. While he was president the Republican party gradually accepted the economic program once sponsored by Hamilton and opposed by Jefferson: a second Bank of the United States, a protective tariff, and a large funded debt. In 1817, Madison retired to his estate at Montpelier to manage his farm, pursue his studies, advise James Monroe, his successor in the White House, and warn against disunion. He died in 1836 at the age of eighty-five.

Questions to consider. In the extract from **The Federalist,** Number Ten, presented below, Madison's argument is carefully organized and closely reasoned and shows great insight into the workings of social groups. Madison began by singling out factions as the chief problem confronting free nations like the United States. How did he define **faction**? He said there are two ways to prevent factions from forming. What are they? Why did he reject both of them? What did he mean by saying that the "latent causes of faction" are found in human nature? Do you think he was right in his statement that "the most common and durable source of factions has been the various and unequal distribution of property"? What examples did he give of various propertied interests? Madison believed there is no real problem in dealing with factions that represent minority interests. The real problem, he said, is with factions that include the majority of the people; majority factions, he feared, would pose a threat to private rights and the public good. Madison did not think a "pure democracy" could handle the "mischief of faction." Why not? How did he distinguish a republic from a democracy? Why did he think a republican form of government, such as outlined in the U.S. Constitution, could deal effectively with the problem of factions?

The Federalist, Number Ten (1787)
James Madison

Among the numerous advantages promised by a well-constructed Union, none deserves to be more accurately developed than its tendency to break and control the violence of faction. The friend of popular governments never finds himself so much alarmed for their character and fate as when he contemplates their propensity to this dangerous vice. He will not fail, therefore, to set a due value on any plan which, without violating the principles to which he is attached, provides a proper cure for it. . . .

By a faction I understand a number of citizens, whether amounting to a majority or minority of the whole, who are united and actuated by some common impulse of passion, or of interest, adverse to the rights of other citizens, or to the permanent and aggregate interests of the community.

There are two methods of curing the mischiefs of faction: the one, by removing its causes; the other, by controlling its effects.

There are again two methods of removing the causes of faction: the one, by destroying the liberty which is essential to its existence; the other, by giving to every citizen the same opinions, the same passions, and the same interests.

It could never be more truly said than of the first remedy that it was worse than the disease. Liberty is to faction what air is to fire, an aliment without which it instantly expires. But it could not be a less folly to abolish liberty, which is essential to political life, because it nourishes faction than it would be to wish the annihilation of air, which is essential to animal life, because it imparts to fire its destructive agency.

The second expedient is as impracticable as the first would be unwise. As long as the reason of man continues fallible, and he is at liberty to exercise it,

From **The Federalist** (Colonial Press, New York, 1901), 44–52.

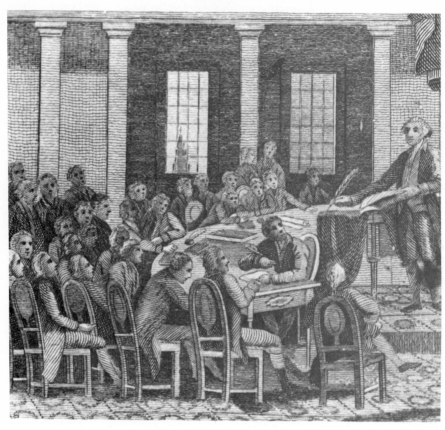

Washington presiding over the Constitutional Convention. In May 1787, the Constitutional Convention, made up of delegates from every state except Rhode Island, met in Philadelphia to revise the Articles of Confederation. The states sent some of their ablest men to Philadelphia: George Washington, James Madison (who played such an important role there that he was called the "Father of the Constitution"), George Mason (author of the Virginia Bill of Rights), Alexander Hamilton, and Benjamin Franklin. Absent were Thomas Jefferson and John Adams, who were on missions abroad, and Samuel Adams and Patrick Henry, who opposed changing the Articles of Confederation. Very early in their deliberations the delegates decided to scrap the Articles and draft an entirely new framework of government. (Library Company of Philadelphia)

different opinions will be formed. As long as the connection subsists between his reason and his self-love, his opinions and his passions will have a reciprocal influence on each other; and the former will be objects to which the latter will attach themselves. The diversity in the faculties of men, from which the rights of property originate, is not less an insuperable obstacle to a uniformity of interests. The protection of these faculties is the first object of government. From the protection of different and unequal faculties of acquiring property, the possession of different degrees and kinds of property immediately results; and from the influence of these on the sentiments and views of the respective proprietors ensues a division of the society into different interests and parties.

The latent causes of faction are thus sown in the nature of man; and we see them everywhere brought into different degrees of activity, according to the different circumstances of civil society. A zeal for different opinions concerning religion, concerning government, and many other points, as well of speculation as of practice; an attachment to different leaders ambitiously contending for pre-eminence and power; or to persons of other descriptions whose fortunes have been interesting to the human passions, have, in turn, divided mankind into parties, inflamed them with mutual animosity, and rendered them much more disposed to vex and oppress each other than to co-operate for their common good. So strong is this propensity of mankind to fall into mutual animosities that where no substantial occasion presents itself the most frivolous and fanciful distinctions have been sufficient to kindle their unfriendly passions and excite their most violent conflicts. But the most common and durable source of factions has been the various and unequal distribution of property. Those who hold and those who are without property have ever formed distinct interests in society. Those who are creditors, and those who are debtors, fall under a like discrimination. A landed interest, a manufacturing interest, a mercantile interest, a moneyed interest, with many lesser interests, grow up of necessity in civilized nations, and divide them into different classes, actuated by different sentiments and views. . . .

. . . Shall domestic manufacturers be encouraged, and in what degree, by restrictions on foreign manufacturers? are questions which would be differently decided by the landed and the manufacturing classes, and probably by neither with a sole regard to justice and the public good. The apportionment of taxes on the various descriptions of property is an act which seems to require the most exact impartiality; yet there is, perhaps, no legislative act in which greater opportunity and temptation are given to a predominant party to trample on the rules of justice. Every shilling with which they overburden the inferior number is a shilling saved to their own pockets.

It is in vain to say that enlightened statesmen will be able to adjust these clashing interests and render them all subservient to the public good. Enlightened statesmen will not always be at the helm. Nor, in many cases, can such an adjustment be made at all without taking into view indirect and remote considerations, which will rarely prevail over the immediate interest which one party may find in disregarding the rights of another or the good of the whole.

The inference to which we are brought is that the *causes* of faction cannot be removed and that relief is only to be sought in the means of controlling its *effects*.

If a faction consists of less than a majority, relief is supplied by the republican principle, which enables the majority to defeat its sinister views by regular vote. It may clog the administration, it may convulse the society; but it will be unable to execute and mask its violence under the forms of the Constitution. When a majority is included in a faction, the form of popular government, on the other hand, enables it to sacrifice to its ruling passion or interest both the public good and the rights of other citizens. To secure the public good and private rights against the danger of such a faction, and at the same time to preserve the spirit and the form of popular government, is then the great object to which our inquiries are directed. . . .

By what means is this object attainable? Evidently by one of two only. Either the existence of the same passion or interest in a majority at the same time must be prevented, or the majority, having such coexistent passion or interest, must be rendered, by their number and local situation, unable to concert and carry into effect schemes of oppression. . . .

. . . [A] pure democracy, by which I mean a society consisting of a small number of citizens, who assemble and administer the government in person, can admit of no cure for the mischiefs of faction. A common passion or interest will, in almost every case, be felt by a majority of the whole; a communication and concert results from the form of government itself; and there is nothing to check the inducements to sacrifice the weaker party or an obnoxious individual. Hence it is that such democracies have ever been spectacles of turbulence and contention; have ever been found incompatible with personal security or the rights of property; and have in general been as short in their lives as they have been violent in their deaths. . . .

A republic, by which I mean a government in which the scheme of representation takes place, opens a different prospect and promises the cure for which we are seeking. Let us examine the points in which it varies from pure democracy, and we shall comprehend both the nature of the cure and the efficacy which it must derive from the Union.

The two great points of difference between a democracy and a republic are: first, the delegation of the government, in the latter, to a small number of citizens elected by the rest; secondly, the greater number of citizens and greater sphere of country over which the latter may be extended.

The effect of the first difference is, on the one hand, to refine and enlarge the public views by passing them through the medium of a chosen body of citizens, whose wisdom may best discern the true interest of their country and whose patriotism and love of justice will be least likely to sacrifice it to temporary or partial considerations. Under such a regulation it may well happen that the public voice, pronounced by the representatives of the people, will be more consonant to the public good than if pronounced by the people themselves, convened for the purpose. On the other hand, the effect may be inverted. Men of factious tempers, of local prejudices, or of sinister designs, may, by intrigue, by corruption, or by other means, first obtain the suffrages, and then betray the interests of the people. . . .

In the first place it is to be remarked that however small the republic may be the representatives must be raised to a certain number in order to guard against the cabals of a few; and that however large it may be they must be limited to a certain number in order to guard against the confusion of a multitude. . . .

In the next place, as each representative will be chosen by a greater number of citizens in the large than in the small republic, it will be more difficult for unworthy candidates to practise with success the vicious arts by which elections are too often carried; and the suffrages of the people being more free, will be more likely to center on men who possess the most attractive merit and the most diffusive and established characters. . . .

The other point of difference is the greater number of citizens and extent of territory which may be brought within the compass of republican than of democratic government; and it is this circumstance principally which renders factious combinations less to be dreaded in the former than in the latter. The smaller the society, the fewer probably will be the distinct parties and interests composing it; the fewer the distinct parties and interests, the more frequently will a majority be found of the same party; and the smaller the number of individuals composing a majority, and the smaller the compass within which they are placed, the more easily will they concert and execute their plans of oppression. Extend the sphere and you take in a greater variety of parties and interests. . . .

The influence of factious leaders may kindle a flame within their particular States but will be unable to spread a general conflagration through the other States. A religious sect may degenerate into a political faction in a part of the Confederacy; but the variety of sects dispersed over the entire face of it must secure the national councils against any danger from that source. A rage for paper money, for an abolition of debts, for an equal division of property, or for any other improper or wicked project, will be less apt to pervade the whole body of the Union than a particular member of it, in the same proportion as such a malady is more likely to taint a particular county or district than an entire State.

In the extent and proper structure of the Union, therefore, we behold a republican remedy for the diseases most incident to republican government.

COUNTERPOINT II

Nationalism, Democracy, and War

The famous documents of the American Revolution—the Declaration of Independence, **Common Sense,** and various issues of **The Crisis,** among others—possess the fine clear ring of nationalist passion and popular government. Jefferson and Paine believed that the documents themselves contributed mightily to these nationalist and republican sentiments, that the Declaration and **The Crisis** galvanized, persuaded, and inspired at least as much as they reflected and expressed. They believed these documents, along with the experience of fighting and winning a war, helped make people more American, more devoted to popular government, and (as that generation phrased it) more "jealous of their liberties."

But did these documents foster patriotism? And if so, then to what extent? To address the issue of rising nationalism, Richard Merritt analyzed what he calls the "symbol content" of colonial and revolutionary writing. Merritt studied seven colonial newspapers from the period 1735–1775 to discover what share of their total news references ("symbols") belonged to one of three categories: (1) "American place" events, or events occurring somewhere in the area that later became the United States; (2) nonlocal "continental place" events, or events occurring in the area that later became the United States but not in the papers' home colonies; and (3) events involving people called Americans, American colonists, or continentals rather than simply colonists, British, and so forth.

The results are striking (see figure A). Both the "American place" share of the total symbols and the "continental" share of the American place symbols rose sharply after 1763 and sharply again after 1773. By 1775, half the total newspaper symbols referred to "American place" events, and of these more than half referred to continental events. But far more spectacular is the line showing references to people called "Americans." "Americans" hardly existed before 1763. Afterward they were everywhere. So while Jefferson and Paine may have galvanized or inflamed nationalist feelings, they did not create them. Nationalism was there already, the tinder of restrictive British policy waiting to be fired.

Nationalism, yes. But what about government by the people? Americans of all classes and stripes might rally round the new flag, but did the revolutionary struggle and its rhetoric and ideas draw ordinary citizens into politics—make citizens, that is, of ordinary people? Jackson Turner Main explored this question by comparing the occupations and wealth of members of the legislatures of six colonies with those of members of the same legislatures after the war when the colonies had become states. His findings are significant (see table B.1). In the three northern legislatures (New Hampshire, New York, and New Jersey), farmers and people of moderate wealth more than doubled their representation, and did so almost entirely at the expense of merchants and lawyers and the rich; and even in the southern legislatures (Maryland, Virginia, and South Carolina), the basic trend is the same, although the numbers are not quite so striking. The trend is clear, moreover, even in the second of Main's tables (B.2), where he omits districts formed after the war, which were usually in the west and naturally included more farmers. "Ordinarily citizens increasingly took part in politics," asserts Main, just as "political theorists began to defend popular government." Thanks partly to Jefferson and Paine, this intensely nationalist revolution became, at least for the moment, an intensely participatory one, too.

This was, finally and probably foremost, a revolution for liberty, for John Peter Zenger's right to criticize and to be tried by his peers, as well as for Paine's nationhood and Jefferson's popular government. But here, somewhat unexpectedly, men sensed a potential problem. A free nation could obviously come only from victory on the battlefield, and victory on the battlefield just as obviously required a strong army under strong leadership. Yet every political thinker of the period knew that armies constituted a threat to liberty. Not only did they control the means of violence. Historically, they also consisted overwhelmingly of aristocrats and plebians, "distinct from the rest of the people," and an ominous combination with swords in hand. Were these concerns justified even in the United States, with its fiery rhetoric of liberty and popular government? Mark Edward Lender tried to find out by comparing muster rolls of New Jersey units of the Continental army with state tax lists. His findings, shown in tables C.1 and C.2, suggest that the historical pattern held true: even the army of revolutionary America consisted, it appears, of "aristocrats and plebians." Little wonder that Jefferson feared the army as "dangerous to liberty" and incorporated the militia's right to bear arms in the Bill of Rights.

A. American Community Awareness, 1735–1775

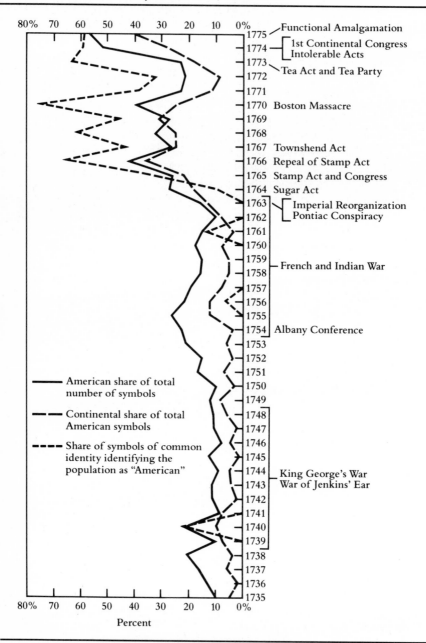

American share of total
number of symbols

Continental share of total
American symbols

Share of symbols of common
identity identifying the
population as "American"

Functional Amalgamation
1775
1774 — 1st Continental Congress
      Intolerable Acts
1773
1772 — Tea Act and Tea Party
1771
1770 Boston Massacre
1769
1768
1767 Townshend Act
1766 Repeal of Stamp Act
1765 Stamp Act and Congress
1764 Sugar Act
1763 — Imperial Reorganization
1762   Pontiac Conspiracy
1761
1760
1759
1758 — French and Indian War
1757
1756
1755
1754 Albany Conference
1753
1752
1751
1750
1749
1748
1747
1746
1745
1744 — King George's War
1743   War of Jenkins' Ear
1742
1741
1740
1739
1738
1737
1736
1735

Percent

SOURCE: From Richard L. Merritt, *Symbols of American Community*, New Haven, Conn., Yale University Press, 1966. Reprinted by permission.

B. Prewar and Postwar Representatives by Economic Status and Occupation

1. Economic Status and Occupations of the Representatives

	N.H., N.Y., and N.J.		Md., Va., and S.C.	
	Prewar	*Postwar*	*Prewar*	*Postwar*
Wealthy	36%	12%	52%	28%
Well-to-do	47	26	36	42
Moderate	17	62	12	30
Merchants and lawyers	43	18	22.5	17
Farmers	23	55	12	26

2. Economic Status and Occupations of the Representatives from Pre-Revolutionary Districts

	N.H., N.Y., and N.J.		Md., Va., and S.C.	
	Prewar	*Postwar*	*Prewar*	*Postwar*
Wealthy	35%	18%	50%	38%
Well-to-do	45	37	38	42
Moderate	20	45	12	20
Merchants and lawyers	41	24	22	18.5
Farmers	25	50	12	22

SOURCE: From Jackson Turner Main, "Government by the People: The American Revolution and the Democratization of the Legislatures," as published in *William and Mary Quarterly* (July 1966). Reprinted by permission.

C. New Jersey's Landowners and Continental Army Members According to Acreage Owned and Degree of Wealth

1. New Jersey Landowners Compared: The General State Population, Continental Army Soldiers, and Officers (late 1770s)

Acres	All New Jersey	Soldiers	Officers
Landless	37.0%	56.7%	2.3%
1–24	12.8	12.5	6.8
25–99	20.5	21.8	20.4
100–199	18.7	7.6	38.6
200–299	6.7	1.4	18.2
300–399	2.1	0.0	4.5
400–	2.2	0.0	9.1

2. New Jersey Continental Army Soldiers and Officers Compared According to Wealth of the General State Population (late 1770s)

Percentage of Enlisted Men from:

Lower Third	Middle Third	Upper Third
61%	29%	10%

Percentage of Officers from:

Lower Third	Middle Third	Upper Third
0	16	84

SOURCE: From *The Military in America: From the Colonial Era to the Present* by Peter Karsten, Ed. Reprinted with permission of Macmillan Publishing Company. Copyright © 1980 by The Free Press, a Division of Macmillan Publishing Company.

The Senate wing of the new Capitol, District of Columbia, 1800. The hill on which the building stood overlooked an area almost the size of New York City, empty except for brick kilns and huts for the laborers. (Watercolor by William R. Birch; Library of Congress)

CHAPTER THREE

Nationalists and Partisans

15.

THE INDUSTRIAL VISION

Under the new Constitution, Congress had the power to tax, borrow, and regulate trade and money. But the president was also important; he could recommend to Congress "such measures" as he thought "necessary and expedient." While George Washington was president, he established many precedents of economic policy and behavior. Probably the most important recommendations made during his presidency came from Secretary of the Treasury Alexander Hamilton. Hamilton's four reports to Congress on economic and financial policies were crucial in shaping the development of the new nation. In them Hamilton sought to make the Constitution's promise of a "more perfect Union" a reality by recommending governmental policies that fostered private enterprise and economic growth.

Hamilton's first three reports had to do with funding the national debt and creating a national bank. Hamilton wanted the federal government to take over the old Revolutionary debt as well as the debts incurred by the states during the Revolution, convert them into bonds, and pay for the interest on the bonds by levying excise taxes on distilled spirits and by imposing customs duties on such imports as tea, coffee, and wine. Congress adopted his funding proposals; it also accepted his plan for a large national bank that could make loans to businesses and issue currency backed by federal bonds. Hamilton's fourth report, "On Manufactures," urged a system of import taxes ("protective tariffs"), better roads and harbors ("internal improvements"), and subsidies ("bounties") in order to spur manufacturing.

Hamilton's four reports, with their emphasis on national rather than state power, on industry rather than agriculture, and on public spending to promote private enterprise, had a tremendous political impact. First, they triggered the birth of the earliest formal party system: Hamiltonian Federalists urging passage of the program and Democratic Republicans, followers of Secretary of State Thomas Jefferson, trying to modify or block it. Second, the reports helped establish the questions of governmental power and the nature of the economy as basic issues of political debate over the next half-century, as urgent for South Carolina in 1828 (Document 21) and Andrew Jackson in 1832 (Document 22) as for the politicians of the 1790s. Finally, Hamilton's reports became a veritable fountainhead for Americans concerned with the enhancement of capitalism and national power. Hamiltonian conservatives did not want an uninvolved government; they wanted to forge a partnership between government and business in which federal policies would actively promote business enterprise.

Congress did not immediately adopt Hamilton's recommendations for manufacturing. Protective tariffs, internal improvements, and bounties came much later and were adopted in a piecemeal fashion. Still, "On Manufactures" is important in its prevision of the future. Hamilton was perceptive in foreseeing that America's destiny was an industrial one. Long after he had passed from the scene, industrialism did overtake and surpass agriculture (with the encouragement of the states as well as of the federal government) as the driving force of the American economy. The observations Hamilton made in 1791 enable us to see the beginnings of the trend toward industrialization and help explain its seemingly inexorable inner logic.

Hamilton himself was concerned more with the political implications of his reports than with their economic effects. His major aim was to strengthen the Union. This strong nationalism probably came from Hamilton's lack of state loyalties. He was born in 1755 in the West Indies (Hamilton claimed 1757). Orphaned at the age of thirteen, he was sent by relatives to the colony of New York in 1772. After preliminary study in New Jersey, he entered King's College (now Columbia University). When war with Britain broke out, he joined the army; in 1777 George Washington made him his aide-de-camp and personal secretary. After the Revolution he studied law, married well, rose rapidly in New York society, and became a dominant force in the Washington administration and the Federalist party. Overbearing and ambitious as well as bright and energetic, he proceeded to alienate important party leaders such as John Adams, and his career declined steadily after Washington left office. In 1804, Vice President Aaron Burr, a long-time political adversary who had just been defeated in the election for governor of New York, demanded a duel of honor with Hamilton because of some alleged derogatory remarks. On July 11, Burr shot Hamilton at their meeting in a field near Weehawken, New Jersey. He died the following day.

Questions to consider. Hamilton's report on manufactures reveals as well as recommends: it provides interesting glimpses into American society in 1791. For example, Hamilton argued for manufacturing on the grounds that it would attract immigrants and employ women and children. What does this prediction tell us about the availability and condition of labor in early America and about the attitudes of American leaders toward the work force? Note, too, that Hamilton argued not just for the specialization of labor but even more for the easier application of machinery that would result from labor specialization. What two models did he suggest for combining machinery and labor, and what does his simultaneous use of these two very different models indicate about the state of American industry at the time he was writing? Again, Hamilton thought that the spirit of capitalist enterprise must be fostered by government. How did Hamilton's spirit of enterprise differ from that of Benjamin Franklin's "Poor Richard" a half-century earlier (Document 11)? Why, if this spirit was so prevalent, did Hamilton feel the need for special measures to promote it? How compatible was Hamilton's economic nationalism with Madison's political federalism (Document 14)?

On Manufactures (1791)
Alexander Hamilton

It is now proper to proceed a step further, and to enumerate the principal circumstances, from which it may be inferred that manufacturing establishments not only occasion a position augmentation of the produce and revenue of the society, but that they contribute essentially to rendering them greater than they could possibly be without such establishments. These circumstances are:

1. The division of labor.
2. An extension of the use of machinery.
3. Additional employment to classes of the community not ordinarily engaged in the business.
4. The promoting of emigration from foreign countries.
5. The furnishing greater scope for the diversity of talents and dispositions, which discriminate men from each other.
6. The affording a more ample and various field for enterprise.
7. The creating, in some instances, a new, and securing, in all, a more certain and steady demand for the surplus produce of the soil.

Each of these circumstances has a considerable influence upon the total mass of industrious effort in a community; together, they add to it a degree of energy and effect which is not easily conceived. . . .

1. As to the Division of Labor

It has justly been observed, that there is scarcely any thing of greater moment in the economy of a nation than the proper division of labor. The separation of occupations causes each to be carried to a much greater perfection than it could possibly acquire if they were blended. This arises principally from three circumstances:

1st. The greater skill and dexterity naturally resulting from a constant and undivided application to a single object. It is evident that these properties must increase in proportion to the separation and simplification of objects, and the steadiness of the attention devoted to each; and must be less in proportion to the complication of objects, and the number among which the attention is distracted.

2nd. The economy of time, by avoiding the loss of it, incident to a frequent transition from operation to another of a different nature. This depends on various circumstances; the transition itself, the orderly disposition of the implements, machines, and materials employed in the operation to be relinquished, the preparatory steps to the commencement of a new one, the interruption of the impulse which the mind of the workman acquires from being engaged in a particular operation, the distractions, hesitations, and reluctances which attend the passage from one kind of business to another.

3rd. An extension of the use of machinery. A man occupied on a single object will have it more in his power, and will be more naturally led to exert his imagination, in devising methods to facilitate and abridge labor, than if he were perplexed by a variety of independent and dissimilar operations. Besides this, the fabrication of machines, in numerous instances, becoming itself a distinct trade, the artist who follows it has all the advantages which have been enumerated, for improvement in his particular art; and, in both ways, the invention and application of machinery are extended.

And from these causes united, the mere separation of the occupation of the cultivator from that of the artificer has the effect of augmenting the productive powers of labor, and with them, the total mass of the produce or revenue of a country. In this single view of the subject, therefore, the utility of artificers or manufacturers, towards promoting an increase of productive industry, is apparent.

2. As to an Extension of the Use of Machinery, A Point Which, Though Partly Anticipated, Requires to Be Placed in One or Two Additional Lights

The employment of machinery forms an item of great importance in the general mass of national industry. It is an artificial force brought in aid of the natural force of man; and, to all the purposes of labor, is an increase of hands, an accession of strength, unencumbered too by the expense of maintaining the laborer. . . .

The cotton mill, invented in England, within the last twenty years, is a signal illustration of the general proposition which has been just advanced. In consequence of it, all the different processes for spinning cotton are performed by means of machines, which are put in motion by water, and attended chiefly by women and children—and by a smaller number of persons, in the whole, than are requisite in the ordinary mode of spinning. And it is an advantage of great moment, that the operations of this mill continue with convenience during the night as well as through the day. The prodigious effect of such a machine is easily conceived. To this invention is to be attributed, essentially, the immense progress, which has been so suddenly made in Great Britain, in the various fabrics of cotton.

3. As to the Additional Employment of Classes of the Community Not Originally Engaged in the Particular Business

This is not among the least valuable of the means by which manufacturing institutions contribute to augment the general stock of industry and production. In places where those institutions prevail, besides the persons regularly engaged in them, they afford occasional and extra employment to industrious individuals and families, who are willing to devote the leisure resulting from the intermissions of their ordinary pursuits to collateral labours, as a resource for multiplying their acquisitions or their enjoyments. The husbandman himself experiences a new source of profit and support from the increased industry of his wife and daughters, invited and stimulated by the demands of the neighboring manufactories.

Besides this advantage of occasional employment to classes having different occupations, there is another, of a nature allied to it, and of a similar tendency. This is the employment of persons who would otherwise be idle, and in many cases a burthen on the community, either from the bias of temper, habit, infirmity of body, or some other cause, indisposing or disqualifying them for the toils of the country. It is worthy of particular remark that, in general, women and children are rendered more useful, and the latter more early useful by manufacturing establishments, than they would otherwise be. Of the number of persons employed in the cotton manufactories of Great Britain, it is computed that four sevenths nearly are women and children, of whom the greatest proportion are children, and many of them of a very tender age. . . .

4. As to the Promoting of Emigration from Foreign Countries

Men reluctantly quit one course of occupation and livelihood for another, unless invited to it by very apparent and proximate advantages. Many who would go from one country to another, if they had a prospect of continuing

Secretary of the Treasury Alexander Hamilton. The most influential and, to many, the most brilliant figure of the Washington administration, Alexander Hamilton could also be mischievous, not to say conniving. Faced in 1796 with a Federalist presidential candidate, John Adams, whom he disliked, Hamilton maneuvered to control the electoral college and put Adams's running mate, Thomas Pinckney of South Carolina, into the presidency. The plan, however, backfired. Not only did Adams win; Hamilton's machinations cost Pinckney the vice presidency—which went instead to Hamilton's angular nemesis, Thomas Jefferson. (Portrait by Charles Willson Peale; Independence National Historical Park Collection)

with more benefit the callings to which they have been educated, will often not be tempted to change their situation by the hope of doing better in some other way. Manufacturers who, listening to the powerful invitations of a better price for their fabrics, or their labor, of greater cheapness of provisions and raw materials, of an exemption from the chief part of the taxes, burthens and restraints, which they endure in the Old World, of greater personal independence and consequence, under the operation of a more equal government, and of what is far more precious than mere religious toleration, a perfect equality of religious privileges, would probably flock from Europe to the United States to pursue their own trades or professions, if they were once made sensible of the advantages they would enjoy, and were inspired with an assurance of encouragement and employment, will with difficulty, be induced to transplant themselves, with a view to becoming cultivators of Land.

If it be true, then, that it is in the interest of the United States to open every possible avenue to immigration from abroad, it affords a weighty argument for the encouragement of manufactures; which, for the reasons just assigned, will have the strongest tendency to multiply the inducements to it. . . .

5. As to the Furnishing Greater Scope for the Diversity of Talents and Dispositions, Which Discriminate Men from Each Other

This is a much more powerful means of augmenting the fund of national industry, than may at first sight appear. It is a just observation, that minds of the strongest and most active powers for their proper objects, fall below mediocrity, and labor without effect, if confined to uncongenial pursuits. And it is thence to be inferred, that the results of human exertion may be immensely increased by diversifying its objects. When all the different kinds of industry obtain in a community, each individual can find his proper element, and can call into activity the whole vigor of his nature. And the community is benefited by the services of its respective members, in the manner in which each can serve it with most effect.

If there be any thing in a remark often to be met with, namely, that there is, in the genius of the people of this country, a peculiar aptitude for mechanic improvements, it would operate as a forcible reason for giving opportunities to the exercise of that species of talent, by the propagation of manufactures.

6. As to the Affording a More Ample and Various Field for Enterprise

. . . To cherish and stimulate the activity of the human mind, by multiplying the objects of enterprise, is not among the least considerable of the expedients by which the wealth of a nation may be promoted. Even things in themselves not positively advantageous sometimes become so, by their tendency to provoke exertion. Every new scene which is opened to the busy nature of man to rouse and exert itself, is the addition of a new energy to the general stock of effort.

The spirit of enterprise, useful and prolific as it is, must necessarily be contracted or expanded, in proportion to the simplicity or variety of the occupations and productions which are to be found in a society. It must be less in a nation of mere cultivators, than in a nation of cultivators and merchants; less in a nation of cultivators and merchants, than in a nation of cultivators, artificers and merchants.

7. As to the Creating, in Some Instances, a New, and Securing in All, a More Certain and Steady Demand for the Surplus Produce of the Soil

This is among the most important of the circumstances which have been indicated. It is a principal means by which the establishment of manufactures contributes to an augmentation of the produce or revenue of a country, and has an immediate and direct relation to the prosperity of agriculture.

It is evident that the exertions of the husbandman will be steady or fluctuating, vigorous or feeble, in proportion to the steadiness or fluctuation, adequateness or inadequateness, of the markets on which he must depend for the vent [selling] of the surplus which may be produced by his labor; and that such surplus, in the ordinary course of things, will be greater or less in the same proportion.

For the purpose of this vent, a domestic market is greatly to be preferred to a foreign one; because it is, in the nature of things, far more to be relied upon.

16.

A CALL FOR UNITY

The election of 1800 was a stormy one. During the campaign Democratic-Republican Thomas Jefferson was called a dangerous radical and Federalist John Adams a high-toned royalist. The House of Representatives, voting by states in February 1801, finally picked Jefferson as president on the thirty-sixth ballot. Jefferson called his election "the revolution of 1800." Reacting against what he regarded as monarchical tendencies in the Federalists, he insisted on "republican simplicity" in his administration. He stopped using the fancy carriage of state and rode horseback through the streets of Washington like any other citizen. He refused to wear "court dress" when receiving foreign diplomats, and his casual demeanor shocked some of the diplomatic corps. The British minister was so outraged by the informality of dinners at the Executive Mansion that he began refusing invitations to dine with the president.

Jefferson's first inaugural address, given on March 4, 1801, was a beautifully phrased exposition of his republican philosophy. The American republic, he declared, was founded on the sacred principle of majority rule; but the majority, he added, must respect the rights of the minority. He went on to make an appeal for the restoration of good feeling between the Federalists and the Republicans after the bitter campaign of 1800. The two parties differed on many points, he acknowledged, but they agreed on their devotion to the basic principles of the American system of government: equal justice for all; peace and friendship with all nations; support of the state governments in their rights; the right of election by the people; the supremacy of the civil over military authority; freedom of religion, freedom of the press, and freedom of person, under the protection of habeas corpus; and trial by juries impartially selected. "Sometimes," said Jefferson, "it is said that man can not be trusted with government of himself. Can he, then, be trusted with the government of others? Or have we found angels in the form of kings to govern him? Let history answer this question." History, Jefferson thought, showed the failure of undemocratic governments. He placed his faith in the future in governments resting on the consent of the people.

Thomas Jefferson was born in 1743 on his father's Virginia tobacco plantation. After he graduated from William and Mary College in 1762, he studied law and entered politics, joining the Virginia House of Burgesses in 1769. In 1775 he became a delegate to the Continental Congress and was chosen to draft the Declaration of Independence. He served as governor of Virginia from 1779 to 1781 and as U.S. minister to France from 1785 to 1789. Insistent, in his correspondence with James

Madison, on the necessity of adding a Bill of Rights to the Constitution, he became increasingly disturbed by the policies of Hamilton and Washington and saw his election as president as partial vindication of his own views on the importance of land, liberty, and localism in the new republic. His reputation as a scholar and architect flourished after his retirement from office in 1809, although his personal finances did not. He died, deeply revered as the Sage of Monticello but still an indebted slaveholder, at his Monticello estate on July 4, 1826, fifty years to the day after the adoption of his Declaration of Independence. On the same day John Adams died in Quincy, Massachusetts. Jefferson and Adams had been friends at the time of the American Revolution but became political enemies during the early years of the American republic. They became reconciled later in life and entered into a lively correspondence that has delighted generations of Americans. Just before he died Adams exclaimed: "Thomas Jefferson survives!"

Questions to consider. In reading Jefferson's address several questions come at once to mind. In what ways did Jefferson perceive the United States as different from the countries of Europe? What did he mean by saying that "every difference of opinion is not a difference of principle"? After the bitter political strife of the 1790s, how could Jefferson argue that "we are all Republicans, we are all Federalists"? What role did the accidents of geography—physical separation from Europe and what Jefferson called "a chosen country, with room enough for our descendants"—play in his optimistic expectations? Did any of the themes appearing in Jefferson's inaugural address clash with those put forth by Federalists like Hamilton in 1791 (Document 15) and John Marshall in 1803 (Document 17)? Is it possible to summarize Jefferson's "essential principles of our Government" even more than he was able or willing to do? In view of these principles, how could a Massachusetts Federalist like John Adams believe that Jefferson's election as president would produce "the loathsome steam of human victims offered in sacrifice"?

First Inaugural Address (1801)
Thomas Jefferson

Called upon to undertake the duties of the first executive office of our country, I avail myself of the presence of that portion of my fellow-citizens which is here assembled to express my grateful thanks for the favor with which they

From James D. Richardson, ed., *A Compilation of the Messages and Papers of the Presidents* (Government Printing Office, Washington, D.C., 1897–1907), I: 309–312.

have been pleased to look toward me, to declare a sincere consciousness that the task is above my talents, and that I approach it with those anxious and awful presentiments which the greatness of the charge and the weakness of my powers so justly inspire. A rising nation, spread over a wide and fruitful land, traversing all the seas with the rich productions of their industry, engaged in commerce with nations who feel power and forget right, advancing rapidly to destinies beyond the reach of mortal eyes—when I contemplate these transcendent objects, and see the honor, the happiness, and the hopes of this beloved country committed to the issue and the auspices of this day, I shrink from the contemplation, and humble myself before the magnitude of the undertaking. Utterly, indeed, should I despair did not the presence of many whom I here see remind me that in the other high authorities provided by our Constitution I shall find resources of wisdom, of virtue, and of zeal on which to rely under all difficulties. To you, then, gentlemen, who are charged with the sovereign functions of legislation, and to those associated with you, I look with encouragement for that guidance and support which may enable us to steer with safety the vessel in which we are all embarked amidst the conflicting elements of a troubled world.

During the contest of opinion through which we have passed the animation of discussions and of exertions has sometimes worn an aspect which might impose on strangers unused to think freely and to speak and to write what they think; but this being now decided by the voice of the nation, announced according to the rules of the Constitution, all will, of course, arrange themselves under the will of the law, and unite in common efforts for the common good. All, too, will bear in mind this sacred principle, that though the will of the majority is in all cases to prevail, that will to be rightful must be reasonable; that the minority possess their equal rights, which equal law must protect, and to violate would be oppression. Let us, then, fellow-citizens, unite with one heart and one mind. Let us restore to social intercourse that harmony and affection without which liberty and even life itself are but dreary things. And let us reflect that, having banished from our land that religious intolerance under which mankind so long bled and suffered, we have yet gained little if we countenance a political intolerance as despotic, as wicked, and capable of as bitter and bloody persecutions. During the throes and convulsions of the ancient world, during the agonizing spasms of infuriated man, seeking through blood and slaughter his long-lost liberty, it was not wonderful that the agitation of the billows should reach even this distant and peaceful shore; that this should be more felt and feared by some and less by others, and should divide opinions as to measures of safety. But every difference of opinion is not a difference of principle. We have called by different names brethren of the same principle. We are all Republicans, we are all Federalists. If there be any among us who would wish to dissolve this Union or to change its republican form, let them stand undisturbed as monuments of the safety with which error of opinion may be tolerated where reason is left free to combat it. I know, indeed, that some honest men fear that a republican government can not be strong, that this Government is not strong enough; but would the honest patriot, in the full tide of successful experiment, abandon a government which has so far kept us free and firm on the theoretic and visionary fear that this Government, the world's best hope, may by possibility want energy to preserve itself? I trust not. I believe this, on the contrary, the strongest Government on earth. I believe it the only one where every man, at the call of the law, would fly to the standard of the law, and would meet invasions of the public order as his own personal concern. Sometimes it is said that man can not be trusted with government of himself. Can he, then, be trusted with the government of others? Or have we found angels in the forms of kings to govern him? Let history answer this question.

Let us, then, with courage and confidence pursue our own Federal and Republican principles, our attachment to union and representative government. Kindly separated by nature and a wide ocean from the exterminating havoc of one quarter of the globe; too high-minded to endure the degradations of the others; possessing a chosen country, with room enough for our descendants to the thousandth and thousandth generation; entertaining a due sense of our own faculties, to the acquisitions of our own industry, to honor and confidence from our fellow-citizens, resulting not from birth, but from our actions and their sense of them; enlightened by a benign religion, professed, indeed, and practiced in various forms, yet all of them inculcating honesty, truth, temperance, gratitude, and the love of man; acknowledging and adoring an overruling Providence, which by all its dispensations proves that it delights in the happiness of man here and his greater happiness hereafter—with all these blessings, what more is necessary to make us a happy and prosperous people? Still one thing more, fellow-citizens—a wise and frugal Government, which shall restrain men from injuring one another, shall leave them otherwise free to regulate their own pursuits of industry and improvement, and shall not take from the mouth of labor the bread it has earned. This is the sum of good government, and this is necessary to close the circle of our felicities.

About to enter, fellow-citizens, on the exercise of duties which comprehend everything dear and valuable to you, it is proper you should understand what I deem the essential principles of our Government, and consequently those which ought to shape its Administration. I will compress them within the narrowest compass they will bear, stating the general principle, but not all its limitations. Equal and exact justice to all men, of whatever state or persuasion, religious or political; peace, commerce, and honest friendship with all nations, entangling alliances with none; the support of the State governments in all their rights, as the most competent administrations for our domestic concerns and the surest bulwarks against antirepublican tendencies; the preservation of the General Government in its whole constitutional vigor, as the sheet anchor of our peace at home and safety abroad; a jealous care of the right of election by the people—a mild and safe corrective of abuses which are lopped by the sword of revolution where peaceable remedies are unprovided; absolute acquiescence in the decisions of the majority, the vital principle

Thomas Jefferson.   Third president of the United States and the first to be inaugurated in Washington, Jefferson was one of the most gifted men in America. There was almost nothing in human affairs that did not attract his eager attention, and he acquired an expert knowledge in an amazing variety of fields. He spoke or read seven languages and was familiar with both ancient and modern literature. He wrote an essay on English poetry, a book on rules for debate in the Senate, and a long article on standards of weights and measures. He collected paintings, played the violin, and took a serious interest in both science and religion. He was also a distinguished architect and designed his home at Monticello in Virginia. (Sketch by Benjamin H. Latrobe, c. 1799; Maryland Historical Society)

of republics, from which is no appeal but to force, the vital principle and immediate parent of despotism; a well-disciplined militia, our best reliance in peace and for the first moments of war, till regulars may relieve them; the supremacy of the civil over the military authority; economy in the public expense, that labor may be lightly burthened; the honest payment of our debts and sacred preservation of the public faith; encouragement of agriculture, and of commerce as its handmaid; the diffusion of information and arraignment of all abuses at the bar of the public reason; freedom of religion; freedom of the press, and freedom of person under the protection of the habeas corpus, and trial by juries impartially selected. These principles form the bright constellation which has gone before us and guided our steps through an age of revolution and reformation. The wisdom of our sages and blood of our heroes have been devoted to their attainment. They should be the creed of our political faith, the text of civic instruction, the touchstone by which to try the services of those we trust; and should we wander from them in moments of error or of alarm, let us hasten to retrace our steps and to regain the road which alone leads to peace, liberty, and safety.

I repair, then, fellow-citizens, to the post you have assigned me. With experience enough in subordinate offices to have seen the difficulties of this the greatest of all, I have learnt to expect that it will rarely fall to the lot of imperfect man to retire from this station with the reputation and the favor which bring him into it. Without pretentions to that high confidence you reposed in our first and greatest revolutionary character, whose preeminent services had entitled him to the first place in his country's love and destined for him the fairest page in the volume of faithful history, I ask so much confidence only as may give firmness and effect to the legal administration of your affairs. I shall often go wrong through defect of judgment. When right, I shall often be thought wrong by those whose positions will not command a view of the whole ground. I ask your indulgence for my own errors, which will never be intentional, and your support against the errors of others, who may condemn what they would not if seen in all its parts. The approbation implied by your suffrage is a great consolation to me for the past, and my future solicitude will be to retain the good opinion of those who have bestowed it in advance, to conciliate that of others by doing them all the good in my power, and to be instrumental to the happiness and freedom of all.

Relying, then, on the patronage of your good will, I advance with obedience to the work, ready to retire from it whenever you become sensible how much better choice it is in your power to make. And may that infinite Power which rules the destinies of the universe lead our councils to what is best, and give them a favorable issue for your peace and prosperity.

17.

THE CONSTITUTION PROTECTED

Marbury v. **Madison** was the first case in which the Supreme Court exercised the right of "judicial review" over laws passed by Congress. In February 1803, Chief Justice John Marshall, a staunch Federalist, speaking for the majority of justices on the Supreme Court, announced his opinion in the case. William Marbury had been appointed justice of the peace for the District of Columbia by John Adams in the last hours of his administration. But because Marbury was a Federalist, James Madison, Jefferson's secretary of state, withheld the commission from him. Marbury appealed to the Supreme Court for a writ of mandamus, that is, a court order compelling Madison to deliver the commission.

Marshall did not believe that Madison was justified in denying Marbury his commission as justice of the peace. But in his opinion he declared that the Supreme Court could not force Madison to deliver the commission. The Constitution, he said, in defining the original jurisdiction of the Supreme Court, did not include the issue of writs to executive officers. Nonetheless, section 13 of the Judiciary Act of 1789 did give the Supreme Court the power to issue such writs, and it was under this law that Marbury had applied to the Court. Marshall, however, declared that section 13 of the Judiciary Act was unconstitutional and that therefore the Court could not render judgment. He then went on to assert the right of the Supreme Court to pass on the constitutionality of laws passed by Congress. "It is a proposition too plain to be contested," he declared, "that the constitution controls any legislative act repugnant to it" and that "a legislative act contrary to the constitution is not law." He added, "It is emphatically the province and duty of the judicial department to say what the law is." And he concluded that "a law repugnant to the constitution is void, and that courts, as well as other departments, are bound by that instrument." By claiming for the Court the duty of deciding whether acts of Congress were constitutional, Marshall upheld the prestige of the judiciary, even though he was unable to do anything for Marbury. But it was not until the **Dred Scott** case (Document 31), more than half a century later, that the Supreme Court invalidated a Congressional act for the second time.

Born in 1755 to well-to-do Virginians, John Marshall received little formal schooling. He studied law, however, and eventually became active in state politics. His service in the army during the American Revolution helped develop his nationalistic outlook. A distant cousin of Thomas Jefferson but a devoted Federalist nonetheless, Marshall served on a commission to France in 1797 and was elected to Congress in 1799. In 1801 President John Adams named him to the U.S. Supreme Court, where he served as chief justice for the next thirty-four years. Among his notable decisions besides **Marbury** v. **Madison** were **McCulloch** v. **Maryland** (1819) (Document 19), which protected federal agencies such as the Bank of the United States from state taxes; **Dartmouth College** v. **Woodward** (1819), which upheld the sanctity of contracts; and **Gibbons** v. **Ogden** (1824), which established federal authority over interstate and foreign commerce. In these and other cases Marshall sought to protect the rights of property, increase the power of the federal government, and raise the prestige of the federal judiciary. Personally convivial, gossipy, courtly with women, and in general, reveling in the social life of the slaveholding gentry, Marshall in public remained a figure of controversy throughout his career. He died in Philadelphia in 1835.

Questions to consider. Why, according to Chief Justice Marshall, should the Constitution and its principles be considered permanent? How important was it to Marshall's argument that the U.S. Constitution was written? What alternative did he have in mind, and why did he feel compelled to assert the special character of a written document? Why did he single out the legislative branch as opposed to the executive (or judiciary) as the chief danger to the permanence of the Constitution and its principles? On what grounds, according to Marshall, did the judiciary become the final arbiter of constitutional quarrels with the right to annul legislation? How persuasive do you find Marshall's examples of the centrality of the courts and the Constitution in the American system? Why, finally, was Marshall's decision seen as a political victory for the Federalist party?

Marbury *v.* Madison (1803)

. . . The question whether an act repugnant to the constitution can become the law of the land is a question deeply interesting to the United States; but, happily not of an intricacy proportioned to its interest. It seems only necessary to recognize certain principles supposed to have been long and well established, to decide it.

That the people have an original right to establish for their future government such principles as, in their opinion, shall most conduce to their own

From 1 Craven 137 (1803).

happiness, is the basis on which the whole American fabric has been erected. The exercise of this original right is a very great exertion, nor can it nor ought it to be frequently repeated. The principles therefore so established are deemed fundamental. And as the authority from which they proceed is supreme and can seldom act, they are designed to be permanent.

This original and supreme will organizes the government, and assigns to different departments their respective powers. It may either stop here or establish certain limits not to be transcended by those departments.

The government of the United States is of the latter description. The powers of the legislature are defined and limited; and that those limits may not be mistaken or forgotten, the constitution is written. To what purpose are powers limited, and to what purpose is that limitation committed to writing, if these limits may, at any time, be passed by those intended to be restrained? The distinction between a government with limited and unlimited powers is abolished if those limits do not confine the persons on whom they are imposed and if acts prohibited and acts allowed are of equal obligation. It is a proposition too plain to be contested, that the constitution controls any legislative act repugnant to it, or, that the legislature may alter the constitution by an ordinary act.

Between these alternatives there is no middle ground. The constitution is either a superior paramount law, unchangeable by ordinary means, or it is on a level with ordinary legislative acts, and, like other acts, is alterable when the legislature shall please to alter it.

If the former part of the alternative be true, then a legislative act contrary to the constitution is not law; if the latter part be true, then written constitutions are absurd attempts, on the part of the people, to limit a power in its own nature illimitable.

Certainly all those who have framed written constitutions contemplate them as forming the fundamental and paramount law of the nation, and consequently the theory of every such government must be that an act of the legislature repugnant to the Constitution is void.

This theory is essentially attached to a written constitution, and is consequently to be considered, by this court, as one of the fundamental principles of our society. It is not, therefore, to be lost sight of in the further consideration of this subject.

If an act of the legislature repugnant to the constitution is void, does it, notwithstanding its invalidity, bind the courts and oblige them to give it effect? Or, in other words, though it be not law, does it constitute a rule as operative as if it was a law? This would be to overthrow in fact what was established in theory, and would seem, at first view, an absurdity too gross to be insisted on. It shall, however, receive a more attentive consideration.

It is emphatically the province and duty of the judicial department to say what the law is. Those who apply the rule to particular cases must of necessity expound and interpret that rule. If two laws conflict with each other, the courts must decide on the operation of each.

So if a law be in opposition to the constitution; if both the law and the constitution apply to a particular case, so that the court must either decide that case conformably to the law, disregarding the constitution, or conformably to the constitution, disregarding the law, the court must determine which of these conflicting rules governs the case. This is of the very essence of judicial duty.

If, then, the courts are to regard the constitution, and the constitution is superior to any ordinary act of the legislature, the constitution, and not such ordinary act, must govern the case to which they both apply.

Those, then, who controvert the principle that the constitution is to be considered in court as a paramount law, are reduced to the necessity of maintaining that courts must close their eyes on the constitution and see only the law.

This doctrine would subvert the very foundation of all written constitutions. It would declare that an act which, according to the principles and theory of our government, is entirely void, is yet, in practice, completely obligatory. It would declare that if the legislature shall do what is expressly forbidden, such act, notwithstanding the express prohibition, is in reality effectual. It would be giving to the legislature a practical and real omnipotence with the same breath which professes to restrict their powers within narrow limits. It is prescribing limits and declaring that those limits may be passed at pleasure.

That it thus reduces to nothing what we have deemed the greatest improvement on political institutions, a written constitution, would of itself be sufficient, in America, where written constitutions have been viewed with so much reverence, for rejecting the construction. But the peculiar expressions of the constitution of the United States furnish additional arguments in favor of its rejection.

The judicial power of the United States is extended to all cases arising under the constitution.

Could it be the intention of those who gave this power to say that in using it the constitution should not be looked into? That a case arising under the constitution should be decided without examining the instrument under which it arises?

This is too extravagant to be maintained.

In some cases, then, the constitution must be looked into by the judges. And if they can open it at all, what part of it are they forbidden to read or to obey?

There are many other parts of the constitution which serve to illustrate this subject.

It is declared that "no tax or duty shall be laid on articles exported from any state." Suppose a duty on the export of cotton, of tobacco, or of flour, and a suit instituted to recover it, ought judgment to be rendered in such a case? Ought the judges to close their eyes on the constitution, and only see the law?

The constitution declares "that no bill of attainder of *ex post facto* law shall be passed." If, however, such a bill should be passed, and a person should be prosecuted under it, must the court condemn to death those victims whom the constitution endeavors to preserve?

"No person," says the constitution, "shall be convicted of treason unless on the testimony of two witnesses to the same overt act, or on confession in open court."

Here the language of the constitution is addressed especially to the courts. It prescribes, directly for them, a rule of evidence not to be departed from. If the legislature should change that rule, and declare one witness, or a confession out of court, sufficient for conviction, must the constitutional principle yield to the legislative act?

From these, and many other selections which might be made, it is apparent that the framers of the constitution contemplated that instrument as a rule for the government of *courts,* as well as of the legislature. Why otherwise does it direct the judges to take an oath to support it? This oath certainly applies in an especial manner to their conduct in their official character. How immoral to impose it on them if they were to be used as the instruments, and the knowing instruments, for violating what they swear to support!

The oath of office, too, imposed by the legislature, is completely demonstrative of the legislative opinion on this subject. It is in these words: "I do solemnly swear that I will administer justice without respect to persons, and do equal right to the poor and to the rich; and that I will faithfully and impartially discharge all the duties incumbent on me as ———, according to the best of my abilities and understanding, agreeably to *the constitution* and laws of the United States." Why does a judge swear to discharge his duties agreeably to the constitution of the United States, if that constitution forms no rule for his government—if it is closed upon him, and cannot be inspected by him?

If such be the real state of things, this is worse than solemn mockery. To prescribe, or to take this oath, becomes equally a crime.

It is also not entirely unworthy of observation, that in declaring what shall be the *supreme* law of the land, the constitution itself is first mentioned, and not the laws of the United States generally, but those only which shall be made in *pursuance* of the constitution, have that rank.

Thus, the particular phraseology of the constitution of the United States confirms and strengthens the principle, supposed to be essential to all written constitutions, that a law repugnant to the constitution is void, and that courts, as well as other departments, are bound by that instrument.

18.

THE WIDE MISSOURI

Thomas Jefferson's presidency did not usher in the wild-eyed revolutionary radicalism that some Federalist party orators had warned against, but "Long Tom" did prove reluctant to have the central government promote trade and manufacturing. More solicitous of states' rights than the Federalists, Jefferson hesitated to assert the government's authority in economic matters. More solicitous of farming than of industry as a way of life, he also hesitated to encourage commerce as opposed to agriculture. Ironically enough, it was precisely this agrarian vision, this belief that America should remain predominantly rural, that led Jefferson to purchase the Louisiana Territory from France in 1803, thus doubling the nation's size by means of a maneuver that some observers felt was unconstitutional and underhanded.

This vision of America as a land of farmers also prompted the president to sponsor the exploration of the upper Louisiana Territory and the great Columbia River region beyond. Jefferson's interest in the West was long-standing—he asked Congress to authorize an expedition into the Pacific Northwest months before the United States actually bought the Louisiana Territory—and besides, he never lost an opportunity to slake his immense thirst for scientific knowledge. What better opportunity could arise? Ever the politician, however, he was also careful to stress (for the benefit of stray Federalist voters) that the venture might open vast new trading horizons as well as vast new agricultural regions.

The leaders of this first expedition were U.S. Army captains Meriwether Lewis, a noted woodsman who had once been Jefferson's private secretary, and William Clark, an Indian fighter from Kentucky. In the spring of 1804, Lewis and Clark started from St. Louis up the Missouri River with a large party in three well-stocked boats "under a gentle breeze"; Lewis, in nominal command, fully shared responsibility with Clark. After wintering in present-day North Dakota in 40°-below temperatures, nine hand-picked men plus a Shoshone and a French-Canadian guide traversed the Rocky Mountains; they survived on horse meat and tallow, and in November reached "this great Pacific Ocean. O the joy!" Back in St. Louis by the following September, Lewis sent the eagerly awaited letter excerpted below, the party's first communication with government and country in a year. Enthusiastically received, this report whetted American interest in the new territory to a keen edge, leading not only to more exploration and extensive fur trading but to formal U.S. interest in the Oregon Territory and its ultimate wresting in 1845 from the grip of long-time foe Great Britain.

Meriwether Lewis, the youthful head of the great expedition, was born in 1774 in Albemarle County, Virginia, not far from Jefferson's home. Although his family eventually settled in the state of Georgia, Lewis returned alone at age thirteen to Virginia where, after sporadic private study, he enlisted in the local militia in time to be sent to help suppress the Pennsylvania Whisky Rebellion in 1794. The next year, lacking better prospects and having acquired a taste for bivouacking, Lewis joined the regular army. But when President Jefferson offered to make him presidential secretary, he eagerly, and wisely, accepted. So close did the two men become that for two years Lewis lived in the executive mansion, helping plan the expedition. He prepared himself to lead it by studying mapmaking, firearms design, and other skills. In late 1806, on the heels of his remarkable expeditionary triumph, Jefferson appointed Lewis governor of the Louisiana Territory. In 1809 while journeying to Washington on administrative business, Lewis died under mysterious circumstances near Nashville, Tennessee.

Questions to consider. Because Meriwether Lewis was eager to send word to the East, he could not in this first letter afford to compile a full report. He had to make decisions, in other words, about what information to include and what not to include. Are you in any way surprised at the letter's contents? What might he have emphasized but did not? What impression of the journey and the territory was he trying to leave with his reader? Although addressed to Jefferson personally, the letter was quickly publicized and widely read throughout the United States. Does Lewis seem to have anticipated this? Was he writing, that is, for other eyes as well as Jefferson's? If so, whose? Do you think Lewis understood the implications of his message for future American development and future U.S. foreign policy?

———————

Report on the Missouri and Columbia Rivers (1806)
Meriwether Lewis

It is with pleasure that I announce to you the safe arrival of myself and party at 12 o'clock today at this place with our papers and baggage. In obedience to your orders we have penetrated the continent of North America to the

From Reuben Gold Thwaites, ed., **Original Journals of the Lewis and Clark Expedition** (New York, 1904–05), VII: 334–337.

Pacific Ocean, and sufficiently explored the interior of the country to affirm with confidence that we have discovered the most practicable route which does exist across the continent by means of the navigable branches of the Missouri and Columbia Rivers. . . .

We view this passage across the continent as affording immense advantages to the fur trade, but fear that the advantages which it offers as a communication for the productions of the East Indies to the United States and thence to Europe will never be found equal on an extensive scale to that by way of the Cape of Good Hope; still we believe that many articles not bulky, brittle nor of a very perishable nature may be conveyed to the United States by this route with more facility and at less expense than by that at present practiced.

The Missouri and all its branches from the Cheyenne upwards abound more in beaver and common otter, than any other streams on earth, particularly that proportion of them lying within the Rocky Mountains. The furs of all this immense tract of country including such as may be collected on the upper portion of the River St. Peters, Red River, and the Assinniboin with the immense country watered by the Columbia, may be conveyed to the mouth of the Columbia by the 1st of August in each year and from thence be shipped to, and arrive in Canton [China] earlier than the furs at present shipped from Montreal annually arrive in London. The British N. West Company of Canada were they permitted by the United States might also convey their furs collected in the Athabaske, on the Saskashawan, and south and west of Lake Winnipic by that route within the period before mentioned. The productions of nine-tenths of the most valuable fur country of America could be conveyed by the route proposed to the East Indies.

In the infancy of the trade across the continent, or during the period that the trading establishments shall be confined to the Missouri and its branches, the men employed in this trade will be compelled to convey the furs collected in that quarter as low on the Columbia as tide water [near the ocean], in which case they could not return to the falls of the Missouri until about the 1st of October, which would be so late in the season that there would be considerable danger of the river being obstructed by ice before they could reach this place and consequently that the commodities brought from the East Indies would be detained until the following spring; but this difficulty will at once vanish when establishments are also made on the Columbia, and a sufficient number of men employed at them to convey annually the productions of the East Indies to the upper establishment on the Kooskooske, and there exchange them with the men of the Missouri for their furs in the beginning of July. By this means the furs not only of the Missouri but those also of the Columbia may be shipped to the East Indies by the season before mentioned, and the commodities of the East Indies arrive at St. Louis or the mouth of the Ohio by the last of September in each year.

Although the Columbia does not as much as the Missouri abound in beaver and otter, yet it is by no means despicable in this respect, and would

The Lewis and Clark Expedition.   In this depiction, Meriwether Lewis stands at the door of a tepee, with William Clark, musket in hand, to his right. Inside the shelter is Sacajawea, a Shoshone woman hired with her husband, a French-Canadian named Charbonneau, as interpreters and guides. At the far left is York, Clark's slave, an accomplished linguist whose labor in winning the good will of the Indian tribes encountered by the group was invaluable. (Montana State Capitol Building)

furnish a valuable fur trade distinct from any other consideration in addition to the otter and beaver which it could furnish. There might be collected considerable quantities of the skins of three species of bear affording a great variety of colours and of superior delicacy, those also of the tiger cat, several species of fox, martin and several others of an inferior class of furs, besides the valuable sea otter of the coast.

If the government will only aid, even in a very limited manner, the enterprise of her citizens I am fully convinced that we shall shortly derive the benefits of a most lucrative trade from this source, and that in the course of ten or twelve years a tour across the continent by the route mentioned will be undertaken by individuals with as little concern as a voyage across the Atlantic is at present.

The British N. West Company of Canada has for several years carried on a partial trade with the Minnetares, Ahwayhaways and Mandans on the Missouri from their establishments on the Assinniboin at the entrance of Mouse River; at present I have good reason for believing that they intend shortly to form an establishment near those nations with a view to engross the fur trade of the Missouri. The known enterprise and resources of this company, latterly strengthened by an union with their powerful rival the X. Y. Company, renders them formidable in that distant part of the continent to all other traders; and in my opinion if we are to regard the trade of the Missouri as an object of importance to the United States, the strides of this company towards the Missouri cannot be too vigilantly watched nor too firmly and speedily opposed by our government. The embarrassments under which the navigation of the Missouri at present labours from the unfriendly dispositions of the Kancez, the several bands of Tetons, Assinniboins, and those tribes that resort to the British establishments on the Saskashawan is also a subject which requires the earliest attention of our government. As I shall shortly be with you I have deemed it unnecessary here to detail the several ideas which have presented themselves to my mind on those subjects, more especially when I consider that a thorough knowledge of the geography of the country is absolutely necessary to their being understood, and leisure has not yet permitted us to make but one general map of the country which I am unwilling to risk by the mail. . . .

I have brought with me several skins of the sea otter, two skins of the native sheep of America, five skins and skeletons complete of the Bighorn or mountain ram, and a skin of the mule deer besides the skins of several other quadrapeds and birds native of the countries through which we have passed. I have also preserved a pretty extensive collection of plants, and collected nine other vocabularies [of Indian tribes].

I have prevailed on the great chief of the Mandan nation to accompany me to Washington; he is now with my friend and colleague Capt. Clark at this place, in good health and spirits, and very anxious to proceed. . . .

The route by which I purpose traveling from hence to Washington is by way of Cahokia, Vincennes, Louisville, Ky., the Crab Orchard, Abington, Fincastle, Stanton and Charlottesville. Any letters directed to me at Louisville ten days after the receipt of this will most probably meet me at that place. I am very anxious to learn the state of my friends in Albemarle, particularly whether my mother is yet living. I am with every sentiment of esteem your Obt. and very Humble servant.

19.

EMPOWERING CONGRESS

Before the American Revolution, England had prevented the colonies from setting up their own banking institutions, hoping in this way to force them to rely chiefly on British creditors. It was natural, then, that with independence came efforts by local merchants to establish American banks, three of which were in operation by the 1780s. But since these seemed inadequate to finance the kind of economic growth many northern businessmen wanted for the new country, Alexander Hamilton, Washington's secretary of the treasury, persuaded Congress in 1791 to charter a massive Bank of the United States (BUS), with huge reserves and numerous branch offices. Thomas Jefferson's followers never liked the idea of a giant federal bank, though, because it seemed too favorable to commercial interests and too forceful a use of federal power. So when the bank's charter expired in 1811, Congress, with President James Madison's support, refused to renew it.

Killing Hamilton's bank necessarily meant killing a crucial source of business credit. By now, though, the economy had advanced to a point where state-chartered banks (approximately twenty by 1815) could fill much of the gap. It was somewhat ironic, therefore, that when President James Monroe, last of the Jeffersonian "Virginia Dynasty" presidents, persuaded Congress to charter a second Bank of the United States in 1816, some of its strongest opponents were not southerners or farmers but supporters of these thriving state institutions. Accordingly, when the BUS opened a branch in Baltimore, the Maryland legislature levied a stiff tax on it. James McCulloch, cashier of the BUS's threatened Baltimore branch, refused to pay the tax, whereupon Maryland sued, McCulloch countersued, and the case wound up in the Supreme Court, Chief Justice John Marshall presiding.

The case was tricky. Did the central government have the right to sponsor economic and cultural entities such as banks? Did the federal system allow states to punish creations and instruments of the central government? John Marshall had not hesitated to assert the Court's authority to review legislation in 1803, and he did not hesitate to grapple with the issues raised here either. Indeed, so forcefully did he grapple with them that his opinion in **McCulloch** v. **Maryland** may have been the most important of his long tenure, and the one in which he gave fullest expression to his ardent Federalist faith in central authority.

Questions to consider. Of the two questions considered by Marshall—congressional authority to create and a state's right to tax these creations—which does he seem to have considered the more important? Was it necessary to consider congressional authority first? On which of these two questions do you find him more persuasive? Would an agrarian democrat such as Thomas Jefferson have agreed that the "power of the purse" implies the power to create a federal bank? How would slaveholders such as John C. Calhoun (Document 21) (and Jefferson) have reacted? Was **McCulloch,** as some have argued, actually the first step on the road to the Civil War?

═══════

McCulloch *v*. Maryland (1819)

. . . The first question made in this cause is, has Congress power to incorporate a bank? . . .

In discussing this question, the counsel for the State of Maryland have deemed it of some importance, in the construction of the constitution, to consider that instrument not as emanating from the people, but as the act of sovereign and independent States. The powers of the general government, it has been said, are delegated by the States, who alone are truly sovereign; and must be exercised in subordination to the States, who alone possess supreme dominion.

It would be difficult to sustain this proposition. The convention which framed the constitution was, indeed, elected by the State legislatures. But the instrument, when it came from their hands, was a mere proposal, without obligation, or pretensions to it. It was reported to the then existing Congress of the United States, with a request that it might "be submitted to a convention of Delegates chosen in each State, by the people thereof, under the recommendation of its legislature, for their assent and ratification." This mode of proceeding was adopted; and by the Convention, by Congress, and by the State Legislatures, the instrument was submitted to the people. They acted upon it, in the only manner in which they can act safely, effectively, and wisely, on such a subject, by assembling in Convention. It is true, they assembled in their several States; and where else should they have assembled? . . .

From these Conventions the constitution derives its whole authority. The government proceeds directly from the people; is "ordained and established" in the name of the people; and is declared to be ordained, "in order to form

From 4 Wheaton, 316.

a more perfect union, establish justice, insure domestic tranquillity, and secure the blessings of liberty to themselves and to their posterity." The assent of the States, in their sovereign capacity, is implied in calling a Convention, and thus submitting that instrument to the people. But the people were at perfect liberty to accept or reject it; and their act was final. It required not the affirmance, and could not be negatived, by the State governments. The constitution, when thus adopted, was of complete obligation, and bound the State sovereignties. . . .

If any one proposition could command the universal assent of mankind, we might expect it would be this: that the government of the Union, though limited in its powers, is supreme within its sphere of action. This would seem to result necessarily from its nature. It is the government of all; its powers are delegated by all; it represents all, and acts for all. Though any one State may be willing to control its operations, no State is willing to allow others to control them. The nation, on those subjects on which it can act, must necessarily bind its component parts. But this question is not left to mere reason: the people have, in express terms, decided it, by saying, "this constitution, and the laws of the United States, which shall be made in pursuance thereof," "shall be the supreme law of the land," and by requiring that the members of the State legislatures, and the officers of the executive and judicial departments of the States, shall take the oath of fidelity to it.

The government of the United States, then, though limited in its powers, is supreme; and its laws, when made in pursuance of the constitution, form the supreme law of the land, "anything in the constitution or laws of any State, to the contrary, notwithstanding." . . .

Although, among the enumerated powers of government, we do not find the word "bank," or "incorporation," we find the great powers to lay and collect taxes; to borrow money; to regulate commerce; to declare and conduct a war; and to raise and support armies and navies. The sword and the purse, all the external relations, and no inconsiderable portion of the industry of the nation, are intrusted to its government. It can never be pretended that these vast powers draw after them others of inferior importance, merely because they are inferior. Such an idea can never be advanced. But it may, with great reason, be contended, that a government, intrusted with such ample powers, on the due execution of which the happiness and prosperity of the nation so vitally depends, must also be intrusted with ample means for their execution. The power being given, it is the interest of the nation to facilitate its execution. It can never be their interest, and cannot be presumed to have been their intention, to clog and embarrass its execution by withholding the most appropriate means. . . .

The government which has a right to do an act, and has imposed on it the duty of performing that act, must, according to the dictates of reason, be allowed to select the means; and those who contend that it may not select any appropriate means, that one particular mode of effecting the object is excepted, take upon themselves the burden of establishing that exception. . . .

But the constitution of the United States has not left the right of Congress to employ the necessary means, for the execution of the powers conferred on the government, to general reasoning. To its enumeration of powers is added that of making "all laws which shall be necessary and proper, for carrying into execution the foregoing powers, and all other powers vested by this constitution, in the government of the United States, or in any department thereof." . . .

But the argument on which most reliance is placed, is drawn from the peculiar language of this clause. Congress is not empowered by it to make all laws, which may have relation to the powers conferred on the government, but such only as may be *"necessary and proper"* for carrying them into execution. The word *"necessary"* is considered as controlling the whole sentence, and as limiting the right to pass laws for the execution of the granted powers, to such as are indispensable, and without which the power would be nugatory. That it excludes the choice of means, and leaves to Congress, in each case, that only which is most direct and simple.

Is it true, that this is the sense in which the word "necessary" is always used? Does it always import an absolute physical necessity, so strong, that one thing, to which another may be termed necessary cannot exist without that other? We think it does not. If reference be had to its use, in the common affairs of the world, or in approved authors, we find that it frequently imports no more than that one thing is convenient, or useful, or essential to another. To employ the means necessary to an end, is generally understood as employing any means calculated to produce the end, and not as being confined to those single means, without which the end would be entirely unattainable. Such is the character of human language, that no word conveys to the mind, in all situations one single definite idea; and nothing is more common than to use words in a figurative sense. Almost all compositions contain words, which, taken in their rigorous sense, would convey a meaning different from that which is obviously intended. It is essential to just construction, that many words which import something excessive, should be understood in a more mitigated sense—in that sense which common usage justifies. The word "necessary" is of this description. . . .

. . . The subject [of this case] is the execution of those great powers on which the welfare of a nation essentially depends. It must have been the intention of those who gave these powers, to insure, as far as human prudence could insure, their beneficial execution. This could not be done by confining the choice of means to such narrow limits as not to leave it in the power of Congress to adopt any which might be appropriate, and which were conducive to the end. This provision is made in a constitution intended to endure for ages to come, and, consequently, to be adapted to the various crises of human affairs. To have prescribed the means by which government should, in all future time, execute its powers, would have been to change, entirely, the character of the instrument, and give it the properties of a legal code. It would have been an unwise attempt to provide, by immutable rules, for exigencies which, if foreseen at all, must have been seen dimly, and which can be best provided for as they occur. . . .

If a corporation may be employed indiscriminately with other means to carry into execution the powers of the government, no particular reason can be assigned for excluding the use of a bank, if required for its fiscal operations. To use one, must be within the discretion of Congress, if it be an appropriate mode of executing the powers of government. That it is a convenient, a useful, and essential instrument in the prosecution of its fiscal operations, is not now a subject of controversy. . . .

After the most deliberate consideration, it is the unanimous and decided opinion of this court, that the act to incorporate the Bank of the United States is a law made in pursuance of the constitution, and is a part of the supreme law of the land. . . .

It being the opinion of the Court, that the act incorporating the bank is constitutional; and that the power of establishing a branch in the State of Maryland might be properly exercised by the bank itself, we proceed to inquire—

. . . Whether the State of Maryland may, without violating the constitution, tax that branch?

That the power of taxation is one of vital importance; that it is retained by the States; that it is not abridged by the grant of a similar power to the government of the Union; that it is to be concurrently exercised by the two governments: are truths which have never been denied. But, such is the paramount character of the constitution, that its capacity to withdraw any subject from the action of even this power, is admitted. . . .

. . . [Our] great principle is, that the constitution and the laws made in pursuance thereof are supreme; that they control the constitution and laws of the respective States, and cannot be controlled by them. From this, which may be almost termed an axiom, other propositions are deduced as corollaries, on the truth or error of which, and on their application to this case, the cause has been supposed to depend. These are, 1. That a power to create implies a power to preserve. 2. That a power to destroy, if wielded by a different hand, is hostile to, and incompatible with, these powers to create and preserve. 3. That where this repugnancy exists, that authority which is supreme must control, not yield to that over which it is supreme. . . .

If we apply the principle for which the State of Maryland contends, to the constitution generally, we shall find it capable of changing totally the character of that instrument. We shall find it capable of arresting all the measures of the government, and of prostrating it at the foot of the states. The American people have declared their constitution, and the laws made in pursuance thereof, to be supreme; but this principle would transfer the supremacy, in fact, to the States.

If the States may tax one instrument, employed by the government in the execution of its powers, they may tax any and every other instrument. They may tax the mail; they may tax the mint; they may tax patent rights;

they may tax the papers of the custom-house; they may tax judicial process; they may tax all the means employed by the government, to an excess which would defeat all the ends of government. This was not intended by the American people. They did not design to make their government dependent on the States. . . .

The Court has bestowed on this subject its most deliberate consideration. The result is a conviction that the States have no power, by taxation or otherwise, to retard, impede, burden, or in any manner control, the operations of the constitutional laws enacted by Congress to carry into execution the powers vested in the general government. This is, we think, the unavoidable consequence of that supremacy which the constitution has declared. We are unanimously of opinion, that the law passed by the legislature of Maryland, imposing a tax on the Bank of the United States, is unconstitutional and void.

20.

A HEMISPHERIC INTEREST

In the early part of the nineteenth century, Spain's colonies in Latin America revolted, declared their independence, and received diplomatic recognition from the United States. In 1823, however, a group of European powers known as the Holy Alliance talked of sending an expedition to the New World to restore Spain's control over her former colonies. President James Monroe was alarmed at the prospect. So was George Canning, the British foreign minister, who was afraid that British trade with the new American nations might be disrupted by European intervention. Canning asked the United States to join Britain in a declaration warning the European nations against attempts to retake Spain's former colonies by force.

Monroe liked Canning's proposal, but Secretary of State John Quincy Adams argued forcefully for a unilateral statement by the United States. Not only was Adams concerned about intervention in South America, he was also disturbed by Russian expansion (from Alaska, which Russia owned, southward) on the Pacific Coast. He wanted the United States to make it clear to the European powers that all parts of the New World were closed to further colonization, and he wanted to send direct warnings to all the nations involved.

Adams managed to win Monroe to his views. The president agreed to drop the idea of a joint declaration with England in favor of an independent statement. He also adopted Adams's view that the statement should apply the noncolonization principle to the New World as a whole. But he insisted on making the declaration in a public document rather than in notes sent directly to the nations involved.

The Monroe Doctrine, as the declaration came to be called, appeared in Monroe's annual message to Congress on December 2, 1823. The declaration consisted of two sections. The first was a warning to Russia in the Pacific Northwest and contained the following noncolonization principle: "The American continents, by the free and independent condition which they have assumed and maintain, are henceforth not to be considered as subjects for future colonization by any European power." The second section was directed against the powers that might intervene in South America. It declared that the United States would not interfere with "existing colonies or dependencies of any European power" in the New World, but that any attempt to reconquer the independent republics of Latin America would be considered "the manifestation of an unfriendly disposition toward the United States."

Monroe's message pleased most Americans but irritated Europeans; they knew the young nation was not strong enough to back up its words. The British, whose navy was primarily responsible for keeping Europeans from meddling in America, were particularly irked. They realized Monroe's principles could be used against them as well as against other nations. But Monroe's statement was soon forgotten. The expression **Monroe Doctrine** did not become common until the 1850s. And it was not until the late nineteenth century that the Monroe Doctrine itself came to be regarded as one of the cornerstones of American foreign policy.

Monroe was born in Virginia in 1758. After two years of study at the College of William and Mary, he left to take part in the Revolution and was wounded at the battle of Trenton. After leaving the service, he studied law with Jefferson, served in Congress from 1783 to 1786, and was elected to the new U.S. Senate in 1790. An ally from the start of his friend and sponsor, Thomas Jefferson, he went to France in 1803 to help Robert R. Livingston negotiate the Louisiana Purchase. From 1799 to 1800 and in 1811 he was governor of Virginia. He held a cabinet post during the War of 1812 and easily went on to win election to the presidency in 1816 and again in 1820. The last of the "Virginia dynasty" to occupy the White House and also the last president to wear the wig and small clothes (knee breeches) of eighteenth-century gentlemen, Monroe presided over the nation during a period of reduced sectional and party rivalry known as the Era of Good Feelings, which his moderate outlook and instinct for harmonizing different political interests did much to produce. He retired to Virginia in 1825, where he succeeded Jefferson as regent of the University of Virginia and, also like Jefferson, sank into genteel poverty. He died while visiting New York City on July 4, 1831, the third president (after John Adams and Jefferson) to die on the anniversary of American independence.

Questions to consider. Note the extent to which Monroe's message derives from the notion of American separateness and exceptionalism. Note, too, how Thomas Jefferson's roomy chosen country had become with Monroe a good deal roomier just twenty-two years later. As for the security issue that concerned Monroe, how important was it that the European powers were not merely strong but also had political systems different from that of the United States? Was it an alien system or an alien force, or some combination of the two, that disturbed Monroe? How important, finally, were the wishes of "our southern brethren," meaning the Latin Americans, to U.S. policymakers? Why did Monroe refer to them? Does the reference make the American system more or less justifiable? More or less defensible? More or less open-ended and subject to the vagaries of domestic politics and international upheavals?

The Monroe Doctrine (1823)

At the proposal of the Russian Imperial Government, made through the minister of the Emperor residing here, a full power and instructions have been transmitted to the minister of the United States at St. Petersburg to arrange by amicable negotiation the respective rights and interests of the two nations on the northwest coast of this continent. A similar proposal has been made by His Imperial Majesty to the Government of Great Britain, which has likewise been acceded to. The Government of the United States has been desirous by this friendly proceeding of manifesting the great value which they have invariably attached to the friendship of the Emperor and their solicitude to cultivate the best understanding with his Government. In the discussion to which this interest has given rise and in the arrangements by which they may terminate the occasion has been judged proper for asserting, as a principle in which the rights and interests of the United States are involved, that the American continents, by the free and independent condition which they have assumed and maintain, are henceforth not to be considered as subjects for future colonization by any European power.

It was stated at the commencement of the last session that a great effort was then making in Spain and Portugal to improve the condition of the people of those countries, and that it appeared to be conducted with extraordinary moderation. It need scarcely be remarked that the result has been so far very different from what was then anticipated. Of events in that quarter of the globe, with which we have so much intercourse and from which we derive our origin, we have always been anxious and interested spectators. The citizens of the United States cherish sentiments the most friendly in favor of the liberty and happiness of their fellow-men on that side of the Atlantic. In the wars of the European powers in matters relating to themselves we have never taken any part, nor does it comport with our policy so to do. It is only when our rights are invaded or seriously menaced that we resent injuries or make preparations for our defense. With the movements in this hemisphere we are of necessity more immediately connected, and by causes which must be obvious to all enlightened and impartial observers. The political system of the allied powers is essentially different in this respect from that of America. This difference proceeds from that which exists in their respective Governments; and to the defense of our own, which has been achieved by the loss of so much blood and treasure, and matured by the wisdom of their most enlightened citizens, and under which we have enjoyed unexampled felicity, this whole nation is devoted. We owe it, therefore, to candor and to the amicable relations existing between the United States and those powers to declare that we should consider any attempt on their part to extend their system to any

From James D. Richardson, ed., *A Compilation of the Messages and Papers of the Presidents* (Government Printing Office, Washington, D.C., 1897–1907), II: 786–789.

James Monroe.   Elected president in 1816 and re-elected in 1820, James Monroe, who wore knee breeches, silk stockings, cockade, and sword, was the "last of the cocked hats." His career dated back to the period of the American Revolution, in which he had served as a soldier. After the war he served on several diplomatic missions for the new nation and was James Madison's secretary of state just before becoming president. The United States entered an "Era of Good Feelings" during Monroe's presidency and, with the demise of the Federalist party, party strife on the national level came to an end. For a time, the United States was a one-party state. (National Portrait Gallery, Smithsonian Institution, Washington, D.C.)

portion of this hemisphere as dangerous to our peace and safety. With the existing colonies or dependencies of any European power we have not interfered and shall not interfere. But with the Governments who have declared their independence and maintained it, and whose independence we have, on great consideration and on just principles, acknowledged, we could not view any interposition for the purpose of oppressing them, or controlling in any other manner their destiny, by any European power in any other light than as the manifestation of an unfriendly disposition toward the United States. In the war between those new Governments and Spain we declared our neutrality at the time of their recognition, and to this we have adhered, and shall continue to adhere, provided no change shall occur which, in the judgment of the competent authorities of this Government, shall make a corresponding change on the part of the United States indispensable to their security.

The late events in Spain and Portugal shew that Europe is still unsettled. Of this important fact no stronger proof can be adduced than that the allied powers should have thought it proper, on any principle satisfactory to themselves, to have interposed by force in the internal concerns of Spain. To what extent such interposition may be carried, on the same principle, is a question in which all independent powers whose governments differ from theirs are interested, even those most remote, and surely none more so than the United States. Our policy in regard to Europe, which was adopted at an early stage of the wars which have so long agitated that quarter of the globe, nevertheless remains the same, which is, not to interfere in the internal concerns of any of its powers; to consider the government *de facto* as the legitimate government for us; to cultivate friendly relations with it, and to preserve those relations by a frank, firm, and manly policy, meeting in all instances the just claims of every power, submitting to injuries from none. But in regard to these continents circumstances are eminently and conspicuously different. It is impossible that the allied powers should extend their political system to any portion of either continent without endangering our peace and happiness; nor can anyone believe that our southern brethren, if left to themselves, would adopt it of their own accord. It is equally impossible, therefore, that we should behold such interposition in any form with indifference. If we look to the comparative strength and resources of Spain and those new Governments, and their distance from each other, it must be obvious that she can never subdue them. It is still the true policy of the United States to leave the parties to themselves, in the hope that other powers will pursue the same course. . . .

21.

THE SECTIONAL SPECTER

The first great sectional struggle in the United States (after the Missouri crisis over slavery) was over the tariff. Northern industrialists favored high tariffs to protect their products from foreign competition. But the South was an agricultural region, and Southerners complained that protective tariffs raised the price of manufactured goods and prevented them from importing low-priced goods from abroad. On May 20, 1828, Congress passed a tariff bill with rates so high that South Carolina's John C. Calhoun (vice president at the time) called it a "Tariff of Abominations." He presented a lengthy statement of the Southern position on tariffs in which he developed his theory of nullification.

Calhoun believed in the "compact" theory of the Union. He maintained that the Constitution was a contract into which the states had entered of their own free will. The states retained their sovereignty, and the federal government was merely their agent for general purposes. If the federal government exceeded its authority and encroached on the powers of the states, the states had a right to resist. Calhoun thought the constitutionality of acts of Congress should be decided by state conventions called for that purpose. If such a convention declared an act of Congress in violation of the Constitution, that act became null and void within the borders of that state. Calhoun insisted that the Constitution did not give Congress the right to levy protective tariffs and that the states had a right to nullify tariff legislation.

On December 19, 1828, the South Carolina legislature published Calhoun's statement (without mentioning his name) as "South Carolina Exposition and Protest," together with resolutions, reproduced below, condemning the tariff. For the time being, South Carolina contented itself with making this protest, hoping that the tariff would be revised after Andrew Jackson became president. But in July 1832, when a new tariff bill was passed by Congress and signed by Jackson, South Carolinians decided to put Calhoun's theory into practice. On November 4, 1832, a special state convention met in Columbia, adopted an ordinance declaring the tariffs of 1828 and 1832 unconstitutional, and announced that no tariff duties would be collected in the state after February 1, 1833. Jackson at once denounced South Carolina's action and asked Congress to give him authority to use the army and navy, if necessary, to compel South Carolina to obey the law. South Carolina continued defiant. When Congress passed a compromise bill lowering the tariff rate, the "nullies" (as they were called) repealed the nullification ordinance. But they did not disavow the nullification theory.

Calhoun was born in South Carolina in 1782 to an upcountry farmer. After he graduated from Yale College, he practiced law briefly and then married a wealthy Charleston woman and began a political climb that led to Congress, a post in James Monroe's cabinet, and the vice presidency under both John Quincy Adams and Andrew Jackson. He began as a vigorous nationalist, favoring the protective tariff, but moved to states' rights and an antitariff position when it became clear that South Carolina had more to gain from free trade. During the nullification crisis he resigned from the vice presidency in December 1832 for a seat in the Senate, where he became one of the "great triumvirate" (along with Henry Clay and Daniel Webster), an implacable foe of Jackson, and a staunch supporter of South Carolina, the South, and slavery. He died in Washington, D.C., in early 1850.

Questions to consider. Both economic and political issues are raised by Calhoun in "South Carolina Exposition and Protest." As to the former, why was a protective tariff considered so threatening to the Carolinians? Were they fearful of higher prices for imported goods or of reduced markets for their own product, cotton? Why did the "encouragement of domestic industry," originally urged by Alexander Hamilton in 1791 (Document 15), cause such a fierce blowup in 1828 but not before? Was Calhoun trying to speak for all of American agriculture or only for a certain kind? Was it the threat to agriculture or to something else that most disturbed Calhoun? Which of the eight articles of the "Protest" furnishes the best clue to the situation in South Carolina? As to the political issue, why did Calhoun fear what he called "simple consolidated government" as a threat to freedom? To what extent could he draw support for this idea from the writings of James Madison in 1787 (Document 14) and Thomas Jefferson in 1801 (Document 16)? What would John Marshall (Documents 17 and 19) have made of the theory of nullification? Could the theory have helped in a practical way to resolve constitutional disputes?

South Carolina Exposition and Protest (1828)

John C. Calhoun

The Senate and House of Representatives of South Carolina, now met, and sitting in General Assembly, through the Hon. William Smith and the Hon. Robert Y. Hayne, the representatives in the Senate of the United States, do, in the name and on behalf of the good people of the said commonwealth, solemnly PROTEST against the system of protecting duties, lately adopted by the federal government, for the following reasons:—

1st. *Because* the good people of this commonwealth believe that the powers of Congress were delegated to it in trust for the accomplishment of certain specified objects which limit and control them, and that every exercise of them for any other purpose, is a violation of the Constitution as unwarrantable as the undisguised assumption of substantive, independent powers not granted or expressly withheld.

2d. *Because* the power to lay duties on imports is, and in its very nature can be, only a means of effecting objects specified by the Constitution; since no free government, and least of all a government of enumerated powers, can of right impose any tax, any more than a penalty, which is not at once justified by public necessity, and clearly within the scope and purview of the social compact; and since the right of confining appropriations of the public money to such legitimate and constitutional objects is as essential to the liberty of the people as their unquestionable privilege to be taxed only by their own consent.

3d. *Because* they believe that the tariff law passed by Congress at its last session, and all other acts of which the principal object is the protection of manufactures, or any other branch of domestic industry, if they be considered as the exercise of a power in Congress to tax the people at its own good will and pleasure, and to apply the money raised to objects not specified in the Constitution, is a violation of these fundamental principles, a breach of a well-defined trust, and a perversion of the high powers vested in the federal government for federal purposes only.

4th. *Because* such acts, considered in the light of a regulation of commerce, are equally liable to objection; since, although the power to regulate commerce may, like all other powers, be exercised so as to protect domestic manufactures, yet it is clearly distinguishable from a power to do so *eo nomine,* both in the nature of the thing and in the common acception of the terms; and because the confounding of them would lead to the most extravagant results, since the encouragement of domestic industry implies an absolute control over

Jonathan Elliot, ed., The Debates in the Several State Conventions on the Adoption of the Federal Constitution, &c (5 v., J. B. Lippincott, Philadelphia, 1836), IV: 580–582.

John C. Calhoun. Calhoun, who served as congressman, vice president under Andrew Jackson, and then senator from South Carolina, started out as a strong nationalist and then became one of the most vigorous states' righters in the nation. He insisted that sovereignty (supreme power) resided in "the people of the several states" rather than in the people making up the nation as a whole, and that the people of the states had the right to nullify any federal laws they thought threatened their state's welfare. Calhoun developed his doctrine of nullification as a reaction against protective-tariff measures designed to encourage Northern industries but which he thought hurt South Carolina and other Southern states with little or no manufacturing. He was also a states' righter because he wanted to safeguard the institution of slavery from interference by antislavery crusaders in the North. (National Portrait Gallery, Smithsonian Institution, Washington, D.C.)

all the interests, resources, and pursuits of a people, and is inconsistent with the idea of any other than a simple, consolidated government.

5th. *Because,* from the contemporaneous exposition of the Constitution in the numbers of the *Federalist,* (which is cited only because the Supreme Court has recognized its authority), it is clear that the power to regulate commerce was considered by the Convention as only incidentally connected with the encouragement of agriculture and manufactures; and because the power of laying imposts and duties on imports was not understood to justify in any case, a prohibition of foreign commodities, except as a means of extending commerce, by coercing foreign nations to a fair reciprocity in their intercourse with us, or for some *bona fide* commercial purpose.

6th. *Because,* whilst the power to protect manufactures is nowhere expressly granted to Congress, nor can be considered as necessary and proper to carry into effect any specified power, it seems to be expressly reserved to the states, by the 10th section of the 1st article of the Constitution.

7th. *Because* even admitting Congress to have a constitutional right to protect manufactures by the imposition of duties, or by regulations of commerce, designed principally for that purpose, yet a tariff of which the operation is grossly unequal and oppressive, is such an abuse of power as is incompatible with the principles of a free government and the great ends of civil society, justice, and equality of rights and protection.

8th. *Finally,* because South Carolina, from her climate, situation, and peculiar institutions, is, and must ever continue to be, wholly dependent upon agriculture and commerce, not only for her prosperity, but for her very existence as a state; because the valuable products of her soil—the blessings by which Divine Providence seems to have designed to compensate for the great disadvantages under which she suffers in other respects—are among the very few that can be cultivated with any profit by slave labor; and if, by the loss of her foreign commerce, these products should be confined to an inadequate market, the fate of this fertile state would be poverty and utter desolation; her citizens, in despair, would emigrate to more fortunate regions, and the whole frame and constitution of her civil policy be impaired and deranged, if not dissolved entirely.

Deeply impressed with these considerations, the representatives of the good people of this commonwealth, anxiously desiring to live in peace with their fellow-citizens, and to do all that in them lies to preserve and perpetuate the union of the states, and liberties of which it is the surest pledge, but feeling it to be their bounden duty to expose and resist all encroachments upon the true spirit of the Constitution, lest an apparent acquiescence in the system of protecting duties should be drawn into precedent—do, in the name of the commonwealth of South Carolina, claim to enter upon the Journal of the Senate their *protest* against it as unconstitutional, oppressive, and unjust.

22.

ASSAULTING MONOPOLY

The Second Bank of the United States (BUS), chartered by Congress in 1816 for twenty years, was a powerful institution. It performed several important functions: it served as a depository for government funds, it marketed government securities, it made loans to businesses, and, by maintaining specie payments (gold and silver) on its bank notes, it provided the country with a sound currency. With headquarters in Philadelphia and twenty-nine branches in other cities, the BUS contained private funds as well as government money and controlled one-fifth of the bank notes and one-third of the bank deposits and specie of the country. Advocates of "cheap money"—state bankers, land speculators, and some small businessowners—were hostile to the bank because it restricted the amount of paper money in circulation—they hoped to benefit from an abundance of paper currency. But those who favored "hard money" also disliked the bank. Eastern working people were suspicious of wages paid in paper money and Southern planters and Western farmers also tended to look on any money but gold and silver as dishonest. Andrew Jackson, who had an unpleasant experience with banks as a young man, was a hard-money man and distrustful of all banks.

In the spring of 1832, friends of the BUS in Congress, particularly Henry Clay, urged Nicholas Biddle, the bank's president, to seek a renewal of the bank's charter. The charter did not actually expire until 1836, but Clay was sure that Congress would approve a new charter at once. He was right; after investigating the bank's operations, Congress passed a recharter bill by large majorities. But on July 10, 1832, President Jackson vetoed the bill. In his veto message, he denounced the bank bill as an unconstitutional violation of states' rights as well as an endorsement of a dangerous monopoly whose profits came from "the earnings of the American people" and went to the benefit of foreign stockholders and "a few hundred of our own citizens, chiefly of the richest class."

When Jackson ran for re-election in 1832 the BUS was the main campaign issue. Henry Clay, the candidate of the National Republicans, was a strong supporter of the bank, and so were most eastern merchants and businessmen. They insisted that the bank performed an essential function in managing the country's finances. But working people in the East and farmers in the West tended to support Jackson. They felt that Nicholas Biddle followed policies that favored the rich and powerful at the expense of the plain people. Biddle himself continually boasted about the great powers at his disposal and made no secret of his contempt for popular government. During the 1832 campaign he worked hard to defeat Jackson by lending large sums of money to Jackson's opponents. Biddle's behavior convinced the Jacksonians that the BUS represented a dangerous "concentration of power in the hands of a few men irresponsible to the people."

After his triumphant re-election Jackson decided to move against the bank at once without waiting for its charter to expire. He directed Secretary of the Treasury Roger B. Taney to place government funds in state banks rather than in the BUS, where they were usually deposited. By the end of 1833, some twenty-three state banks, called "pet banks" by Jackson's enemies, were handling funds of the federal government. Jackson's withholding of federal funds effectively killed Biddle's bank. Although it remained in operation until its charter expired in 1836, the BUS was no longer a powerful force. In 1836 it was reorganized as a state bank in Pennsylvania. The decline of the BUS was accompanied by increasing disarray in the nation's economy. In 1837 came a financial panic, followed by the country's worst depression up to that time.

Andrew Jackson was born in 1767 on the Carolina frontier; his parents were poor Scotch-Irish immigrants. But Jackson climbed rapidly to wealth and status through land speculation and law practice. In 1795, before he was thirty, he established the Hermitage, a splendid plantation near Nashville, Tennessee, and he headed for Congress the next year. As major-general of his state's militia, Jackson won a victory over the British at the battle of New Orleans in 1815 that catapulted him to national prominence and led to a Senate seat in 1823 and the presidency in 1828. Known as Old Hickory and famous as a champion of the West and the common man, Jackson quarreled with John C. Calhoun over nullification as well as with Biddle over the BUS. These conflicts added to his popularity and enabled him to build a strong Democratic party based on patronage and personality as well as on appeals to regional and class interests. Having survived the first attempt to assassinate a president when an unemployed housepainter attacked him in 1835, Jackson retired at the end of his second term to the Hermitage, where he died in 1845.

Questions to consider. Jackson, as you will see, opposed the BUS as a monopoly. Why did he attack monopolies so strongly? Were there other monopolies in the country at that time besides the BUS? Did banks in general trouble Jackson, or only this particular bank? How did his castigation of foreign control strengthen Jackson's position with the people? Note, too, the president's concern for the right of states to tax the bank and of state-chartered banks to prosper. Is it surprising that a vigorous chief executive and strong opponent of nullification should here be a champion of states' rights? In assuming this stance, was Jackson acting in the tradition of Thomas Jefferson (Document 16) or of John C. Calhoun (Document 21)? With whom was Jackson quarreling in his remarks near the end of the message about "necessary" and "proper"? Consider, finally, Jackson's championing of the low and poor against the high and rich. Did this appeal to class differences, as opposed to occupational or sectional ones, signal a new turn in American politics? If so, why do you suppose it occurred in 1832 rather than, say, in 1816 or 1824? Who were Jackson's poor, anyway?

Bank Veto Message (1832)

Andrew Jackson

The bill "to modify and continue" the act entitled "An act to incorporate the subscribers to the Bank of the United States" was presented to me on the 4th July instant. Having . . . come to the conclusion that it ought not to become a law, I herewith return it to the Senate, in which it originated, with my objections.

A bank of the United States is in many respects convenient for the Government and useful to the people. Entertaining this opinion, and deeply impressed with the belief that some of the powers and privileges possessed by the existing bank are unauthorized by the Constitution, subversive of the rights of the States, and dangerous to the liberties of the people, I felt it my duty at an early period of my Administration to call the attention of Congress to the practicability of organizing an institution combining all its advantages and obviating these objections. I sincerely regret that in the act before me I can perceive none of these modifications of the bank charter which are necessary, in my opinion, to make it compatible with justice, with sound policy, or with the Constitution of our country.

The present corporate body . . . enjoys an exclusive privilege of banking under the authority of the General Government, a monopoly of its favor and support, and, as a necessary consequence, almost a monopoly of the foreign and domestic exchange. The powers, privileges, and favors bestowed upon it in the original charter, by increasing the value of the stock far above its par value, operated as a gratuity of many millions to the stockholders. . . .

The act before me proposes another gratuity to the holders of the same stock. . . . On all hands it is conceded that its passage will increase at least 20 or 30 per cent more the market price of the stock, subject to the payment of the annuity of $200,000 per year secured by the act, thus adding in a moment

From James D. Richardson, ed., **A Compilation of the Messages and Papers of the Presidents** (Government Printing Office, Washington, D. C., 1897–1907), II: 217–218.

General Jackson, president-elect, on his way to Washington.   Andrew Jackson was one of the most popular presidents ever to occupy the White House. On his way to Washington for his inauguration on March 4, 1829, he was greeted by crowds of enthusiastic people everywhere. Backwoodsmen, hunters, farmers, woodcutters, teamsters, and steamboat captains poured into Washington to see their hero take the oath of office. After his inaugural address men, women, and children rushed past the police and up the steps to shake hands with him. Jackson finally managed to get away, mounted his horse, and started for the White House followed by a wildly cheering throng. When the crowd reached the White House, people poured into the reception rooms, through windows as well as doors, and the building became so jammed that one could hardly move. The attempt to serve refreshments almost led to a riot. Waiters emerging from the kitchen with loaded trays were pushed to the floor by the crowd, china and glassware were smashed, and gallons of punch spilled on the carpets. (Library of Congress)

one-fourth to its par value. It is not our own citizens only who are to receive the bounty of our Government. More than eight millions of the stock of this bank are held by foreigners. By this act the American Republic proposes virtually to make them a present of some millions of dollars. For these gratuities to foreigners and to some of our own opulent citizens the act secures no equivalent whatever. . . .

Every monopoly and all exclusive privileges are granted at the expense of the public, which ought to receive a fair equivalent. The many millions which this act proposes to bestow on the stockholders of the existing bank must come directly or indirectly out of the earnings of the American people. It is due to them, therefore, if their Government sell monopolies and exclusive privileges, that they should at least exact for them as much as they are worth in open market. . . .

The modifications of the existing charter proposed by this act are not such, in my view, as make it consistent with the rights of the States or the liberties of the people. The qualification of the right of the bank to hold real estate, the limitation of its power to establish branches, and the power reserved to Congress to forbid the circulation of small notes are restrictions comparatively of little value or importance. All the objectionable principles of the existing corporation, and most of its odious features, are retained without alleviation. . . .

Is there no danger to our liberty and independence in a bank that in its nature has so little to bind it to our country? The president of the bank has told us that most of the State banks exist by its forbearance. Should its influence become concentrated, as it may under the operation of such an act as this, in the hands of a self-elected directory whose interests are identified with those of the foreign stockholders, will there not be cause to tremble for the purity of our elections in peace and for the independence of our country in war? Their power would be great whenever they might choose to exert it; but if this monopoly were regularly renewed every fifteen or twenty years on terms proposed by themselves, they might seldom in peace put forth their strength to influence elections or control the affairs of the nation. But if any private citizen or public functionary should interpose to curtail its powers or prevent a renewal of its privileges, it can not be doubted that he would be made to feel its influence. . . .

If we must have a bank with private stockholders, every consideration of sound policy and every impulse of American feeling admonishes that it should be *purely American*. Its stockholders should be composed exclusively of our own citizens, who at least ought to be friendly to our Government and willing to support it in times of difficulty and danger. . . .

The principle is conceded that the States can not rightfully tax the operations of the General Government. They can not tax the money of the Government deposited in the State banks, nor the agency of those banks in remitting it; but will any man maintain that their mere selection to perform this public service for the General Government would exempt the State banks and their ordinary business from State taxation? Had the United States, instead of establishing a bank at Philadelphia, employed a private banker to keep and transmit their funds, would it have deprived Pennsylvania of the right to tax his bank and his usual banking operations? . . .

It can not be *"necessary"* to the character of the bank as a fiscal agent of the Government that its private business should be exempted from that taxation to which all the State banks are liable, nor can I conceive it *"proper"* that the substantive and most essential powers reserved by the State shall be thus attacked and annihilated as a means of executing the powers delegated to the General Government. It may be safely assumed that none of those sages who had an agency in forming or adopting our Constitution ever imagined that any portion of the taxing power of the States not prohibited to them nor delegated to Congress was to be swept away and annihilated as a means of executing certain powers delegated to Congress. . . .

The bank is professedly established as an agent of the executive branch of the Government, and its constitutionality is maintained on that ground. Neither upon the propriety of present action nor upon the provisions of this act was the Executive consulted. It has had no opportunity to say that it neither needs nor wants an agent clothed with such powers and favored by such exemptions. There is nothing in its legitimate functions which makes it necessary or proper. Whatever interest or influence, whether public or private, has given birth to this act, it can not be found either in the wishes or necessities of the executive department, by which present action is deemed premature, and the powers conferred upon its agent not only unnecessary, but dangerous to the Government and country. . . .

There are no necessary evils in government. Its evils exist only in its abuse. If it would confine itself to equal protection, and, as Heaven does its rains, shower its favors alike on the high and the low, the rich and the poor, it would be an unqualified blessing. In the act before me there seems to be a wide and unnecessary departure from these just principles. . . .

Experience should teach us wisdom. Most of the difficulties our Government now encounters and most of the dangers which impend over our Union have sprung from an abandonment of the legitimate objects of Government by our national legislation, and the adoption of such principles as are embodied in this act. Many of our rich men have not been content with equal protection and equal benefits, but have besought us to make them richer by act of Congress. By attempting to gratify their desires we have in the results of our legislation arrayed section against section, interest against interest, and man against man, in a fearful commotion which threatens to shake the foundations of our Union. It is time to pause in our career to review our principles, and if possible revive that devoted patriotism and spirit of compromise which distinguished the sages of the Revolution and the fathers of our Union.

23.

THE TRAIL OF TEARS

American attitudes toward the Indian nations varied widely in the first part of the nineteenth century. Some people urged a policy of assimilation; others proposed the voluntary removal of the Indians to lands in the West. But land-hungry Americans in the South and West wanted to push the Indians off their ancestral lands by force, and a few people even favored extermination. When Andrew Jackson, an old Indian fighter, became president in March 1829, he adopted a policy of forcing the Indian tribes to move to the trans-Mississippi West. The Removal Act of 1830, passed by Congress with his encouragement, ordered the Indians to trade their tribal lands in the United States for new homes in federal territory west of the Mississippi River.

Indians everywhere objected to the removal policy, but there was little they could do about it. In Illinois and Florida the Indians put up forceful resistance, but after several years of bloody warfare they were finally subdued. In Georgia, the Cherokees, an Indian nation in the northwestern part of the state, tried to protect their rights peacefully. Belying the average white's contention that Indians were "savages," the Cherokees had become skilled in agriculture, built fine homes and roads, accepted Christian missionaries, adopted a constitution, and published books in an alphabet invented by Sequoya, a talented hunter who had become a silversmith and a scholar. The Cherokees had treaty commitments from the U.S. government, but neither President Jackson nor the state of Georgia was willing to respect them. In July 1830, when Georgia decided to take over their lands, the Cherokees made a moving appeal to the American people to respect their "national and individual rights" and permit them "to remain on the land of our fathers."

The Cherokees' appeal was in vain. Although some northeastern humanitarians sympathized with the Cherokees, and the Supreme Court in two decisions written by Chief Justice John Marshall ruled in the Cherokees' favor, the state of Georgia asserted its sovereignty over their territory, and Jackson sent an army of 7,000 to drive the Indians westward at bayonet point. Over 4,000 of the 15,000 Cherokees who went west along the Trail of Tears in 1838 perished en route. By the time Jackson left office he could boast that his removal policy was rapidly nearing completion. The "shotgun removal," as it was called, shocked Ralph Waldo Emerson, one of America's greatest writers. "Such a dereliction of all faith and virtue," he cried, "such a denial of justice, and such deafness to screams for mercy were never heard of in time of peace and in the dealing of a nation with its own allies and wards, since the earth was made."

Questions to consider. In the first part of their appeal the Cherokees reviewed the history of their relations with American presidents, beginning with George Washington, called attention to the "solemn treaties" guaranteeing their rights, as well as the oral and written promises made to them by high U.S. officials, discussed their own efforts to "become civilized," and expressed gratitude for the petitions on their behalf pouring into Congress from every part of the United States. In the final section of the appeal, which appears below, note the style in which the Cherokees state their case. Is it coolly argued or does it contain deep-seated feelings? How united were the Cherokees? What rights did they cite? What were their major objections to moving to a new location?

Appeal of the Cherokee Nation (1830)

We are aware that some persons suppose it will be for our advantage to remove beyond the Mississippi. We think otherwise. Our people universally think otherwise. Thinking that it would be fatal to their interests, they have almost to a man sent their memorial to Congress, deprecating the necessity of a removal. This question was distinctly before their minds when they signed their memorial. Not an adult person can be found, who has not an opinion on the subject; and if the people were to understand distinctly, that they could be protected against the laws of the neighboring States, there is probably not an adult person in the nation, who would think it best to remove; though possibly a few might emigrate individually. There are doubtless many who would flee to an unknown country, however beset with dangers, privations and sufferings, rather than be sentenced to spend six years in a Georgia prison for advising one of their neighbors not to betray his country. And there are others who could not think of living as outlaws in their native land, exposed to numberless vexations, and excluded from being parties or witnesses in a court of justice. It is incredible that Georgia should ever have enacted the oppressive laws to which reference is here made, unless she had supposed that something extremely terrific in its character was necessary, in order to make the Cherokees willing to remove. We are not willing to remove; and if we could be brought to this extremity, it would be, not by argument;

From E. C. Tracy, **Memoir of the Life of Jeremiah Evarts** (Boston, 1845), 149–158.

The Trail of Tears. In Robert Lindneux's dramatic painting, the Cherokee move toward reservation territory west of the Mississippi River in 1838. Some 4,000 of the 15,000 who began the trip died. But 15,000 was actually only a small portion of the 100,000 Indians driven out of the southeastern United States between 1820 and 1845, and 4,000 was only a small portion of the 25,000 to 30,000 killed in the process. (Woolaroc Museum of Oklahoma)

not because our judgment was satisfied; not because our condition will be improved—but only because we cannot endure to be deprived of our national and individual rights, and subjected to a process of intolerable oppression.

We wish to remain on the land of our fathers. We have a perfect and original right to claim this, without interruption or molestation. The treaties with us, and laws of the United States made in pursuance of treaties, guaranty our residence, and our privileges, and secure us against intruders. Our only request is, that these treaties may be fulfilled, and these laws executed.

But if we are compelled to leave our country, we see nothing but ruin before us. The country west of the Arkansas territory is unknown to us. From what we can learn of it, we have no prepossessions in its favor. All the inviting parts of it, as we believe, are preoccupied by various Indian nations, to which it has been assigned. They would regard us as intruders, and look upon us with an evil eye. The far greater part of that region is, beyond all controversy, badly supplied with wood and water; and no Indian tribe can live as agriculturists without these articles. All our neighbors, in case of our removal, though crowded into our near vicinity, would speak a language totally different from ours, and practice different customs. The original possessors of that region are now wandering savages, lurking for prey in the neighborhood. They have always been at war, and would be easily tempted to turn their arms against peaceful emigrants. Were the country to which we are urged much better than it is represented to be, and were it free from the objections which we have made to it, still it is not the land of our birth, nor of our affections. It contains neither the scenes of our childhood, nor the graves of our fathers.

24.

TO THE FARTHEST SHORES

When James K. Polk ran for president in 1844, the Democrats campaigned for the reannexation of Texas and the reoccupation of Oregon. Texas, they insisted, had been acquired by the Louisiana Purchase of 1803 and had been unwisely returned to Spain in a later treaty. The Oregon country, too, they maintained, had become part of the United States by virtue of American settlements there in the early nineteenth century; they felt that British claims there were unjustified. Polk agreed heartily with the Democratic platform on both issues. In May 1844 he declared, "Let Texas be reannexed and the authority and laws of the United States be established and maintained within her limits, as also in the Oregon Territory, and let the fixed policy of our government be, not to permit Great Britain or any other foreign power to plant a colony or hold dominion over any portion of the people or territory of either."

Polk compromised with Britain on Oregon, signing a treaty in 1846 fixing the boundary there at the 49th parallel. But his administration went to war with Mexico from 1846 to 1848 over Texas and ended by acquiring California and the Southwest for the United States. Polk's territorial conquests produced a lively debate over the meaning of expansionism for the United States. Some people, especially in New England, thought the Mexican War had been inspired by Southern planters (like Polk himself) greedy for new lands into which to extend slavery. Others saw both Oregon and the Southwest as tokens in a Northern drive for more farmland and for harbors on the West Coast for the China trade. Another group, perhaps the largest, saw expansion in terms of "manifest destiny," the right of a teeming, vigorous American nation to fill up a continent either empty or held by "inferior" peoples and thus destined almost by nature itself to be absorbed.

One of the most articulate representatives of the manifest destiny school was Senator Thomas Hart Benton of Missouri, a long-time supporter of Jackson, Polk, and the Democratic party. Benton was a tireless promoter of midwestern agricultural and commercial interests that looked favorably on the acquisition of new lands and ports. But he also took the "higher" ground of national destiny. Benton, born in North Carolina in 1782, briefly attended the University of North Carolina before moving to Tennessee, where he practiced law and served in the militia under Andrew Jackson. In 1815 he moved to St. Louis, Missouri, on the raw frontier. Here Benton prospered as a lawyer, newspaper editor, and land speculator. In 1820 he was elected to the Senate, where he remained, a champion of the Midwest and of Jackson and the Democratic party, until 1850. In that year his growing opposition to slavery cost him his Senate seat. The same stand also cost him the Missouri governor's race in 1856, the year in which he published his masterpiece of political autobiography, **Thirty Years' View.** A loyal Democrat to the end, Benton refused to bolt his party even after the Republicans nominated his son-in-law, John C. Frémont, for president in 1856. He died in Washington, D.C., in 1858.

    Questions to consider. Several questions are raised in a reading of "The Destiny of the Race." First, by placing expansionism within a context of age-old population movements, did Benton make it seem inevitable and irresistible and therefore not really open to political criticism? Second, by explaining expansionism in terms of white superiority, did he encourage Americans to think according to racial categories about all issues, including slavery and political rights for dark-skinned people in the United States? Finally, did he encourage Americans to pursue their destiny still further? Did his trans-Pacific vision involve conquest and colonization as well as trade? In what sense would Americans and Asians be common foes of the "great Powers of Europe"? How, precisely, would the "van of the Caucasian race" wake up the "torpid body of old Asia"? Does this somewhat surprising prediction in any way modify Benton's racism?

The Destiny of the Race (1846)
Thomas Hart Benton

Since the dispersion of man upon earth, I know of no human event, past or present, which promises a greater, a more beneficent change upon earth than the arrival of the van of the Caucasian race (the Celtic-Anglo-Saxon division) upon the border of the sea which washes the shore of eastern Asia. The Mongolian, or Yellow race, is there, four hundred million in number, spreading almost to Europe; a race once the foremost of the human family in the arts of civilization, but torpid and stationary for thousands of years. It is a race far above the Ethiopian, or Black—above the Malay, or Brown (if we must admit five races)—and above the American Indian, or Red; it is a race

From the **Congressional Globe,** May 28, 1846.

far above all these, but still, far below the White; and, like all the rest, must receive an impression from the superior race whenever they come in contact. It would seem that the White race alone received the divine command, to subdue and replenish the earth! for it is the only race that has obeyed it—the only one that hunts out new and distant lands, and even a New World, to subdue and replenish. Starting from western Asia, taking Europe for their field, and the Sun for their guide, and leaving the Mongolians behind, they arrived, after many ages, on the shores of the Atlantic, which they lit up with the lights of science and religion, and adorned with the useful and the elegant arts. Three and a half centuries ago, this race, in obedience to the great command, arrived in the New World, and found new lands to subdue and replenish. For a long time, it was confined to the border of the new field (I now mean the Celtic-Anglo-Saxon division); and even fourscore years ago the philosophic Burke was considered a rash man because he said the English colonists would top the Alleghenies, and descend into the valley of the Mississippi, and occupy without parchment if the Crown refused to make grants of land.

What was considered a rash declaration eighty years ago, is old history, in our young country, at this day. Thirty years ago I said the same thing of the Rocky Mountains and the Columbia: it was ridiculed then: it is becoming history to-day. The venerable Mr. Macon [North Carolina senator] has often told me that he remembered a line low down in North Carolina, fixed by a royal governor as a boundary between the whites and the Indians: where is the boundary now? The van of the Caucasian race now top the Rocky Mountains, and spread down to the shores of the Pacific. In a few years a great population will grow up there, luminous with the accumulated lights of European and American civilization. Their presence in such a position cannot be without its influence upon eastern Asia. The sun of civilization must shine across the sea: socially and commercially, the van of the Caucasians, and the rear of the Mongolians, must intermix. They must talk together, and trade together, and marry together. Commerce is a great civilizer—social intercourse as great—and marriage greater. The White and Yellow races can marry together, as well as eat and trade together. Moral and intellectual superiority will do the rest: the White race will take the ascendant, elevating what is susceptible of improvement—wearing out what is not. The Red race has disappeared from the Atlantic coast: the tribes that resisted civilization, met extinction. This is a cause of lamentation with many. For my part, I cannot murmur at what seems to be the effect of divine law. I cannot repine that this Capitol has replaced the wigwam—this Christian people, replaced the savages—white matrons, the red squaws—and that such men as Washington, Franklin, and Jefferson, have taken the place of Powhattan, Opechonecanough, and other red men, howsoever respectable they may have been as savages.

Civilization, or extinction, has been the fate of all people who have found themselves in the track of the advancing Whites, and civilization, always the preference of the Whites, has been pressed as an object, while extinction has

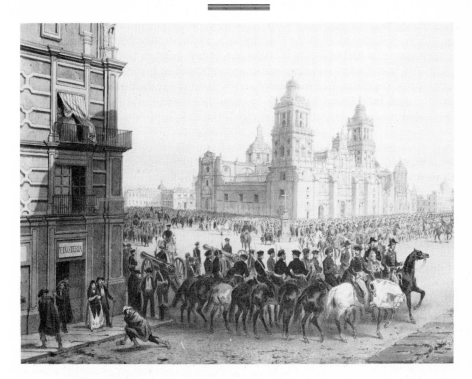

American troops enter Mexico City. In March 1847, General Winfield Scott landed at Vera Cruz on the Gulf coast of Mexico, and fought his way along the same path taken by Cortés in 1519 to the Mexican capital. "Old Fuss and Feathers" then put on a full dress uniform and, in a ceremony captured in this painting, led his forces into the central plaza. Although Scott's occupation impressed most U.S. citizens, Mexicans, including the woman in the bottom left corner with stone in hand, saw it differently—as an unforgettable cataclysmic blow to their morale as a nation and people. (Library of Congress)

followed as a consequence of its resistance. The Black and the Red races have often felt their ameliorating influence. The Yellow race, next to themselves in the scale of mental and moral excellence, and in the beauty of form, once their superiors in the useful and elegant arts, and in learning, and still respectable though stationary; this race cannot fail to receive a new impulse from the approach of the Whites, improved so much since so many ages ago they left the western borders of Asia. The apparition of the van of the Caucasian race, rising upon them in the east after having left them on the west, and after having completed the circumnavigation of the globe, must wake up and reanimate the torpid body of the old Asia. Our position and policy will commend us to their hospitable reception: political considerations will aid the action of social and commercial influences. Pressed upon by the great Powers of Europe—the same that press upon us—they must in our approach see the advent of friends, not of foes—of benefactors, not of invaders. The moral and intellectual superiority of the White race will do the rest: and thus the youngest people, and the newest land, will become the reviver and the regenerator of the oldest.

COUNTERPOINT III

Politics and Money

In the famous message that accompanied Andrew Jackson's 1832 veto of the bill to recharter the Bank of the United States (Document 22), the president claimed to be championing "the people" against "the opulent" and to be seeking "equal protection" for "the high and the low, the rich and the poor." This claim unnerved numerous well-to-do Whigs, members of the party that opposed a strong executive, particularly in view of Jackson's disreputable frontier background, his rugged, aggressive manner, and the apparent popularity among ordinary voters of his actions. But historians have been divided over just what, if anything, Jacksonian democracy and President Jackson himself actually represented. Some largely agree with Jackson's own assessment. Some see Democrats and Whigs as basically the same. Some question Jackson's political and economic impact whatever his intention.

Did the ascendance of Jackson and his party tend in fact to divide party politics along economic lines? Was there really a difference between Democrats and Whigs? In an effort to find out, Frank Gattell analyzed the party affiliations of several hundred rich New Yorkers taking into account their amount of wealth and their affiliation by presidential term for the period 1828–1851 (see table A). Most of these men did apparently support the Whigs, not the Jacksonians, and the wealthier they were the likelier they were to be Whigs. Furthermore, the later the presidential term, the more Whiggish wealthy New Yorkers became (see table A.2). Gattell's numbers indicate, in other words, that Jackson's actions, rhetoric, and reputation probably did affect the politics of the New York upper class, and that the longer he was president the greater the effect. So Jacksonian politics may indeed have had some class basis, just as Jackson himself often claimed.

But claims are one thing, results another. Did Jackson's pose as a champion of the "common people" actually bring them significant political or economic benefits? Did he democratize, for example, officeholding? Edward Pessen studied local officeholders from 1825 to 1837 (table B.1) and from 1838 to 1850 (table B.2) to see whether businessmen and professionals lost representation to humbler occupations in the Jacksonian era. His answer seems to be maybe, at least in some places. In New York City and Boston, merchants, physicians, and attorneys apparently declined while manufacturers and artisans increased, and Philadelphia "gentlemen," bankers, and businessmen lost some representation to shopkeepers. Did changes of this kind constitute a

Jacksonian democratization of elective offices? Modestly, perhaps. But the changes were not great. In Brooklyn, a newer city, they actually seem to have run the other way. So while Andy Jackson's bank war undoubtedly had local political consequences, there is apparently no compelling reason to credit the Democrats with more than modest changes in the pattern of local representation.

Remember, however, that Jackson's veto message was economic as well as political. He was not championing more political offices for "the people" but greater economic opportunity. Did, then, Jackson's policies and actions affect the distribution of American wealth? Did the struggle for more equal opportunity produce more equal results? Stuart Blumin tried to answer this question by examining the distribution of wealth in Philadelphia in 1860 (see figure C). According to his distribution curve, as of 1860 the bottom third of all Philadelphians owned no property. As shown in the population curve, Blumin found that the bottom 80 percent of Philadelphians owned just 3 percent of the city's wealth. The wealthiest 10 percent owned 90 percent, however, and the top 1 percent owned half! Andrew Jackson may have caused rich New Yorkers to support the Whigs, and he may have inspired some urban artisans to run successfully for municipal office. But if the distribution of wealth is any measure, what he assuredly did not do was achieve a more equitable American economy.

A. Party Affiliations of Wealthy New Yorkers

1. Party Affiliation by Amount of Wealth, 1844–45

	Total	Politics Identified		Whigs		Democrats	
$5,000,000 or more	4	4	(100.0%)	4	(100.0%)	0	(0.0%)
$1,000,000 to $4,999,000	18	13	(72.2)	12	(92.3)	1	(7.7)
$500,000 to $999,000	80	59	(73.8)	54	(91.5)	5	(8.5)
$400,000 to $499,000	27	25	(92.6)	23	(92.0)	2	(8.0)
$300,000 to $399,000	101	67	(66.3)	50	(74.6)	17	(25.4)
$250,000 to $299,000	63	47	(74.6)	37	(78.7)	10	(21.3)
$200,000 to $249,000	162	110	(67.9)	98	(89.1)	12	(10.9)
Total	455	325	(71.4)	278	(85.5)	47	(14.5)

2. Party Affiliation by Time Period

	Total	Politics Identified		Whigs		Democrats	
1828–31	909[a]	90	(9.9%)	48	(53.4%)	42	(46.6%)
1832–35	909	379	(41.9)	291	(76.8)	88	(23.2)
1836–39	905	298	(32.9)	244	(81.9)	54	(18.1)
1840–43	900	324	(36.0)	270	(83.4)	54	(16.6)
1844–47	892	190	(21.3)	156	(82.2)	34	(17.8)
1848–51	880	134	(15.2)	106	(79.2)	28	(20.8)

[a]Twenty-nine wealthy citizens died between 1828 and 1847.

SOURCE: From Frank Otto Gatell, "Money and Party in Jacksonian America," *Political Science Quarterly* 82 (June 1967), pp. 244, 247. Reprinted by permission.

B. Occupations of City Officials from New York, Brooklyn, Boston, and Philadelphia

1. Occupations of City Councils and Boards of Aldermen, 1825–1837[a]

Occupation	New York	Brooklyn	Boston	Philadelphia
Merchants	28%	34%	65%	54%
"Gentlemen"	—	—	—	25
Bankers, insur. co. executives, brokers	2	—	10	6
Businessmen, publishers	13	2	31	9
Owners of yards, bldgs., wharves, bldrs., shipbuilders	4	10	10	4
Manufacturers	3	13	7	14
Attorneys	20	10	26	36
Physicians	3	—	5	5
Officials, military and naval officers, ship captains	1	2	6	4
Engineers, accountants, printers	1	2	1	—
Grocers, distillers, butchers, bakers, druggists, retailers	14	16	9	20
Artisan-entrepreneurs	6	—	8	8
Artisans, mechanics	6	8	10	13
Farmers	—	2	—	—

2. Occupations of City Councils and Boards of Aldermen, 1838–1850[b]

Occupation	New York	Brooklyn	Boston	Philadelphia
Merchants	15.0%	42%	57%	79%
"Gentlemen"	—	—	—	8
Bankers, insur. co. executives, brokers	3	—	7.5	1
Businessmen, publishers	18	4	37	6
Owners of yards, bldgs., wharves, bldrs., shipbuilders	6	14	10	—
Manufacturers	9	7	10	16
Attorneys	11	13	18.5	41
Physicians	1	—	2.5	2
Officials, military and naval officers, ship captains	4	—	7	3
Engineers, accountants, printers	1	—	4	—
Grocers, distillers, butchers, bakers, druggists, retailers	14	18	7.5	31
Artisan-entrepreneurs	7.5	1	21	4
Artisans, mechanics	10	1	18	10
Laborers, farmers	—	—	—	—

[a]To 1840 for Philadelphia. Since fractions were not included, totals do not always sum to 100%.
[b]1840–1850 for Philadelphia. Totals do not always sum to 100%.

SOURCE: From Edward Pessen, *Riches, Class, and Power Before the Civil War*, Lexington, Mass.: D.C. Heath and Company, 1973, pp. 285, 287. Reprinted by permission of the author.

C. Distribution of Wealth in Philadelphia, 1860

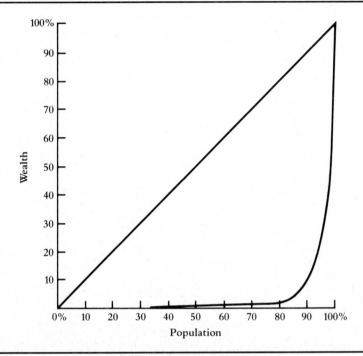

SOURCE: From Stuart Blumin, "Mobility and Change in Ante-Bellum Philadelphia," in *Nineteenth-Century Cities,* Stephen Thernstrom and Richard Sennett, eds., New Haven, Conn.: Yale University Press, 1969. Reprinted by permission.

An 1851 temperance banner promotes the domestic rewards of abstention from alcohol.   (Library of Congress)

CHAPTER FOUR

The Age of Reform

25.

A CALL TO ARMS

With the publication in Boston of the first issue of William Lloyd Garrison's **Liberator** in January 1831, the antislavery movement turned toward militancy. But Garrison's call for immediate emancipation was preceded by David Walker's **Appeal to the Coloured Citizens of the World,** published in September 1829. In one place in his impassioned pamphlet, not appearing in the excerpt below, Walker called American blacks the "most wretched, degraded and abject sort of beings that ever lived since the world began," blasted American whites for their condescension, insensitivity, and cruelty, and demanded that they end slavery and begin treating blacks as human beings with all the rights of other citizens. "Treat us like men," he cried, "and we will be friends."

In composing his **Appeal** Walker knew whereof he wrote. A free black born in North Carolina in 1785, he managed to get an education. He traveled widely in the South observing slavery before he settled in Boston in 1827 and opened a shop that sold old clothes. When **Freedom's Journal,** the first American black newspaper, began publication in New York in 1827, Walker began contributing articles to it; he also lectured against slavery to small groups in Boston. He wrote his **Appeal** at high speed, printed it at his own expense, and saw to it that copies made their way into the South. The reaction to the **Appeal** was not surprising. Prominent Southerners demanded its suppression; even Bostonians called it "wicked and inflammatory." Garrison himself praised its "impassioned and determined spirit," but regretted its publication; later he changed his mind and reprinted most of it in the **Liberator.** Though there were threats on his life, Walker prepared new editions of his **Appeal.** But on June 28, 1830, he was found dead near the doorway of his shop, possibly the victim of poisoning.

Questions to consider. Walker's **Appeal** shocked even those whites opposed to slavery. Why do you suppose this was so? To whom was he addressing his plea: to slaves, to free blacks, or to whites? Do you think he was exaggerating the misery of blacks in the United States? How radical does his **Appeal** sound today? What kind of action did he call upon American blacks to take? What part did religion play in his view of things?

Appeal to the Coloured Citizens
of the World (1829)
David Walker

I know that the blacks, take them half enlightened and ignorant, are more humane and merciful than the most enlightened and refined European that can be found in all the earth. Let no one say that I assert this because I am prejudiced on the side of my colour, and against the whites or Europeans. For what I write, I do it candidly, for my God and the good of both parties: Natural observations have taught me these things; there is a solemn awe in the hearts of the blacks, as it respects *murdering* men; whereas the whites (though they are great cowards) where they have the advantage, or think that there are any prospects of getting it, they murder all before them, in order to subject men to wretchedness and degradation under them. This is the natural result of pride and avarice. . . . Should the lives of such creatures be spared? Are God and Mammon in league? What has the Lord to do with a gang of desperate wretches, who go *sneaking about the country like robbers*—light upon his people wherever they can get a chance, binding them with chains and handcuffs, beat and murder them as they would *rattle-snakes?* Are they not the Lord's enemies? Ought they not to be destroyed? Any person who will save such wretches from destruction, is fighting against the Lord, and will receive his just recompense. . . . The whites have had us under them for more than three centuries, murdering, and treating us like brutes; and, as Mr. Jefferson wisely said, they have never *found us out*—they do not know, indeed, that there is an unconquerable disposition in the breasts of the blacks, which, when it is fully awakened and put in motion, will be subdued, only with the destruction of the animal existence. Get the blacks started, and if you do not have a gang of tigers and lions to deal with, I am a deceiver of the blacks and of the whites.

Now, I ask you, had you not rather be killed than to be a slave to a tyrant, who takes the life of your mother, wife, and dear little children? Look upon your mother, wife and children, and answer God Almighty; and believe this, that it is no more harm for you to kill a man, who is trying to kill you, than it is for you to take a drink of water when thirsty; in fact, the man who will stand still and let another murder him, is worse than an infidel, and, if he has common sense, ought not to be pitied. . . . Oh! coloured people of these United States, I ask you, in the name of that God who made us, have we, in consequence of oppression, nearly lost the spirit of man, and, in no very trifling degree, adopted that of brutes? Do you answer, no? I ask you, then, what set of men can you point me to, in all the world, who are so abjectedly

From David Walker, **Walker's Appeal, in Four Articles; Together with a Preamble to Coloured Citizens of the World** (D. Walker, Boston, 1830), 11–87.

employed by their oppressors, as we are by our *natural enemies*? How can, Oh! how can those enemies but say that we and our children are not of the HUMAN FAMILY, but were made by our Creator to be an inheritance to them and theirs for ever? How can the slaveholders but say that they can bribe the best coloured person in the country, to sell his brethren for a trifling sum of money, and take that atrocity to confirm them in their avaricious opinion, that we were made to be slaves to them and their children? . . .

I aver, that when I look over these United States of America, and the world, and see the ignorant deceptions and consequent wretchedness of my brethren, I am brought ofttimes solemnly to a stand, and in the midst of my reflections I exclaim to my God, "Lord didst thou make us to be slaves to our brethren, the whites?" But when I reflect that God is just, and that millions of my wretched brethren would meet death with glory—yea, more, would plunge into the very mouths of cannons and be torn into particles as minute as the atoms which compose the elements of the earth, in preference to a mean submission to the lash of tyrants, I am with streaming eyes, compelled to shrink back into nothingness before my Maker, and exclaim again, thy will be done, O Lord God Almighty.

Men of colour, who are also of sense, for you particularly is my APPEAL designed. Our more ignorant brethren are not able to penetrate its value. I call upon you therefore to cast your eyes upon the wretchedness of your brethren, and to do your utmost to enlighten them—*go to work and enlighten your brethren!* — Let the Lord see you doing what you can to rescue them and yourselves from degradation. Do any of you say that you and your family are free and happy, and what have you to do with the wretched slaves and other people? So can I say, for I enjoy as much freedom as any of you, if I am not quite as well off as the best of you. Look into our freedom and happiness, and see of what kind they are composed!! They are of the very lowest kind—they are the very *dregs!*—they are the most servile and abject kind, that ever a people was in possession of! If any of you wish to know how FREE you are, let one of you start and go through the southern and western States of this country, and unless you travel as a slave to a white man (a servant is a *slave* to the man whom he serves) or have your free papers (which if you are not careful they will get from you) if they do not take you up and put you in jail, and if you cannot give good evidence of your freedom, sell you into eternal slavery, I am not a living man: or any man of colour, immaterial who he is, or where he came from, if he is *the fourth from the negro race!!* (as we are called) the white Christian of America will serve him the same they will sink him into wretchedness and degradation for ever while he lives. And yet some of you have the hardihood to say that you are free and happy! May God have mercy on your freedom and happiness!! I met a coloured man in the street a short time since, with a string of boots on his shoulders; we fell into conversation, and in the course of which, I said to him, what a miserable set of people we are! He asked, why?—Said I, we are so subjected under the whites, that we cannot obtain the comforts of life, but by cleaning their boots and shoes,

> # CASH!
>
> **All persons that have SLAVES to dispose of, will do well by giving me a call, as I will give the**
>
> ## HIGHEST PRICE FOR
>
> # Men, Women, &
>
> ## CHILDREN.
>
> **Any person that wishes to sell, will call at Hill's tavern, or at Shannon Hill for me, and any information they want will be promptly attended to.**
>
> ### *Thomas Griggs.*
> **Charlestown, May 7, 1835.**
>
> PRINTED AT THE FREE PRESS OFFICE, CHARLESTOWN.

Broadside, Charleston, 1835. The African slave trade ended in 1808, but the domestic trade continued to flourish. Breeding slaves for the market became a lucrative business in the South in the four decades before the Civil War. Cried one European after observing an auction in the nation's capital: "You call this the land of liberty, and every day that passes things are done in it at which the despotisms of Europe would be horror-struck and disgusted!" (Library of Congress)

old clothes, waiting on them, shaving them &c. Said he, (with the boots on his shoulders) "I am completely happy!!! I never want to live any better or happier than when I get a plenty of boots and shoes to clean!!!" Oh! how can those who are actuated by avarice only, but think, that our Creator made us to be an inheritance to them for ever, when they see that our greatest glory is centered in such mean and low objects? Understand me, brethren, I do not mean to speak against the occupations by which we acquire enough and sometimes scarcely that, to render ourselves and families comfortable through life. I am subjected to the same inconvenience, as you all. — My objections are, to our *glorying* and being *happy* in such low employments; for if we are men, we ought to be thankful to the Lord for the past, and for the future. Be looking forward with thankful hearts to higher attainments than *wielding the razor* and *cleaning boots and shoes.* The man whose aspirations are not *above,* and even *below* these, is indeed, ignorant and wretched enough. I advanced it therefore to you, not as a *problematical,* but as an unshaken and for ever immovable *fact,* that your full glory and happiness, as well as all other coloured people under Heaven, shall never be fully consummated, but with the *entire emancipation of your enslaved brethren all over the world.* You may therefore, go to work and do what you can to rescue, or join in with tyrants to oppress them and yourselves, until the Lord shall come upon you all like a thief in the night. For I believe it is the will of the Lord that our greatest happiness shall consist in working for the salvation of our whole body. When this is accomplished a burst of glory will shine upon you, which will indeed astonish you and the world. Do any of you say this never will be done? I assure you that God will accomplish it—if nothing else will answer, he will hurl tyrants and devils into *atoms* and make way for his people. But O my brethren! I say unto you again, you must go to work and prepare the way of the Lord.

26.

CHRISTIANITY AND FREEDOM

David Walker's militant call to arms in 1829 (Document 25) failed to influence most white abolitionists, who at this stage of the struggle over slavery sought to persuade people by nonviolent means to oppose and eventually to end the system. Persuading significant numbers of slaveholders to free their slaves seemed hopelessly daunting after the rapid spread of the Cotton Kingdom had made slavery so profitable, and it was virtually impossible after Southern states began to make it illegal to manumit (voluntarily free) one's slaves.

Furthermore, it was almost as difficult to persuade Northerners as Southerners to support nonviolent abolitionism, not only because it appeared hopeless but also because most white Northerners considered blacks inferior and did not want them around free or otherwise. The American Colonization Society had tried with little success to encourage manumission by raising money to send freed slaves to Africa. Yet the problem remained, so that when William Lloyd Garrison began to publish his militant antislavery journal, **The Liberator,** in Boston in 1831, it still sought on the one hand to reassure readers as to its nonviolence and on the other to persuade them that free blacks would make acceptable citizens and neighbors.

Though resisted at first, sometimes with ropes and torches, Garrison's message slowly gained a little better hearing and won growing numbers of converts, especially in New England and New York. By 1833, buoyed by these small gains and also by the example of the British West Indies where slavery had just been abolished by Parliament, Garrison felt confident enough to try to organize the movement nationwide. The result was the American Anti-Slavery Society, whose constitution, penned by Garrison, is reprinted below.

William Lloyd Garrison, the chief architect of the American Anti-Slavery Society, was born in 1805 in Massachusetts, where he obtained an education mainly through the reading he was able to do as an apprentice to a local printer. In the 1820s Garrison briefly edited a temperance journal and wrote for a Quaker reform paper. But it was **The Liberator,** with his stirring pledge "I will not excuse—I will not retreat a single inch—**and I will be heard,**" that made him a major voice in nineteenth-century reform. His support for women's rights, which angered most men, and his attacks on the U.S. Constitution as a "pact with evil" (namely slavery) compounded Garrison's already difficult work. Some urged him to moderate his strident rhetoric—to which he invariably rejoined, "No! No! Tell a man whose house is on fire to give a moderate alarm or to moderately rescue his wife from the hands of the ravisher!" During the 1850s Garrison's antislavery activities were eclipsed by those of politicians such as Charles Sumner and zealots such as John Brown. Yet he persevered to become a backer of Abraham Lincoln and continued publishing **The Liberator** and guiding the American Anti-Slavery Society until the Thirteenth Amendment finally ended the system. He died in New York City in 1879.

Questions to consider. The American Anti-Slavery Society set out its credo in a long preamble modeled after the Declaration of Independence. But in the Society's constitution Garrison mixed religious sentiments with arguments based on natural rights far more than Jefferson had in 1776 (Document 12). Does this sound like a tactic more likely to be effective in the 1830s? Might it also reveal something important about the temperament of the early abolitionists? Assuming the Society's constitution was intended partly as propaganda, to whom does it seem to have been addressed? What did Garrison mean by saying toward the end of the preamble that his approach would "prevent a general convulsion"? Were readers likely to find this reassuring? Do you find the statement on goals in Article II clear and persuasive? Was Article III essential to the document? How would nonviolent black abolitionists have responded? How would David Walker have felt (Document 25)?

The Constitution of the American Anti-Slavery Society (1833)

William Lloyd Garrison

Whereas the Most High God "hath made of one blood all nations of men to dwell on all the face of the earth," and hath commanded them to love their neighbors as themselves;

and whereas, our National Existence is based upon this principle, as recognized in the Declaration of Independence, "that all mankind are created equal, and that they are endowed by their Creator with certain inalienable rights, among which are life, liberty, and the pursuit of happiness";

and whereas, after the lapse of nearly sixty years, since the faith and honor of the American people were pledged to this avowal, before Almighty

From **Platform of the American Anti-Slavery Society and Its Auxiliaries** (New York, 1860), p. 3.

William Lloyd Garrison and The Liberator.   A pivotal year for the antislavery movement was 1831, when William Lloyd Garrison, an ex-Baptist from Newburyport, Massachusetts, published the first issue of **The Liberator,** whose ringing slogan appears on the banner to the right. But not everyone approved, as leading men of Boston showed in 1835 when "howling with rage" they pulled Garrison from a lecture hall, roped him by the waist, and pulled him, "faces distorted by malice and passion," through the streets as a warning to his kind. The mayor probably saved Garrison's life by arresting him for "disturbing the peace"! Deciding the next morning that discretion was the better part of valor, Garrison took a train to Providence, Rhode Island. (Left, Sophia Smith Collection; right, Massachusetts Historical Society)

God and the World, nearly one-sixth part of the nation are held in bondage by their fellow-citizens;

and whereas, Slavery is contrary to the principles of natural justice, of our republican form of government, and of the Christian religion, and is destructive of the prosperity of the country, while it is endangering the peace, union, and liberties of the States;

and whereas, we believe it the duty and interest of the masters immediately to emancipate their slaves, and that no scheme of expatriation, either voluntary or by compulsion, can remove this great and increasing evil;

and whereas, we believe that it is practicable, by appeals to the consciences, hearts, and interests of the people, to awaken a public sentiment throughout the nation that will be opposed to the continuance of Slavery in any part of the Republic, and by effecting the speedy abolition of Slavery, prevent a general convulsion;

and whereas, we believe we owe it to the oppressed, to our fellow-citizens who hold slaves, to our whole country, to posterity, and to God, to do all that is lawfully in our power to bring about the extinction of Slavery, we do hereby agree, with a prayerful reliance on the Divine aid, to form ourselves into a society, to be governed by the following Constitution:—

ART. I.—This Society shall be called the AMERICAN ANTI-SLAVERY SOCIETY.

ART. II.—The object of this Society is the entire abolition of Slavery in the United States. While it admits that each State, in which Slavery exists, has, by the Constitution of the United States, the exclusive right to *legislate* in regard to its abolition in said State, it shall aim to convince all our fellow-citizens, by arguments addressed to their understandings and consciences, that Slaveholding is a heinous crime in the sight of God, and that the duty, safety, and best interests of all concerned, require its *immediate abandonment,* without expatriation. The Society will also endeavor, in a constitutional way to influence Congress to put an end to the domestic Slave trade, and to abolish Slavery in all those portions of our common country which come under its control, especially in the District of Columbia,—and likewise to prevent the extension of it to any State that may be hereafter admitted to the Union.

ART. III.—This Society shall aim to elevate the character and condition of the people of color, by encouraging their intellectual, moral, and religious improvement, and by removing public prejudice, and thus they may, according to their intellectual and moral worth, share an equality with the whites, of civil and religious privileges; but this Society will never, in any way, countenance the oppressed in vindicating their rights by resorting to physical force.

ART. IV.—Any person who consents to the principles of this Constitution, who contributes to the funds of this Society, and is not a Slaveholder, may be a member of this Society, and shall be entitled to vote at the meetings. . . .

27.

RISING GENERATIONS

The era from the 1830s until the Civil War was marked by intense reform movements, especially in the Northeast. "In the history of the world," exclaimed Ralph Waldo Emerson, "the doctrine of Reform had never such a scope as at the present hour." Most reformers were deeply religious; they took seriously Christianity's emphasis on the spiritual equality of all human beings and Jesus' special concern for the lowly and humble. They were also inspired by the Declaration of Independence with its insistence on inalienable rights, and were eager to make its social and political ideas a reality. Many reformers believed that human nature was perfectible, and that with better social arrangements men and women would be able to live more fully and freely than they ever had before.

During the Age of Reform the antislavery movement became important; so did the temperance movement (against alcohol consumption), the struggle for women's rights, more humane prisons and asylums, and improved conditions for working people. Horace Mann, a Boston lawyer and politician, took an interest in all these reforms, but he was especially interested in the development of public elementary education, or the "common schools." So absorbed did Mann become with expanding and improving the schools that he stunned his friends by quitting the law and resigning from the Massachusetts senate to become secretary of the state's fledgling board of education.

At the time Mann began his labors, Massachusetts already had a notable educational tradition deriving chiefly from the Puritan insistence that as many people as possible should be able to read the Bible. By the early 1800s most districts of the state had rudimentary schools and a fair amount of somewhat haphazard instruction. But reformers, finding this thoroughly unsatisfactory, worked assiduously to persuade towns and villages to build more and better schools; to fill them with comfortable desks, blackboards, books, maps, blocks, and writing materials; to establish standards and train professional (mostly female) teachers; and to make elementary education compulsory.

The common (public) school "revivalists," as they called themselves, had little power save persuasion. Public schools then as now were almost wholly the responsibility of local governments. Yet the revivalists were astoundingly successful, particularly in the North. By the time of the Civil War, the United States, even with meager results in the South, had educated more of its children for a longer period than any other country in the world, with the possible exception of Prussia. But the United States, unlike Prussia and most other countries, accomplished this widespread education almost wholly through local initiative—prodded, to be sure, by Horace Mann and his fellow reformers but local nonetheless.

The fact that the so-called schoolmen usually had to persuade local districts to do something might help explain why their writing seems overblown and excessive to modern ears. Horace Mann achieved real impact only by painting a dire picture of the schools, and he was obviously not at all reluctant to do so. But something else was going on here, too. The nineteenth century was a golden age of American oratory, a period in which public figures—politicians, ministers, and reformers alike—took tremendous pride in entertaining and moving throngs of listeners. Public speakers worked hard on producing and delivering noteworthy speeches, and tried, usually with success, to have them published with all their original rhetorical flourishes intact. Most of the famous essays of Ralph Waldo Emerson were public lectures before they were works of literature, and Senator Daniel Webster, the "Godlike Dan'l" himself, once captivated 40,000 Bostonians with a two-hour address on municipal water systems! Horace Mann clearly reveled in this kind of expressive rhetoric. But what sounds ridiculously overheated to us would have seemed just comfortably warm in the nineteenth century.

Mann, most famous and influential of the school reformers, was born in the village of Franklin, Massachusetts, in 1796. Although his family was poor, Horace was able to pursue his education by means of various scholarships and eventually graduated from Brown University at the age of twenty-three. After serving for twelve years as secretary of the Massachusetts board of education, the post for which he gave up politics and the law, he left to replace John Quincy Adams in the U.S. House of Representatives for a term. In 1852 he became the first president of Antioch College in Ohio, where he died in 1859.

Questions to consider. In this report, Mann was trying to describe society as he saw it and also to suggest what the future might bring without major school reform. What features of Massachusetts society— its economy, its institutions, its class structure, the habits and viewpoints of its people, and its tensions and conflicts—emerge most clearly from Mann's report? Are you surprised at any of the topics he included? Is anything missing that might be there? What special problems did he perceive in the education of factory children as opposed to farm children, and of girls as opposed to boys? Why did he consider it so important for girls to have access to good books? When Mann peered into the future, what did he see? Why did he seem to hold the English city of Manchester in such horror? What did he mean by "barbarism"?

Report on the Public Schools (1840)
Horace Mann

I feel fully justified in affirming, that the prospects of the rising generation are daily growing brighter, by means of the increasing light which is shed upon them from our Common Schools. . . . Stronger feelings and firmer convictions of the importance of our Common Schools are taking possession of the public mind, and where they have not yet manifested themselves in any outward and visible improvement, they are silently and gradually working to that end. . . .

It must not, however, be inferred, that the most extensive reform is not still necessary in regard to those edifices, where the business of education, for the great mass of the children in the State, is carried on. By what I have learned from authentic sources, and have seen, in three annual circuits through all parts of the Commonwealth, respecting its three thousand schoolhouses, I am convinced that there is no other class of buildings within our limits, erected either for the permanent or the temporary residence of our native population, so inconvenient, so uncomfortable, so dangerous to health by their construction within, or so unsightly and repulsive in their appearance without. Every other class of edifices, whether public or private, has felt the hand of reform. Churches, courthouses, even jails and prisons, are rebuilt, or remodelled, great regard being paid, in most cases to ornament, and in all cases to health, to personal convenience and accommodation. But the schoolhouse, which leads directly towards the church, or rather may be considered as its vestibule, and which furnishes to the vast majority of our children, the only public means they will ever enjoy, for qualifying themselves to profit by its counsels, its promises, its warnings, its consolations;—the schoolhouse, which leads directly from the courthouse, from the jail and from the prison, and is, for the mass of our children, the great preventive and safeguard against being called or forced into them, as litigants or as criminals;— this class of buildings, all over the State, stands in afflicting contrast with all the others. The courthouses, which are planned and erected under the advice and control of the county authorities, and of the leading men in the county for themselves and in which they spend but a few terms in the year, and the meeting-houses, where the parents spend but a few hours in a week, are provided with costly embellishments, and with every appurtenance, that can gratify taste or subserve comfort; but the houses, where the children, in the most susceptible period of their lives, spend from thirty to forty hours in a week, seem to be deserted by all public care, and abandoned to cheerlessness and dilapidation. . . .

If, in a portion of the manufacturing districts, in the State, a regular and systematic obedience is paid to the law, while, in other places, it is regularly

From Horace Mann, **Third Annual Report of the Secretary of the Board of Education** (Boston: Dutton and Wentworth, 1840), 35–36, 39–40, 43–48, 96.

and systematically disregarded, the inevitable consequences to the latter will be obvious, upon a moment's reflection. The neighborhood or town where the law is broken will soon become the receptacle of the poorest, most vicious and abandoned parents, who are bringing up their children to be also as poor, vicious and abandoned as themselves. The whole class of parents, who cannot obtain employment for their children, at one place, but are welcomed at another, will circulate through the body politic, until at last, they will settle down as permanent residents, in the latter; like the vicious humors of the natural body, which, being thrown off by every healthy part, at last accumulate and settle upon a diseased spot. Every breach of this law, therefore, inflicts direct and positive injustice, not only upon the children employed, but upon all the industrious and honest communities in which they are employed; because its effect will be to fill those communities with paupers and criminals;— or, at least, with a class of persons, who, without being absolute, technical paupers, draw their subsistence in a thousand indirect ways, from the neighborhood, where they reside; and without being absolute criminals in the eye of the law, still commit a thousand injurious, predatory acts, more harassing and annoying to the peace and security of a village, than many classes of positive crimes.

While water-power only is used for manufacturing purposes, a natural limit is affixed, in every place, to the extension of manufactories. The power being all taken up, in any place, the further investment of capital and the employment of an increased number of operatives, must cease. While we restrict ourselves to the propulsion of machinery by water, therefore, it is impossible, that we should have such an extensive manufacturing district as, for instance, that of Manchester in England, because we have no streams of sufficient magnitude for the purpose. But Massachusetts is already the greatest manufacturing State in the Union. Her best sites are all taken up, and yet her disposition to manufacture appears not to be checked. Under such circumstances, it seems not improbable, that steam-power will be resorted to. Indeed this is already done to some extent. Should such improvements be made in the use of steam, or such new markets be opened for the sale of manufactured products, that capitalists, by selecting sites where the expense of transportation, both of the raw material and of the finished article, may be so reduced as, on the whole, to make it profitable to manufacture by steam, then that agency will be forthwith employed; and, if steam is employed, there is no assignable limit to the amount of a manufacturing population, that may be gathered into a single manufacturing district. If, therefore, we would not have, in any subsequent time, a population like that of the immense city of Manchester, where great numbers of the laboring population live in the filthiest streets, and mostly in houses, which are framed back to back, so that in no case is there any yard behind them, but all ingress and egress, for all purposes, is between the front side of the house and the public street,—if we would not have such a population, we must not only have preventive laws, but we must see that no cupidity, no contempt of the public welfare for the sake of private gain, is allowed openly to violate or clandestinely to evade them. It would, indeed, be most lamentable and self-contradictory, if, with all our institutions devised and prepared on the hypothesis of common intelligence and virtue, we should rear a class of children, to be set apart and, as it were, dedicated to ignorance and vice. . . .

. . . It is obvious, that children of ten, twelve, or fourteen years of age, may be steadily worked in our manufactories, without any schooling, and that this cruel deprivation may be persevered in for six, eight, or ten years, and yet, during all this period, no very alarming outbreak shall occur to rouse the public mind from its guilty slumber. The children are in their years of minority, and they have no control over their own time, or their own actions. The bell is to them, what the water-wheel and the main shaft are to the machinery, which they superintend. The wheel revolves and the machinery must go; the bell rings and the children must assemble. In their hours of work, they are under the police of the establishment; at other times, they are under the police of the neighborhood. Hence this state of things may continue for years, and the peace of the neighborhood remain undisturbed, except, perhaps, by a few nocturnal or sabbath-day depredations. The ordinary movements of society may go on without any shocks or collisions,—as, in the human system, a disease may work at the vitals and gain a fatal ascendancy there, before it manifests itself on the surface. But the punishment for such an offence, will not be remitted, because its infliction is postponed. The retribution, indeed, is not postponed, it only awaits the full completion of the offence; for this is a crime of such magnitude, that it requires years for the criminal to perpetrate it in, and to finish it off thoroughly, in all its parts. But when the children pass from the condition of restraint to that of freedom,—from years of enforced but impatient servitude to that independence for which they have secretly pined, and to which they have looked forward, not merely as the period of emancipation, but of long-delayed indulgence;—when they become strong in the passions and propensities that grow up spontaneously, but are weak in the moral powers that control them, and blind in the intellect which foresees their tendencies;—when, according to the course of our political institutions, they go, by one bound, from the political nothingness of a child, to the political sovereignty of a man,—then, for that people, who so cruelly neglected and injured them, there will assuredly come a day of retribution. It scarcely needs to be added, on the other hand, that if the wants of the spiritual nature of a child, in the successive stages of its growth, are duly supplied; then a regularity in manual employment, is converted from a servitude into a useful habit of diligence, and the child grows up in a daily perception of the wonder-working power of industry, and in the daily realization of the trophies of victorious labor. A majority of the most useful men who have ever lived, were formed under the happy necessity of mingling bodily with mental exertion.

But by far the most important subject, respecting which I have sought for information, during the year, remains to be noticed. While we are in little danger of over-estimating the value of Common Schools, yet we shall err egregiously, if we regard them as ends, and not as means. A forgetfulness of this distinction would send the mass of our children of both sexes into the

New England schoolroom, 1857. Horace Mann's reform efforts succeeded to an astonishing degree in the towns and villages of the Northern states. By modern standards, however, even the new and newly refurbished schools were sometimes stark and gloomy, as this photograph of a girls' class suggests. Even when teachers were better trained and paid, they relied on strict discipline and drill to educate their students. (The Metropolitan Museum of Art)

world, scantily provided either with the ability or the disposition to perform even the most ordinary duties of life. Common Schools derive their value from the fact, that they are an instrument, more extensively applicable to the whole mass of the children, than any other instrument ever yet devised. They are an instrument, by which the good men in society can send redeeming influences to those children, who suffer under the calamity of vicious parentage and evil domestic associations. The world is full of lamentable proofs, that the institution of the family may exist for an indefinite number of generations, without mitigating the horrors of barbarism. But the institution of Common Schools is the offspring of an advanced state of civilization, and is incapable of coexisting with barbarian life, because, should barbarism prevail, it would destroy the schools, should the schools prevail, they would destroy barbarism. They are the only civil institution, capable of extending its beneficent arms to embrace and to cultivate in all parts of its nature, every child that comes into the world. . . .

. . . Young men, it may be said, have a larger circle of action; they can mingle more in promiscuous society,—at least, they have a far wider range of business occupations,—all of which stimulate thought, suggest inquiry and furnish means for improvement. But the sphere of females is domestic. Their life is comparatively secluded. The proper delicacy of the sex forbids them from appearing in the promiscuous marts of business, and even from mingling, as actors, in those less boisterous arenas, where mind is the acting agent, as well as the object to be acted upon. If then, she is precluded from these sources of information, and these incitements to inquiry; if, by the unanimous and universal opinion of civilized nations, when she breaks away from comparative seclusion and retirement, she leaves her charms behind her; and if, at the same time she is debarred from access to books, by what means, through what channels, is she to obtain the knowledge so indispensable for the fit discharge of maternal and domestic duties, and for rendering herself an enlightened companion for intelligent men? Without books, except in cases of extraordinary natural endowment, she will be doomed to relative ignorance and incapacity. . . .

The State, in its sovereign capacity, has the deepest interest in this matter. If it would spread the means of intelligence and self-culture over its entire surface, making them diffusive as sunshine, causing them to penetrate into every hamlet and dwelling, and, like the vernal sun, quickening into life the seeds of usefulness and worth, wherever the prodigal hand of nature may have scattered them;—it would call into existence an order of men, who would establish a broader basis for its prosperity, and give a brighter lustre to its name,—who would improve its arts, impart wisdom to its counsels, and extend the beneficent sphere of its charities. Yet, not for its own sake only, should it assume this work. It is a corollary from the axioms of its constitution, that every child, born within its borders, shall be enlightened. In its paternal character, the government is bound, even to those who can make no requital. Sacredly is it bound to develop all the existing capacities, and to ensure the utmost attainable welfare, of that vast crowd and throng of men, who, without being known, during life, beyond their neighboring hills,—without leaving any enduring name behind them after death, still, by their life-long industry, fill up, as it were, drop by drop, the mighty stream of the country's prosperity. In the heart of this multitude, dwell capacities of good, and possibilities of evil, wholly transcending the power of finite imagination to conceive. Here are an inconceivable extent and magnitude of interests, sympathies, obligations;—here are all the great instincts of humanity, working out their way to a greater or less measure of good, according to the light they enjoy;—and, compared with this wide and deep mass of unrecorded life, all that emerges into history and is seen of man, is as nothing.

28.

THE UTOPIANS

The Brook Farm Association was estabished in 1841 in a rural area nine miles from Boston. One of many utopian communities that sprang up in the United States in the first part of the nineteenth century, Brook Farm was an experiment in cooperative living. Of the two hundred cooperative colonies that flowered from New England to Utah during this period, Brook Farm was probably the most famous because of its proximity to a large city and because many well-known literary people were associated with it. The "Farmers," dedicated to "plain living and high thinking," engaged in agriculture, lived communally, operated an excellent school, and held dances, games, picnics, plays, lectures, and discussions. It was, said one visitor, "rich in cheerful buzz." Praised by Ralph Waldo Emerson for their experimentalism, but disparaged by Henry David Thoreau for their conformity, the Brook Farmers, like other uto- pians, emphasized the equality of the sexes and the rights and dignity of labor. In 1844, the association adopted Fourierism, a socialist doctrine originating in France, introduced more organization into their commu- nity, and published the **Harbinger,** a Fourierist journal with a nationwide circulation. In 1847 a fire destroyed the main building at Brook Farm; the association, which was heavily in debt, disbanded soon after.

The constitution of the Brook Farm Association was written chiefly by George Ripley, who was born in Greenfield, Massachusetts, in 1802. He studied at the Harvard Divinity School and served as a Unitarian minister in Boston for more than a decade. He also edited the **Christian Register,** was a member of the informal Transcendental Club, to which Emerson also belonged, and became increasingly preoccupied with literary matters. In 1841 he left the Unitarian church, helped edit the **Dial,** an organ of transcendental writers, and, with the help of his wife, launched the Brook Farm Institute of Agriculture and Education, com- monly called "Mr. Ripley's community," in East Roxbury. With the col- lapse of Brook Farm he moved to Long Island and became literary critic for Horace Greeley's **New York Tribune.** For thirty-one years Rip- ley reviewed books for the **Tribune,** including Nathanial Hawthorne's **Scarlet Letter** and Charles Darwin's **Origin of Species;** he was also editor of the literary department of **Harper's New Monthly Magazine.** He died in 1880.

Questions to consider. Ripley was a close friend of such transcen- dentalists as Emerson and Thoreau and infused his association with the transcendentalist belief in the spirituality of physical nature and the superiority of intuitive insight to logical reasoning. What objectives were announced in the Brook Farm constitution's preamble? What do these objectives reveal about American society in 1841? What does the constitution say about religion? How much freedom was there to be in the new community? Would you characterize Brook Farm as capitalistic, socialistic, or communistic? How democratic was the community?

The Constitution of the Brook Farm Association (1841)

In order more effectually to promote the great purposes of human culture; to establish the external relations of life on a basis of wisdom and purity; to apply the principles of justice and love to our social organization in accordance with the laws of Divine Providence; to substitute a system of brotherly cooperation for one of selfish competition; to secure to our children and those who may be entrusted to our care, the benefits of the highest physical, intellectual and moral education, which in the progress of knowledge the resources at our command will permit; to institute an attractive, efficient, and productive system of industry; to prevent the exercise of worldly anxiety, by the competent supply of our necessary wants; to diminish the desire of excessive accumulation, by making the acquisition of individual property subservient to upright and disinterested uses; to guarantee to each other forever the means of physical support, and of spiritual progress; and thus to impart a greater freedom, simplicity, truthfulness, refinement, and moral dignity, to our mode of life;—we the undersigned do unite in a voluntary Association, and adopt and ordain the following articles of agreement, to wit:

Article I

Sec. 1 The name of this Association shall be "THE BROOK-FARM ASSOCIATION FOR INDUSTRY AND EDUCATION." All persons who shall hold one or more shares in its stock, or whose labor and skill shall be considered an equivalent for capital, may be admitted by the vote of two-thirds of the Association, as members thereof.

Sec. 2 No member of the Association shall ever be subjected to any religious test; nor shall any authority be assumed over individual freedom of opinion

From O. B. Frothingham, **Transcendentalism in New England** (G. P. Putnam's Sons, New York, 1876), 159–164.

by the Association, nor by any one member over another; nor shall any one be held accountable to the Association, except for such overt acts, omissions of duty, as violate the principles of justice, purity, and love, on which it is founded; and in such cases the relation of any member may be suspended, or discontinued, at the pleasure of the Association.

Article II

Sec. 1 The members of this Association shall own and manage such real and personal estate in joint stock proprietorship, divided into shares of one hundred dollars, each, as may from time to time be agreed on. . . .

Sec. 4 The shareholders on their part, for themselves, their heirs and assigns, do renounce all claim on any profits accruing to the Association for the use of their capital invested in the stock of the Association, except five percent interest on the amount of stock held by them, payable in the manner described in the preceding section.

Article III

Sec. 1 The Association shall provide such employment for all its members as shall be adapted to their capacities, habits, and tastes; and each member shall select and perform such operations of labor, whether corporal or mental, as shall be deemed best suited to his own endowments, and the benefit of the Association.

Sec. 2 The Association guarantees to all its members, their children, and family dependents, house-rent, fuel, food, and clothing, and the other necessaries of life, without charge, not exceeding a certain fixed amount to be decided annually by the Association; no charge shall ever be made for support during inability to labor from sickness or old age, or for medical or nursing attendance, except in case of shareholders, who shall be charged therefor . . . but no charge shall be made to any members for education or the use of library and public rooms. . . .

Article V

Sec. 1 The government of the Association shall be vested in a board of Directors, divided into four departments as follows: 1st, General Direction; 2d, Direction of Education; 3d, Direction of Industry; 4th, Direction of Finance; consisting of three persons each. . . .

Sec. 5 The departments of Education and Finance shall be under the control each of its own Direction, which shall select, and in concurrence with the

General Direction, shall appoint such teachers, officers, and agents, as shall be necessary to the complete and systematic organization of the department. No Directors or other officers shall be deemed to possess any rank superior to the other members of the Association, nor shall they receive any extra remuneration for their official services.

Sec. 6 The department of Industry shall be arranged in groups and series, as far as practicable, and shall consist of three primary series; to wit, Agricultural, Mechanical, and Domestic Industry. The chief of each series shall be elected every two months by the members thereof. . . .

29.

WOMEN'S FREEDOM

In March 1776, when the Continental Congress in Philadelphia was beginning to contemplate independence from Britain, Abigail Adams wrote her husband, John, from Braintree, Massachusetts: "I long to hear that you have declared an independency. And, by the way," she added, "in the new code of laws which I suppose it will be necessary for you to make, I desire you would remember the ladies and be more generous and favorable to them than your ancestors. Do not put unlimited power into the hands of the husbands. Remember, all men would be tyrants if they could. If particular care and attention is not paid to the ladies, we are determined to foment a rebellion, and will not hold ourselves bound by any laws in which we have no voice or representation. That your sex are naturally tyrannical is a truth so thoroughly established as to admit of no dispute. . . ." Adams wrote back good-humoredly. "We are obliged to go fairly and softly," he told his wife, "and, in practice, you know we are the subjects. We have only the name of masters, and rather than give this up, which would completely subject us to the despotism of the petticoat, I hope General Washington and all our brave heroes would fight. . . ."[1]

Adams wasn't being accurate. American men had more than "the name of masters." The status of women in Adams's day and for many years afterward was distinctly inferior. Sir William Blackstone, the great eighteenth-century British legal authority, set the standard for the American view. "The husband and wife are one," he proclaimed, "and that one is the husband." Women were regarded as the wards of their husbands, were barred from professions like the law, medicine, and the ministry, and had few opportunities for higher education. According to a little verse composed in 1844:

> The father gives his kind command
> The mother joins, approves,
> And children all attentive stand,
> Then each, obedient, moves.

Abigail Adams wasn't the only woman to chafe at the situation. In 1832 Lydia Maria Child published a two-volume **History of the**

---

[1] Charles Francis Adams, ed., **Familiar Letters of John Adams and His Wife During the Revolution** (New York, 1876), 149–150, 155.

Condition of Woman in All Ages, deploring woman's subservience, and in 1843 Margaret Fuller published a long essay, later expanded and published as **Woman in the Nineteenth Century,** in which she declared: "What woman needs is not as a woman to act or rule, but as a nature to grow, as an intellect to discern, as a soul to live freely and unimpeded, to unfold such powers as were given her when we left our common home."

Born near Boston in 1810 to parents who emphasized intellectual development, Margaret Fuller became one of the most learned Americans of her time despite the fact that academies and colleges did not then admit women. Fuller taught school in the Boston area, wrote for literary journals, and conducted highly popular public "conversations" on the education of women while still in her twenties, and in 1840 she became an editor of the **Dial.** In 1844 she took a position as a literary critic at the **New York Tribune,** and she soon earned the reputation as leading American critic of the decade. After the publication of **Women in the Nineteenth Century** in 1843 and **Papers on Literature and Art** in 1846, Fuller sailed for Europe, where she married Angelo Ossoli, an Italian revolutionary. In July 1850, the ship on which she and her husband and child were returning to the United States foundered off the coast of Long Island, drowning all passengers.

Questions to consider. What aspect of women's position most distressed Margaret Fuller? How specifically did she expect that position to be changed? Did she believe men **could** not speak effectively on behalf of women, or that they **would** not? What audience does she seem to have been addressing in this passage? How important was religion in her argument? Was this statement conservative or radical in its implications? Would Fuller have endorsed the Seneca Falls Declaration of 1848 (Document 30)?

Woman in the Nineteenth Century (1845)

Margaret Fuller

. . . The gain of creation consists always in the growth of individual minds, which live and aspire as flowers bloom and birds sing in the midst of morasses; and in the continual development of that thought, the thought of human destiny, which is given to eternity adequately to express, and which ages of failure only seemingly impede. Only seemingly; and whatever seems to the contrary, this country is as surely destined to elucidate a great moral law as Europe was to promote the mental culture of Man. . . .

. . . Knowing that there exists in the minds of men a tone of feeling toward women as toward slaves, such as is expressed in the common phrase, "Tell that to women and children"; that the infinite soul can only work through them in already ascertained limits; that the gift of reason, Man's highest prerogative, is allotted to them in much lower degree; that they must be kept from mischief and melancholy by being constantly engaged in active labor, which is to be furnished and directed by those better able to think, &c., &c.—we need not multiply instances, for who can review the experience of last week without recalling words which imply, whether in jest or earnest, these views or views like these—knowing this, can we wonder that many reformers think that measures are not likely to be taken in behalf of women, unless their wishes could be publicly represented by women?

"That can never be necessary," cry the other side. "All men are privately influenced by women; each has his wife, sister, or female friends, and is too much biased by these relations to fail of representing their interests; and if this is not enough, let them propose and enforce their wishes with the pen. The beauty of home would be destroyed, the delicacy of the sex be violated, the dignity of halls of legislation degraded by an attempt to introduce them there. Such duties are inconsistent with those of a mother"; and then we have ludicrous pictures of ladies in hysterics at the polls, and senate chambers filled with cradles.

But if in reply we admit as truth that Woman seems destined by nature rather for the inner circle, we must add that the arrangements of civilized life have not been as yet such as to secure it to her. Her circle, if the duller, is not the quieter. If kept from "excitement," she is not from drudgery. Not only the Indian squaw carries the burdens of the camp, but the favorites of Louis XIV accompany him in his journeys, and the washerwoman stands at her tub and carries home her work at all seasons and in all states of health. Those who think the physical circumstances of Woman would make a part in the affairs of national government unsuitable are by no means those who think it impos-

From S. Margaret Fuller, **Woman in the Nineteenth Century** (New York: Greeley & McElrath, 1845), 14–15, 23–28, 52.

sible for Negresses to endure field work even during pregnancy, or for seamstresses to go through their killing labors. . . .

. . . While we hear from men who owe to their wives not only all that is comfortable or graceful but all that is wise in the arrangement of their lives the frequent remark, "You cannot reason with a woman"—when from those of delicacy, nobleness, and poetic culture falls the contemptuous phrase "women and children," and that in no light sally of the hour, but in works intended to give a permanent statement of the best experiences—when not one man in the million, shall I say? no, not in the hundred million, can rise above the belief that Woman was made *for Man*—when such traits as these are daily forced upon the attention, can we feel that Man will always do justice to the interests of Woman? Can we think that he takes a sufficiently discerning and religious view of her office and destiny *ever* to do her justice, except when prompted by sentiment—accidentally or transiently, that is, for the sentiment will vary according to the relations in which he is placed? The lover, the poet, the artist are likely to view her nobly. The father and the philosopher have some chance of liberality; the man of the world, the legislator for expediency none.

Under these circumstances, without attaching importance in themselves to the changes demanded by the champions of Woman, we hail them as signs of the times. We would have every arbitrary barrier thrown down. We would have every path laid open to Woman as freely as to Man. Were this done and a slight temporary fermentation allowed to subside, we should see crystallizations more pure and of more various beauty. We believe the divine energy would pervade nature to a degree unknown in the history of former ages, and that no discordant collision but a ravishing harmony of the spheres would ensue.

Yet then and only then will mankind be ripe for this, when inward and outward freedom for Woman as much as for Man shall be acknowledged as a *right,* not yielded as a concession. As the friend of the Negro assumes that one man cannot by right hold another in bondage, so should the friend of Woman assume that Man cannot by right lay even well-meant restrictions on Woman. If the Negro be a soul, if the woman be a soul, appareled in flesh, to one Master only are they accountable. There is but one law for souls, and if there is to be an interpreter of it, he must come not as man or son of man, but as son of God.

Were thought and feeling once so far elevated that Man should esteem himself the brother and friend, but nowise the lord and tutor, of Woman— were he really bound with her in equal worship—arrangements as to function and employment would be of no consequence. What Woman needs is not as a woman to act or rule, but as a nature to grow, as an intellect to discern, as a soul to live freely and unimpeded to unfold such powers as were given her when we left our common home. If fewer talents were given her, yet if allowed the free and full employment of these, so that she may render back to the giver his own with usury, she will not complain; nay, I dare to say she will bless and rejoice in her earthly birthplace, her earthly lot. . . .

It is not the transient breath of poetic incense that women want; each can receive that from a lover. It is not lifelong sway; it needs but to become a coquette, a shrew, or a good cook to be sure of that. It is not money nor notoriety nor the badges of authority which men have appropriated to themselves. If demands made in their behalf lay stress on any of these particulars, those who make them have not searched deeply into the need. The want is for that which at once includes these and precludes them; which would not be forbidden power, lest there be temptation to steal and misuse it; which would not have the mind perverted by flattery from a worthiness of esteem; it is for that which is the birthright of every being capable of receiving it—the freedom, the religious, the intelligent freedom of the universe to use its means, to learn its secret as far as Nature has enabled them, with God alone for their guide and their judge.

Ye cannot believe it, men; but the only reason why women ever assume what is more appropriate to you, is because you prevent them from finding out what is fit for themselves. Were they free, were they wise fully to develop the strength and beauty of Woman; they would never wish to be men or manlike. The well-instructed moon flies not from her orbit to seize on the glories of her partner. No, for she knows that one law rules, one heaven contains, one universe replies to them alike. . . .

30.

WOMEN'S RIGHTS

In the first part of the nineteenth century, women in increasing numbers began asking for equality before the law and asserting their right to be educated, enter the professions, and participate in public affairs along with men. Some women became active in reform, participating in the temperance movement, the fight against slavery, and the crusade for world peace. But even as reformers they were required to take a subordinate position. When a woman tried to speak at a temperance convention in New York she was shouted down. One man yelled, "Shame on the woman, shame on the woman!" And when several women attended the World Anti-Slavery Convention in London in 1840, men refused to seat them as delegates and made them sit in a curtained enclosure out of the public view. Two delegates—Lucretia Mott and Elizabeth Cady Stanton—began talking of holding a convention to battle for their own rights.

In July 1848 the first organized meeting for women's rights ever held met in Seneca Falls, New York, attended by two hundred delegates, including thirty-two men. Stanton drew up the Declaration of Sentiments, using the Declaration of Independence as a model. She also drafted a series of resolutions that were adopted by the convention. Only one of her demands ran into trouble: the right to vote. Woman suffrage still seemed so outlandish that it took the eloquence of Frederick Douglass, a black abolitionist and journalist, to persuade the delegates to adopt it by a small majority. Many people were shocked by the Seneca Falls convention. They denounced the "Reign of Petticoats" and warned against the "Insurrection among Women." But many distinguished Americans—including Ralph Waldo Emerson, John Greenleaf Whittier, and William Lloyd Garrison—supported the movement.

Elizabeth Cady Stanton, who drafted the Seneca Falls Declaration, was born in Johnstown, New York, in 1815. She attended Emma Willard's seminary in Troy, and while studying law with her father, became aware of the injustices suffered by women from American legal practices. When she married the abolitionist lawyer Henry B. Stanton in 1840, she insisted that the word **obey** be omitted from the ceremony. At an antislavery convention that she attended with her husband the same year, she got to know Lucretia Mott, and the two of them began working together for women's rights. Following the Seneca Falls Conference, Stanton joined Mott (and later Susan B. Anthony) in sponsoring conventions, writing articles, delivering lectures, and appearing before legislative bodies on behalf of the cause. Despite Stanton's grace and charm, she was considered a dangerous radical for espousing woman suffrage and easier divorce laws for women. During the Civil War she helped organize the Women's Loyal National League and urged emancipation. After the war she resumed her work for woman suffrage, became president of the National Woman Suffrage Association, lectured on family life, wrote for **Revolution,** a women's rights weekly, and contributed to the three-volume **History of Woman Suffrage,** published in the 1880s. One of the most distinguished feminist leaders in the country, she died in New York City in 1902.

Questions to consider. Many years passed before the women's rights movement in America began achieving some of its objectives. But the Seneca Falls convention marks the formal beginning of the organized movement to advance women's position, so it merits careful study. Do you think there were any advantages in using the Declaration of Independence (Document 12) as a model for the Declaration of Sentiments? How do the grievances listed by Stanton compare with those cited by Jefferson? Where does the emphasis of the Seneca Falls Declaration lie: in legal, economic, or political rights? Were any rights overlooked by Stanton? The demand for suffrage raised the biggest storm; some of those who signed the declaration withdrew their names when the suffrage resolution met with ridicule. Why do you suppose this happened? How radical do the Seneca Falls demands seem today? Which demands have been met by legislation since 1848?

The Seneca Falls Declaration of 1848

When, in the course of human events, it becomes necessary for one portion of the family of man to assume among the people of the earth a position different from that which they have hitherto occupied, but one to which the laws of nature and of nature's God entitle them, a decent respect to the opinions of mankind requires that they should declare the causes that impel them to such a course.

We hold these truths to be self-evident: that all men and women are created equal; that they are endowed by their Creator with certain inalienable

From Susan B. Anthony, Elizabeth Cady Stanton, and Matilda Joslyn Gage, eds., **History of Woman Suffrage** (3 v., Susan B. Anthony, Elizabeth Cady Stanton, and Matilda Joslyn Gage, Rochester, N.Y., 1889), I: 75–80.

Lydia Maria Child

Susan B. Anthony

Lucretia Mott

Elizabeth Cady Stanton

Representative women.   These four women were all ardent reformers. Lydia Maria Child (1802–1880) was active in the antislavery movement, published many articles and pamphlets depicting the moral and economic evils of slavery, and with her husband edited the **National Anti-Slavery Standard** in New York. Susan B. Anthony (1820–1906), an independent-minded Quaker, started out as a temperance reformer but soon became an energetic women's rights crusader with a special interest in woman suffrage. Lucretia Coffin Mott (1793–1880), also a Quaker, started out as an antislavery worker and then, like Elizabeth Cady Stanton (1815–1902), turned to women's rights when the two women were refused recognition as delegates to the World Antislavery Convention in London in 1840. Mott and Stanton were prime movers behind the first women's rights convention, held in Seneca Falls, New York, in July 1848. (Library of Congress) rights; that among these are life, liberty, and the pursuit of happiness; that to secure these rights governments are instituted, deriving their just powers from the consent of the governed. Whenever any form of government becomes destructive of these ends, it is the right of those who suffer from it to refuse allegiance to it, and to insist upon the institution of a new government, laying its foundations on such principles, and organizing its powers in such form, as to them shall seem most likely to effect their safety and happiness. Prudence, indeed, will dictate that governments long established should not be changed for light and transient causes; and accordingly all experience hath shown that mankind are more disposed to suffer, while evils are sufferable, than to right themselves by abolishing the forms to which they were accustomed. But when a long train of abuses and usurpations, pursuing invariably the same object evinces a design to reduce them under absolute despotism, it is their duty to throw off such government, and to provide new guards for their future security. Such has been the patient sufferance of the women under this government, and such is now the necessity which constrains them to demand the equal station to which they are entitled.

The history of mankind is a history of repeated injuries and usurpations on the part of man toward woman, having in direct object the establishment of an absolute tyranny over her. To prove this, let facts be submitted to a candid world.

He has never permitted her to exercise her inalienable right to the elective franchise.

He has compelled her to submit to laws, in the formation of which she had no voice.

He has withheld from her rights which are given to the most ignorant and degraded men—both natives and foreigners.

Having deprived her of this first right of a citizen, the elective franchise, thereby leaving her without representation in the halls of legislation, he has opposed her on all sides.

He has made her, if married, in the eye of the law, civilly dead.

He has taken from her all right in property, even to the wages she earns.

He has made her, morally, an irresponsible being, as she can commit many crimes with impunity, provided they be done in the presence of her husband. In the covenant of marriage, she is compelled to promise obedience to her husband, he becoming, to all intents and purposes, her master—the law giving him power to deprive her of her liberty, and to administer chastisement.

He has so framed the laws of divorce, as to what shall be the proper causes, and in case of separation, to whom the guardianship of the children shall be given, as to be wholly regardless of the happiness of women—the law, in all cases, going upon a false supposition of the supremacy of man, and giving all power into his hands.

After depriving her of all rights as a married woman, if single, and the owner of property, he has taxed her to support a government which recognizes her only when her property can be made profitable to it.

He has monopolized nearly all the profitable employments, and from those she is permitted to follow, she receives but a scanty remuneration. He closes against her all the avenues to wealth and distinction which he considers most honorable to himself. As a teacher of theology, medicine, or law, she is not known.

He has denied her the facilities for obtaining a thorough education, all colleges being closed against her.

He allows her in Church, as well as State, but a subordinate position, claiming Apostolic authority for her exclusion from the ministry, and, with some exceptions, from any public participation in the affairs of the Church.

He has created a false public sentiment by giving to the world a different code of morals for men and women, by which moral delinquencies which exclude women from society, are not only tolerated, but deemed of little account in man.

He has usurped the prerogative of Jehovah himself, claiming it as his right to assign for her a sphere of action, when that belongs to her conscience and to her God.

He has endeavored, in every way that he could, to destroy her confidence in her own powers, to lessen her self-respect, and to make her willing to lead a dependent and abject life.

Now, in view of this entire disfranchisement of one-half the people of this country, their social and religious degradation—in view of the unjust laws above mentioned, and because women do not feel themselves aggrieved, oppressed, and fradulently deprived of their most sacred rights, we insist that they have immediate admission to all the rights and privileges which belong to them as citizens of the United States.

In entering upon the great work before us, we anticipate no small amount of misconception, misrepresentation, and ridicule; but we shall use every instrumentality within our power to effect our object. We shall employ agents, circulate tracts, petition the State and National legislatures, and endeavor to enlist the pulpit and the press in our behalf. We hope this Convention will be followed by a series of Conventions embracing every part of the country.

Resolutions

WHEREAS, The great precept of nature is conceded to be, that "man shall pursue his own true and substantial happiness." Blackstone in his Commentaries remarks, that this law of Nature being coequal with mankind, and dictated by God himself, is of course superior in obligation to any other. It is binding over all the globe, in all countries and at all times; no human laws are of any validity if contrary to this, and such of them as are valid, derive all their force, and all their validity, and all their authority, mediately and immediately, from this original; therefore,

Resolved, That such laws as conflict, in any way, with the true and substantial happiness of woman, are contrary to the great precept of nature and of no validity, for this is "superior in obligation to any other."

Resolved, That all laws which prevent woman from occupying such a station in society as her conscience shall dictate, or which place her in a position inferior to that of man, are contrary to the great precept of nature, and therefore of no force or authority.

Resolved, That woman is man's equal—was intended to be so by the Creator, and the highest good of the race demands that she should be recognized as such.

Resolved, That the women of this country ought to be enlightened in regard to the laws under which they live, that they may no longer publish their degradation by declaring themselves satisfied with their present position, nor their ignorance, by asserting that they have all the rights they want.

Resolved, That inasmuch as man, while claiming for himself intellectual superiority, does accord to woman moral superiority, it is pre-eminently his duty to encourage her to speak and teach, as she has an opportunity, in all religious assemblies.

Resolved, That the same amount of virtue, delicacy, and refinement of behavior that is required of woman in the social state, should also be required of man, and the same transgressions should be visited with equal severity on both man and woman.

Resolved, That the objection of indelicacy and impropriety, which is so often brought against woman when she addresses a public audience, comes with a very ill-grace from those who encourage, by their attendance, her appearance on the stage, in the concert, or in feats of the circus.

Resolved, That woman has too long rested satisfied in the circumscribed limits which corrupt customs and a perverted application of the Scriptures have marked out for her, and that it is time she should move in the enlarged sphere which her great Creator has assigned her.

Resolved, That it is the duty of the women of this country to secure to themselves their sacred right to the elective franchise.

Resolved, That the equality of human rights results necessarily from the fact of the identity of the race in capabilities and responsibilities.

Resolved, therefore, That, being invested by the Creator with the same capabilities, and the same consciousness of responsibility for their exercise, it is demonstrably the right and duty of woman, equally with man, to promote every righteous cause by every righteous means; and especially in regard to the great subjects of morals and religion, it is self-evidently her right to participate with her brother in teaching them, both in private and in public, by writing and by speaking, by any instrumentalities proper to be used, and in any assemblies proper to be held; and this being a self-evident truth growing out of the divinely implanted principles of human nature, any custom or authority adverse to it, whether modern or wearing the hoary sanction of antiquity, is to be regarded as a self-evident falsehood, and at war with mankind.

31.

DEMON RUM

In the early part of the nineteenth century the United States was a hard-drinking nation. European visitors were struck by the amount of alcohol consumed in the young republic. One English observer declared that Americans consumed more "spirits of all kinds" in proportion to the population than any other people in the world.

Distilled spirits were easy to come by in the new nation. Farmers disposed of their surplus fruit and grain by processing them into spirits, which were easily stored and shipped to market. A bushel of corn worth $0.25 yielded two and a half gallons of whiskey worth $1.25 or more. Corn whiskey and apple cider, the most popular beverages, were considered nutritious and healthful; they were far cheaper than coffee or tea, which had to be imported, and preferable to water, which was often impure and shunned as drink fit for pigs. Alcohol was commonly drunk at meals; it made up for the monotonous diet of many Americans. During a good part of the year, people depended on dry, salty foods— parched corn, smoked ham, salt pork—that didn't spoil rapidly. Many Americans ate corn three times a day in the form of johnnycake, corn bread, corn mush, or Indian pudding. They also consumed great quantities of salt pork fried in lard. Whiskey made greasy food taste better; it was also supposed to cure a variety of ailments, including headaches, nausea, and indigestion.

In 1812, Mason Locke ("Parson") Weems, an Episcopalian clergyman and popular writer, published a little temperance tract. Its ebullient title was **The Drunkard's Looking Glass, Reflecting a Faithful Likeness of the Drunkard in Sundry Very Interesting Attitudes, with Lively Representations of the Many Strange Capers which he cuts at different Stages of his Disease; as first, when he has only "a drop in his eye"; second, when he is "half-shaved"; third, when he is getting "a little on the staggers or so"; and fourth and fifth, and so on, till he is "quite capsized"; "Snug under the table with the dogs", and "sticks to the floor without holding on."** Weems was bothered by American drinking habits. He estimated that there were a hundred thousand habitual drunkards in a population of six million. He was not alone in his concern. Clergymen in other denominations, and laymen as well, became increasingly alarmed by the spread of alcoholism in young America. Basil Hall, a British traveler, reported that "a deeper curse never afflicted any nation. The evil is manifested in almost every walk of life, contaminating all it touches."

In 1826, concerned citizens, led by a Congregational clergyman, organized the American Society for the Promotion of Temperance in Boston and dedicated themselves to encouraging abstinence from spiritous liquors. The organization grew rapidly. By 1835 it had attracted more than a million members, established five thousand local branches, and was distributing thousands of tracts and pamphlets picturing the evils of alcohol. The Temperance Society sought pledges of abstinence; it also sponsored "Cold Water Armies" for children. For a time it was the largest of all the reform movements agitating the nation. Hundreds of temperance stories, songs, poems, and plays poured from the press, and a revivalistic fervor permeated the earnest meetings of the temperance advocates.

Eventually the temperance movement split over purposes and procedures. Conservatives favored moderation in drinking and the rejection of distilled spirits but not of wine and beer. Radicals insisted on total abstinence; they also switched from moral suasion to promotion of laws prohibiting the manufacture and sale of intoxicating beverages. In 1846 Maine passed the first prohibition law; in the 1850s several other states did the same. The prohibitionists looked upon liquor as the root of all evil. They insisted that it destroyed the home, encouraged crime and violence, and transformed hard-working, law-abiding citizens into besotted loafers who threatened to make a mockery of the American experiment in self-government.

In 1854 Timothy Shay Arthur published a novel, **Ten Nights in a Bar-Room and What I Saw There,** dramatizing all these points. In Arthur's novel everything goes wrong in Cedarville when the Sickle and Sheaf tavern is opened; diligent workers become shiftless slobs, civility gives way to coarseness, and violence and degradation wreck the lives of several of the town's most promising young men. But there is one bright note. Joe Morgan, the leading drunk in town when the novel opens, decides to reform. When his little girl, Mary (who comes regularly to the tavern to take him home), is mortally wounded in a tavern brawl, Joe takes the pledge.

T. S. Arthur was born in New York City in 1809. Although he did poorly in school, he became a competent magazine editor and prolific writer of children's stories, self-help manuals, and sentimental novels dealing with marital problems. But his most successful books dealt with temperance. He regarded saloons as "nurseries of vice and crime" and waged his fight against them until long after the Civil War. **Ten Nights in a Bar-Room** sold several hundred thousand copies and was made into a play that rivaled a play based on Harriet Beecher Stowe's **Uncle Tom's Cabin** in popularity. Arthur was editor of the **Home Magazine,** which dealt with family problems, when he died in 1885.

Questions to consider. The final chapter of **Ten Nights in a Bar-Room,** reprinted below, has a happy ending. Hargrove, an opponent of taverns from the outset, tells the villagers the sad story of Simon Slade, a once-industrious mill operator who turned to tavern keeping and was eventually killed by his own son. Hargrove, speaking for Arthur, also recommends immediate action. Why does he think that prohibition is the only safeguard against the abuse of alcohol? How does he handle the clash between prohibition laws and the rights of individuals? What does he say about property rights? What does Arthur's chapter reveal about American culture in the 1850s?

Ten Nights in a Bar-Room (1854)
T. S. Arthur

On the day that succeeded the evening of this fearful tragedy, placards were to be seen all over the village, announcing a mass meeting at the "Sickle and Sheaf" that night.

By early twilight, the people commenced assembling. The bar, which had been closed all day, was now thrown open, and lighted; and in this room, where so much of evil had been originated, encouraged, and consummated, a crowd of earnest-looking men were soon gathered. Among them I saw the fine person of Mr. Hargrove. Joe Morgan—or rather Mr. Morgan—was also of the number. The latter I would scarcely have recognized, had not some one near me called him by name. He was well dressed, stood erect, and, though there were many deep lines on his thoughtful countenance, all traces of his former habits were gone. While I was observing him, he arose, and addressing a few words to the assemblage, nominated Mr. Hargrove as chairman of the meeting. To this a unanimous assent was given.

On taking the chair, Mr. Hargrove made a brief address, something to this effect.

"Ten years ago," said he, his voice evincing a light unsteadiness as he began, but growing firmer as he proceeded, "there was not a happier spot in Bolton country than Cedarville. Now, the marks of ruin are everywhere. Ten years ago, there was a kind-hearted, industrious miller in Cedarville, liked by every one, and as harmless as a little child. Now, his bloated, disfigured body lies in that room. His death was violent, and by the hand of his own son!"

Mr. Hargrove's words fell slowly, distinctly, and marked by the most forcible emphasis. There was scarcely one present who did not feel a low shudder run along his nerves, as the last words were spoken in a husky whisper.

From Timothy Shay Arthur, **Ten Nights in a Bar-Room** (J. W. Bradley, Philadelphia, 1860), 68–81.

BLACK VALLEY RAILROAD!

GREAT CENTRAL, BROAD GAUGE, FAST ROUTE,

From Sippington, through Tippleton and Topersville,

VIA

BEGGARSTOWN, DEMONLAND AND BLACK VALLEY,

TO

DESTRUCTION!

ACCIDENTS BY COLLISIONS ENTIRELY AVOIDED AS NO UP TRAINS ARE RUN OVER THE ROAD.

TICKETS SOLD AT ALL LIQUOR SHOPS.

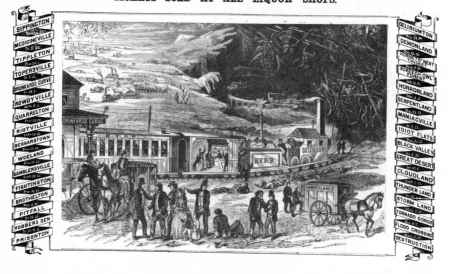

Anti-alcohol poster of the Massachusetts Temperance Alliance, Boston.   Until the antislavery campaign began to gather force in the 1830s, the crusade for temperance was the most popular of all the reform movements before the Civil War. There were numerous temperance organizations at the local and national level and countless temperance meetings, marked by dramatic confessions of reformed alcoholics and by enthusiastic pledge-signings. There were also many corny jokes. A man sees his little girl dipping her doll's dress in a cup, according to a typical temperance tale, and asks what she's doing. "I'm coloring my doll's dress red, Pa," she explains. "With what?" he asks. "With beer, Pa." "You can't color red with beer." "Yes, I can," insists the girl. "Ma said it was beer that colored your nose so red." (Library of Congress)

"Ten years ago," he proceeded, "the miller had a happy wife, and two innocent, glad-hearted children. Now, his wife, bereft of reason, is in a madhouse, and his son the occupant of a felon's cell, charged with the awful crime of patricide!"

Briefly he paused, while his audience stood gazing upon him with half-suspended respiration.

"Ten years ago," he went on, "Judge Hammond was accounted the richest man in Cedarville. Yesterday he was carried, a friendless pauper, to the Almshouse; and to-day he is the unmourned occupant of a pauper's grave! Ten years ago, his wife was the proud, hopeful, loving mother of a most promising son. I need not describe what Willy Hammond was. All here knew him well. Ah! what shattered the fine intellect of that noble-minded woman? Why did her heart break? Where is she? Where is Willy Hammond?"

A low, half repressed groan answered the speaker.

"Ten years ago, you! sir," pointing to a sad-looking old man, and calling him by name, "had two sons—generous, promising, manly-hearted boys. What are they now? You need not answer the question. Too well is their history and your sorrow known. Ten years ago, I had a son—amiable, kind, loving, but weak. Heaven knows how I sought to guard and protect him! But he fell also. The arrows of destruction darkened the very air of our once secure and happy village. And who was safe? Not mine, nor yours!

"Shall I go on? Shall I call up and pass in review before you, one after another, all the wretched victims who have fallen in Cedarville during the last ten years? Time does not permit. It would take hours for the enumeration! No: I will not throw additional darkness into the picture. Heaven knows it is black enough already! But what is the root of this great evil? Where lies the fearful secret? Who understands the disease? A direful pestilence is in the air—it walketh in darkness, and wasteth at noonday. It is slaying the firstborn in our houses, and the cry of anguish is swelling on every gale. Is there no remedy?"

"Yes! yes! There is a remedy!" was the spontaneous answer from many voices.

"Be it our task, then, to find and apply it this night," answered the chairman as he took his seat.

"And there is but one remedy," said Morgan, as Mr. Hargrove sat down. "The accursed traffic must cease among us. You must cut off the fountain, if you would dry up the stream. If you would save the young, the weak, and the innocent—on you God has laid the solemn duty of their protection—you must cover them from the tempter. Evil is strong, wily, fierce, and active in the pursuit of its ends. The young, the weak, and the innocent can no more resist its assaults, than the lamb can resist the wolf. They are helpless, if you abandon them to the powers of evil. Men and brethren! as one who has himself been wellnigh lost—as one who, daily, feels and trembles at the dangers that beset his path—I do conjure you to stay the fiery stream that is bearing every thing good and beautiful among you to destruction. Fathers!

for the sake of your young children, be up now and doing. Think of Willy Hammond, Frank Slade, and a dozen more whose names I could repeat, and hesitate no longer! Let us resolve, this night, that from henceforth, the traffic shall cease in Cedarville. Is there not a large majority of citizens in favour of such a measure? And whose rights or interest can be affected by such a restriction? Who, in fact, has any right to sow disease and death in our community? The liberty, under sufferance, to do so, wrongs the individual who uses it, as well as those who become his victims. Do you want proof of this. Look at Simon Slade, the happy, kind-hearted miller; and at Simon Slade, the tavern-keeper. Was he benefited by the liberty to work harm to his neighbour? No! no! In heaven's name, then, let the traffic cease! To this end, I offer these resolutions:—

"Be it resolved by the inhabitants of Cedarville, That from this day henceforth, no more intoxicating drink shall be sold within the limits of the corporation.

"Resolved, further, That all the liquors in the 'Sickle and Sheath' be forthwith destroyed, and that a fund be raised to pay the creditors of Simon Slade, therefor, should they demand compensation.

"Resolved, That in closing up all other places where liquor is sold, regard shall be had to the right of property which the law secures to every man.

"Resolved, That with the consent of the legal authorities, all the liquor for sale in Cedarville be destroyed; provided the owners thereof be paid its full value out of a fund specially raised for that purpose."

But for the calm, yet resolute opposition of one or two men, these resolutions would have passed by acclamation. A little sober argument showed the excited company that no good end is ever secured by the adoption of wrong means.

There were, in Cedarville, regularly constituted authorities, which alone had the power to determine public measures; or to say what business might or might not be pursued by individuals. And through these authorities they must act in an orderly way.

There was some little chafing at this view of the case. But good sense and reason prevailed. Somewhat modified, the resolution passed, and the more ultra-inclined contented themselves with carrying out the second resolution, to destroy forthwith all liquor to be found on the premises; which was immediately done. After which the people dispersed to their home, each with a lighter heart, and better hopes for the future of their village.

On the next day, as I entered the stage that was to bear me from Cedarville, I saw a man strike his sharp axe into the worn, faded, and leaning post that had, for so many years, borne aloft the "Sickle and Sheaf"; and just as the driver gave word to his horses, the false emblem which had invited so many to enter the way of destruction, fell crashing to the earth.

32.

RACE, SLAVERY, AND
THE CONSTITUTION

The spread of slavery during the early nineteenth century divided the nation and so fanned the flames of sectionalism that the United States was able to remain united only by careful political compromise between North and South. The Missouri Compromise of 1820 admitted Maine, a free state, and Missouri, a slave state, to the Union about the same time, thus preserving the balance between the two sections; it also barred slavery from all territories north of a line (36°30′N) drawn westward from Missouri's southern border. The Compromise of 1850 admitted California as a free state but organized New Mexico and Utah on the principle of popular sovereignty, with slavery left to the inhabitants' decision.

In 1854 Congress violated the Missouri Compromise line. By the Kansas-Nebraska Act of that year, sponsored by Illinois Senator Stephen A. Douglas, who wanted settlers to decide whether or not to have slavery, territory north of 36°30′N was opened to slavery on a "local option" basis. The result was a bloody conflict in Kansas between free-soil settlers opposed to slavery there and those favoring slavery. In 1857, moreover, Chief Justice Roger B. Taney's opinion in the **Dred Scott** case placed the Supreme Court squarely behind the institution of slavery. (A Missouri slave, Dred Scott, had sued his master for freedom, basing his case on the fact that they had lived for a time in free territory.) Speaking for the majority of the justices, Taney announced that blacks could not be American citizens and that Congress could not prohibit slavery even in territories under its direct jurisdiction. The **Dred Scott** decision made all previous compromises over slavery unconstitutional. It also exacerbated sectional tensions. Proslavery Southerners were anxious to extend slavery into new areas; antislavery Northerners were just as determined to do all they could to prevent the further expansion of human bondage despite the Court's ruling. Even Northerners who were not abolitionists opposed Taney's decision. They did not like the idea of Southerners bringing their slaves into the federal territories.

Roger Taney was born in 1777 in Maryland, where he practiced law for a time and then entered politics. An early supporter of Andrew Jackson, he became attorney general in 1831 and helped draft Jackson's message to Congress in 1832 vetoing the recharter bill for the Bank of the United States (Document 22). In 1836 Jackson made Taney chief justice of the Supreme Court. Taney's major opinion before **Dred Scott** was an antimonopoly decision in the **Charles River Bridge** case in 1837. After the **Dred Scott** decision, Taney's prestige declined rapidly, and it all but disappeared after the Republican victory in 1860. He died in Washington four years later.

Scott himself became free because when his master died, the widow married an abolitionist who arranged for Scott's freedom. Scott became a hotel porter in St. Louis and died there of tuberculosis a year after the Supreme Court decision.

Questions to consider. The **Dred Scott** decision purports to cite historical facts as well as advance opinions about those facts. How accurate is Taney's statement that American blacks had never possessed any of the rights and privileges the U.S. Constitution confers on citizens? Why did he make a careful distinction between the rights of citizenship that a state may confer and the rights conferred by the federal Constitution? Do you think Taney's position on the right of states "to confer on whomever it pleased the character of citizen" had implications that he did not intend? Note that Taney insisted that Dred Scott, not being a citizen, was "not entitled to sue in the courts." If he believed this, why did he agree to rule on the case at all? Was he correct in saying that when the nation was founded "no one thought of disputing" the idea that "the negro might justly and lawfully be reduced to slavery"? Do you think his reference to the constitutional provision permitting the slave trade until 1808 strengthened his arguments? Note that in order to find the Missouri Compromise unconstitutional, Taney maintained that the clause in the Constitution giving Congress power to regulate the federal territories applied only to territories belonging to the United States at the time the Constitution was adopted. Do you think he made a convincing case for this assertion? Would Taney's insistence that Congress cannot prohibit slavery in the federal territories logically apply to whites as well as blacks? Was he correct in asserting that the 1787 document made no distinction between property in goods and property in slaves? William Lloyd Garrison called the Constitution a "slaveholder's document," and Taney obviously agreed. But Frederick Douglass, the distinguished black antislavery leader, "abolitionized" the Constitution. He pointed out that the word **slavery** appears nowhere in the Constitution and that the basic purposes of the Union, announced in the preamble, as well as numerous provisions having to do with human rights, categorically rule out slavery. Who do you think was closer to the truth: Taney or Douglass? By 1857, the year of Taney's decision, the Democratic party was the only truly national party. What impact did his decision have on the unity of the party and on such Northern Democrats as Stephen A. Douglas?

Dred Scott *v.* Sanford (1857)

The question is simply this: Can a negro, whose ancestors were imported into this country, and sold as slaves, become a member of the political community formed and brought into existence by the Constitution of the United States, and as such become entitled to all the rights, and privileges, and immunities, guaranteed by that instrument to the citizen? One of which rights is the privilege of suing in a court of the United States in the cases specified in the Constitution.

It will be observed, that the plea applies to that class of persons only whose ancestors were negroes of the African race, and imported into this country, and sold and held as slaves. The only matter in issue before the court, therefore, is, whether the descendants of such slaves, when they shall be emancipated, or who are born of parents who had become free before their birth, are citizens of a State, in the sense in which the word citizen is used in the Constitution of the United States. And this being the only matter in dispute on the pleadings, the court must be understood as speaking in this opinion of that class only, that is of persons who are the descendants of Africans who were imported into this country and sold as slaves. . . .

We proceed to examine the case as presented by the pleadings.

The words "people of the United States" and "citizens" are synonymous terms, and mean the same thing. They both describe the political body who, according to our republican institutions, form the sovereignty, and who hold the power and conduct the government through their representatives. They are what we familiarly call the "sovereign people," and every citizen is one of this people, and a constituent member of this sovereignty. The question before us is, whether the class of persons described in the plea in abatement compose a portion of this people, and are constituent members of this sovereignty? We think they are not, and that they are not included, and were not intended to be included, under the word "citizens" in the Constitution, and can, therefore, claim none of the rights and privileges which that instrument provides for and secures to citizens of the United States. On the contrary, they were at that time considered as a subordinate and inferior class of beings, who had been subjugated by the dominant race, and whether emancipated or not, yet remained subject to their authority, and had no rights or privileges but such as those who held the power and the government might choose to grant them. . . .

In discussing this question, we must not confound the rights of citizenship which a state may confer within its own limits, and the rights of citizenship as a member of the Union. It does not by any means follow, because he has all the rights and privileges of a citizen of a State, that he must be a citizen of the United States. He may have all of the rights and privileges of a State, and yet not be entitled to the rights and privileges of a citizen in any other State. For, previous to the adoption of the Constitution of the United States, every State had the undoubted right to confer on whomsoever it pleased the character of a citizen, and to endow him with all its rights. But this character, of course, was confined to the boundaries of the State, and gave him no rights or privileges in other States beyond those secured to him by the laws of nations and the comity [mutual jurisdiction] of States. Nor have the several States surrendered the power of conferring these rights and privileges by adopting the Constitution of the United States. Each State may still confer them upon an alien, or any one it thinks proper, or upon any class or description of persons; yet he would not be a citizen in the sense in which that word is used in the Constitution of the United States, nor entitled to sue as such in one of its courts, nor to the privileges and immunities of a citizen in the other States. The rights which he would acquire would be restricted to the State which gave them. . . .

The question then arises, whether the provisions of the Constitution, in relation to the personal rights and privileges to which the citizen of a State should be entitled, embraced the negro African race, at that time in this country, or who might afterwards be imported, who had then or should afterwards be made free in any State; and to put it in the power of a single State to make him a citizen of the United States, and endue him with the full rights of citizenship in every other State without their consent. Does the Constitution of the United States act upon him whenever he shall be made free under the laws of a State, and raised there to the rank of a citizen, and immediately clothe him with all the privileges of a citizen in every other State, and in its own courts?

The court think the affirmative of these propositions cannot be maintained. And if it cannot, the plaintiff in error could not be a citizen of the State of Missouri, within the meaning of the Constitution of the United States, and, consequently, was not entitled to sue in its courts. . . .

It is difficult at this day to realize the state of public opinion in relation to that unfortunate race, which prevailed in the civilized and enlightened portions of the world at the time of the Declaration of Independence, and when the Constitution of the United States was framed and adopted. . . .

They had for more than a century before been regarded as beings of an inferior order; and altogether unfit to associate with the white race, either in social or political relations; and so far inferior that they had no rights which the white man was bound to respect; and that the negro might justly and lawfully be reduced to slavery for his benefit. . . . This opinion was at that time fixed and universal in the civilized portion of the white race. It was regarded as an axiom in morals as well as in politics, which no one thought of disputing, or supposed to be open to dispute; and men in every grade and position in society daily and habitually acted upon it in their private pursuits, as well as in matters of public concern, without doubting for a moment the correctness of this opinion. . . .

But there are two clauses in the Constitution which point directly and specifically to the negro race as a separate class of persons, and show clearly that they were not regarded as a portion of the people or citizens of the Government then formed.

One of these clauses reserves to each of the thirteen States the right to import slaves until the year 1808, if he thinks it proper. And the importation which it thus sanctions was unquestionably of persons of the race of which we are speaking, as the traffic in slaves in the United States had always been confined to them. And by the other provision the States pledge themselves to each other to maintain the right of property of the master, by delivering up to him any slave who may have escaped from his service, and be found within their respective territories. . . . And these two provisions show, conclusively, that neither the description of persons therein referred to, nor their descendants, were embraced in any of the other provisions of the Constitution; for certainly these two clauses were not intended to confer on them or their posterity the blessings of liberty, or any of the personal rights so carefully provided for the citizen. . . .

Indeed, when we look to the condition of this race in the several States at the time, it is impossible to believe that these rights and privileges were intended to be extended to them. . . .

The Act of Congress, upon which the plaintiff relies, declares that slavery and involuntary servitude, except as a punishment for crime, shall be forever prohibited in all that part of the territory ceded by France, under the name of Louisiana, which lies north of thirty-six degrees thirty minutes north latitude, and not included within the limits of Missouri. And the difficulty which meets us at the threshold of this part of the inquiry is, whether Congress was authorized to pass this law under any of the powers granted to it by the Constitution; for if the authority is not given by that instrument, it is the duty of this court to declare it void and inoperative, and incapable of conferring freedom upon any one who is held as a slave under the laws of any one of the States.

The counsel for the plaintiff has laid much stress upon that article in the Constitution which confers on Congress the power "to dispose of and make all needful rules and regulations respecting the territory or other property belonging to the United States," but, in the judgment of the court, that provision has no bearing on the present controversy, and the power there given, whatever it may be, is confined, and was intended to be confined, to the territory which at that time belonged to, or was claimed by, the United States, and was within their boundaries as settled by the treaty with Great Britain, and can have no influence upon a territory afterwards acquired from a foreign Government. It was a special provision for a known and particular territory, and to meet a present emergency, and nothing more. . . .

If this clause is construed to extend to territory acquired by the present Government from a foreign nation, outside of the limits of any charter from the British Government to a colony, it would be difficult to say, why it was deemed necessary to give the Government the power to sell any vacant lands

Dred and Harriet Scott. It took eleven years for the federal courts to dispose of the freedom suit of Dred and Harriet Scott. During that time the couple became figures of considerable interest to the readers of popular periodicals, such as **Frank Leslie's Illustrated Newspaper,** where these drawings of the couple appeared. Only two years old when Chief Justice Taney handed down his decision, **Leslie's Illustrated** already had almost a hundred thousand readers, mostly middle-class, who enjoyed how Leslie "seized promptly and illustrated the passing events of the day." In covering the Dred Scott affair, **Leslie's** reported not only on Dred and Harriet but on their two daughters. Northerners greeted Taney's harsh decision with anger due in part to the influence of the popular press. (Library of Congress)

belonging to the sovereignty which might be found within it; and if this was necessary, why the grant of this power should precede the power to legislate over it and establish a Government there; and still more difficult to say, why it was deemed necessary so specially and particularly to grant the power to make needful rules and regulations in relation to any personal or movable property it might acquire there. For the words, *other property* necessarily, by every known rule of interpretation, must mean property of a different description from territory or land. And the difficulty would perhaps be insurmountable in endeavoring to account for the last member of the sentence, which provides that "nothing in this Constitution shall be so construed as to prejudice any claims of the United States or any particular State," or to say how any particular State could have claims in or to a territory ceded by a foreign Government, or to account for associating this provision with the preceding provisions of the clause, with which it would appear to have no connection. . . .

But the power of Congress over the person or property of a citizen can never be a mere discretionary power under our Constitution and form of Government. The powers of the Government and the rights and privileges of the Citizen are regulated and plainly defined by the Constitution itself. And when the Territory becomes a part of the United States, the Federal Government enters into possession in the character impressed upon it by those who created it. It enters upon it with its powers over the citizen strictly defined, and limited by the Constitution, from which it derives its own existence, and by virtue of which alone it continues to exist and act as a Government and sovereignty. It has no power of any kind beyond it; and it cannot, when it enters a Territory of the United States, put off its character, and assume discretionary or despotic powers which the Constitution has denied to it. It cannot create for itself a new character separated from the citizens of the United States, and the duties it owes them under the provisions of the Constitution. The Territory being a part of the United States, the Government and the citizen both enter it under the authority of the Constitution, with their respective rights defined and marked out; and the Federal Government can exercise no power over his person or property, beyond what that instrument confers, nor lawfully deny any right which it has reserved. . . .

The rights of private property have been guarded with equal care. Thus the rights of property are united with the rights of person, and placed on the same ground by the fifth amendment to the Constitution. . . . An Act of Congress which deprives a person of the United States of his liberty or property merely because he came himself or brought his property into a particular Territory of the United States, and who had committed no offense against the laws, could hardly be dignified with the name of due process of law. . . .

And this prohibition is not confined to the States, but the words are general, and extend to the whole territory over which the Constitution gives it power to legislate, including those portions of it remaining under territorial government, as well as that covered by States. It is a total absence of power everywhere within the dominion of the United States, and places the citizen of a territory, so far as these rights are concerned, on the same footing with citizens of the States; and guards them as firmly and plainly against any inroads which the general government might attempt, under the plea of implied or incidental powers. And if Congress itself cannot do this—if it is beyond the powers conferred on the Federal Government—it will be admitted, we presume, that it could not authorize a territorial government to exercise them. It could confer no power on any local government, established by its authority, to violate the provisions of the Constitution.

It seems, however, to be supposed, that there is a difference between property in a slave and other property, and that different rules may be applied to it in expounding the Constitution of the United States. And the laws and usages of nations, and the writings of eminent jurists upon the relation of master and slave and their mutual rights and duties, and the powers which governments may exercise over it, have been dwelt upon in the argument.

But . . . if the Constitution recognizes the right of property of the master in a slave, and makes no distinction between that description of property and other property owned by a citizen, no tribunal, acting under the authority of the United States, whether it be legislative, executive, or judicial, has a right to draw such a distinction, or deny to it the benefit of the provisions and guarantees which have been provided for the protection of private property against the encroachments of the Government.

Now . . . the right of property in a slave is distinctly and expressly affirmed in the Constitution. The right to traffic in it, like an ordinary article of merchandise and property, was guaranteed to the citizens of the United States, in every State that might desire it, for twenty years. And the Government in express terms is pledged to protect it in all future time, if the slave escapes from his owner. . . . And no word can be found in the Constitution which gives Congress a greater power over slave property, or which entitles property of that kind to less protection than property of any other description. The only power conferred is the power coupled with the duty of guarding and protecting the owner in his rights.

Upon these considerations, it is the opinion of the court that the Act of Congress which prohibited a citizen from holding and owning property of this kind in the territory of the United States north of the line therein mentioned, is not warranted by the Constitution, and is therefore void; and that neither Dred Scott himself, nor any of his family, were made free by being carried into this territory; even if they had been carried there by the owner, with the intention of becoming a permanent resident.

33.

LIBERTY AND UNION

The great vehicle for antislavery politics was the Republican party. Founded in Ripon, Wisconsin, in 1854, the new party rapidly absorbed members of earlier, smaller antislavery organizations by pledging itself to oppose the further extension of slavery in the United States. In the election of 1856, the Republicans showed amazing strength: their candidate, John C. Frémont, won 1,339,932 popular and 114 electoral votes to Democratic candidate James Buchanan's 1,832,955 popular and 174 electoral votes. During the next four years the party broadened its appeal so as to attract industrialists and workers as well as farmers, professional people, and religious leaders who were opposed to slavery. It also developed able party leaders and made impressive gains at the state and congressional levels.

The Republican party's 1860 platform not only upheld the Union and reiterated its stand against the extension of slavery but also contained a number of economic planks that would appeal to industrialists in the Northeast and farmers in the West. It favored a protective tariff, the building of a transcontinental railroad, and a homestead act giving free land to settlers. Adopted in Chicago in May 1860, the platform conformed closely to the views of such moderates as William H. Seward and Horace Greeley of New York, Benjamin F. Wade and Salmon P. Chase of Ohio, and its standard-bearer, Abraham Lincoln of Illinois. Only when leading abolitionists threatened to walk out of the convention did Republican leaders incorporate a reaffirmation of the Declaration of Independence into their platform. But though the Republicans took a moderate position in their platform, the victory of Lincoln in the 1860 election triggered secession and civil war.

Questions to consider. To what did the Republican platform refer when it announced that events of the past four years had established the necessity of organizing a new party? Do you agree with the statement that the principles of the Declaration of Independence are "essential to the preservation of our Republican institutions"? And with the assertion that "threats of Disunion" are equivalent to "an avowal of contemplated treason"? In denouncing "the lawless invasion by armed force of the soil of any State or Territory" what did the platform makers have in mind? What did the platform say about Kansas? About the **Dred Scott** decision (Document 32)? What dominated the platform: the slavery issue or economic issues? On balance, to whom was the platform supposed to appeal? With which planks would Alexander Hamilton (Document 15) have agreed? Why?

━━━━━━━

The Republican Party Platform of 1860

Resolved, That we, the delegated representatives of the Republican electors of the United States, in Convention assembled, in discharge of the duty we owe to our constituents and our country, unite in the following declarations:

1. That the history of the nation, during the last four years, has fully established the propriety and necessity of the organization and perpetuation of the Republican party, and that the causes which called it into existence are permanent in their nature, and now, more than ever before, demand its peaceful and constitutional triumph.

2. That the maintenance of the principles promulgated in the Declaration of Independence and embodied in the Federal Constitution, "That all men are created equal; that they are endowed by their Creator with certain inalienable rights; that among these are life, liberty and the pursuit of happiness; that, to secure these rights, governments are instituted among men, deriving their just powers from the consent of the governed," is essential to the preservation of our Republican institutions, and that the Federal Constitution, the Rights of the States, and the Union of the States, must and shall be preserved.

3. That to the Union of the States this nation owes its unprecedented increase in population, its surprising development of material resources, its rapid augmentation of wealth, its happiness at home and its honor abroad; and we hold in abhorrence all schemes for Disunion, come from whatever source they may; And we congratulate the country that no Republican member of Congress has uttered or countenanced the threats of Disunion so often made by Democratic members, without rebuke and with applause from their political associates; and we denounce those threats of Disunion, in case of a popular overthrow of their ascendancy, as denying the vital principles of a free government, and as an avowal of contemplated treason, which it is the imperative duty of an indignant People sternly to rebuke and forever silence.

4. That the maintenance inviolate of the rights of the States, and especially the right of each State to order and control its own domestic institutions according to its own judgment exclusively, is essential to that balance of powers on which the perfection and endurance of our political fabric depends;

From Francis Curtis, **The Republican Party** (2 v., G. P. Putnam's Sons, New York, 1904), I: 355–358.

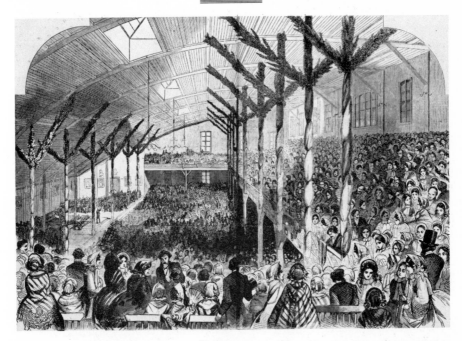

Republican nominating convention, May 1860.   The Republicans, meeting in a huge boxlike structure called the Wigwam in Chicago, adopted a platform opposing the extension of slavery into the federal territories and favoring a protective tariff, the building of a transcontinental railroad, and a homestead act giving free land to settlers. The chief contenders for the nomination were New York Senator William H. Seward and former Illinois Congressman Abraham Lincoln. Seward had long been prominent in national affairs and was far better known than Lincoln, but he had made many political enemies and, although a moderate, had made statements from time to time that made him sound like an outright abolitionist. Lincoln, a newcomer to national politics, had no political enemies and, although he was strongly opposed to the expansion of slavery, he was not an abolitionist. (Library of Congress)

and we denounce the lawless invasion by armed forces of the soil of any State or Territory, no matter under what pretext, as among the gravest of crimes.

5. That the present Democratic Administration has far exceeded our worst apprehensions, in its measureless subserviency to the exactions of a sectional interest, as especially evinced in its desperate exertions to force the infamous Lecompton constitution[1] upon the protesting people of Kansas; in

[1] A proslavery constitution adopted by a proslavery legislature in 1857 and not submitted to a popular vote.—Eds.

construing the personal relation between master and servant to involve an unqualified property in persons; in its attempted enforcement, everywhere, on land and sea, through the intervention of Congress and of the Federal Courts of the extreme pretensions of a purely local interest; and in its general and unvarying abuse of the power intrusted to it by a confiding people. . . .

7. That the new dogma that the Constitution, of its own force, carries Slavery into any or all of the Territories of the United States, is a dangerous political heresy, at variance with the explicit provisions of that instrument itself, with contemporaneous exposition, and with legislative and judicial precedent; is revolutionary in its tendency, and subversive of the peace and harmony of the country.

8. That the normal condition of all the territory of the United States is that of freedom; That as our Republican fathers, when they had abolished slavery in all our national territory, ordained that "no person should be deprived of life, liberty, or property, without due process of law," it becomes our duty, by legislation, whenever such legislation is necessary, to maintain this provision of the Constitution against all attempts to violate it; and we deny the authority of Congress, of a territorial legislature, or of any individuals, to give legal existence to Slavery in any Territory of the United States.

9. That we brand the recent re-opening of the African slave-trade, under the cover of our national flag, aided by perversions of judicial power, as a crime against humanity and a burning shame to our country and age; and we call upon Congress to take prompt and efficient measures for the total and final suppression of that execrable traffic.

10. That in the recent vetoes, by their Federal Governors, of the acts of the Legislatures of Kansas and Nebraska, prohibiting Slavery in those territories, we find a practical illustration of the boasted Democratic principle of Non-Intervention and Popular Sovereignty embodied in the Kansas-Nebraska bill, and a demonstration of the deception and fraud involved therein.

11. That Kansas should, of right, be immediately admitted as a State under the Constitution recently formed and adopted by her people, and accepted by the House of Representatives.

12. That, while providing revenue for the support of the General Government by duties upon imports, sound policy requires such an adjustment of these imposts as to encourage the development of the industrial interests of the whole country; and we commend that policy of national exchanges which secures to the working men liberal wages, to agriculture remunerating prices, to mechanics and manufacturers an adequate reward for their skill, labor and enterprise, and to the nation commercial prosperity and independence.

13. That we protest against any sale or alienation to others of the Public Lands held by actual settlers, and against any view of the Homestead policy which regards the settlers as paupers or supplicants for public bounty; and we demand the passage by Congress of the complete and satisfactory Homestead measure which has already passed the house.

14. That the Republican Party is opposed to any change in our Naturalization Laws or any State legislation by which the rights of our citizenship hitherto accorded to immigrants from foreign lands shall be abridged or impaired; and in favor of giving a full and efficient protection to the rights of all classes of citizens, whether native or naturalized, both at home and abroad.

15. That appropriations by Congress for River and Harbor improvements of a National character, required for the accommodation and security of an existing commerce, are authorized by the Constitution, and justified by the obligations of Government to protect the lives and property of its citizens.

16. That a Railroad to the Pacific Ocean is imperatively demanded by the interests of the whole country; that the Federal Government ought to render immediate and efficient aid in its construction; and that, as preliminary thereto, a daily Overland Mail should be promptly established. . . .

COUNTERPOINT IV

Reform and Violence

Antebellum America saw a tremendous surge of social reform, as the documents in Chapter Four show, but it also experienced a staggering level of violence. An 1813 tavern fight, "a donnybrook of shoving, kicking, eye-gouging, fist-fighting, knifing, and gunfire," involved none other than future President Andrew Jackson and future Senator Thomas Hart Benton; fifteen years later William Cullen Bryant, a distinguished poet, horsewhipped a New York editor on one of the most exclusive streets in the city. But the phenomenon involved more than individual brawls. There also seemed to be a "spirit of riot" and "mob behavior" throughout the country—U.S. mail burnings in South Carolina, multiple hangings of gamblers in Mississippi, and ferocious assaults on Catholic nuns in Massachusetts. In Missouri, vigilantes assaulted Mormons. In Boston a mob dragged William Lloyd Garrison through the streets with a rope around his feet. Often, in fact, reform and violence seemed intertwined, and prominent writers wondered "what this madness means."

Leonard Richards tried to answer this question, in part through the use of statistical methods. Richards's findings generally confirm contemporary impressions. Using newspapers as his source, and defining "mobs" as dozens, sometimes thousands, of people assaulting others and damaging or destroying property, he found that although mobs were commonplace throughout the antebellum era, a crescendo of rioting erupted in the 1830s (see table A). There was a particularly sharp rise between 1835 and 1836 (see figure B). He also found that reform and violence in these key years were indeed linked because almost half the mobs of the era were antiabolitionist mobs (figure B).

What exactly was the link between mobs and reform? What were Garrison and other abolitionists saying or doing that caused this harsh reaction? In part, of course, they were saying what they always said: the slaves should be free from bondage—free to keep their wages and raise Christian families and, by implication, free to live where they liked, even if this included living near white families in Northern communities. The abolitionists' message was not especially welcome to Northern whites, either in the 1830s or later. But neither was it new. Garrison had been propounding it since he founded **The Liberator** in 1831. Richards probed further, this time examining mob activity in fifteen upstate New York counties during the years 1835–1836, when mob action spiked so sharply. He discovered that the riots seemed closely related to the founding of new chapters of the American Anti-Slavery Society. He inferred that it was not the antislavery message itself that provoked violence, but formally organizing to spread it.

With this insight in hand, Richards probed still deeper, using census returns and city directories to identify participants in an 1835 riot in Utica, New York (figure D). The differences between the two sides seemed significant. Mobs had twice as many commercial and professional people—merchants, bankers, lawyers, politicians—as abolitionist groups, and far more rioters were native-born, Episcopalian, or both. Abolitionists, in contrast, included almost four times as many manufacturers and trades-men—representatives from the newest, most modern parts of the economy.

Richards concluded that the mobs represented a traditionalist "establishment" in Utica that felt threatened by the new antislavery groups. They may have felt threatened in part by the abolitionist message to free the slaves. But they also, maybe mainly, feared abolitionists as moderniz-ers—that is, as threats to "old-fashioned" economic and political norms as well as "old-fashioned" white supremacy. On the other hand, once the abolitionists became a familiar part of the community landscape, they became less threatening. And so, then, did the mobs.

Not all mobs assaulted white abolitionists, however. Sometimes, especially in larger cities, they attacked blacks as well, and in particularly violent ways. New York City experienced such a riot in 1834. Did this mob resemble those in upstate New York in composition and motive? Not according to the occupations of those arrested for rioting (see table E). More than four out of five of them were working men (the first three categories in table E), and almost half were skilled laborers and tradesmen, a completely different group from their upstate breth-ren. Nor, obviously, were their stature and leadership threatened, since they possessed neither. By indicating the wards where a high percen-tage of rioters lived and by plotting the locations of their targets (resi-dences and churches of blacks) on a map of lower Manhattan and considering the resulting pattern against the backdrop of abolitionist rhetoric (see figure F), Richards discovered, if not a definitive answer, at least a possible one. Urban artisans of the 1830s, he speculated, felt threatened by economic and social modernization just as the up-state establishment did. But it was not the loss of power and status they feared—it was losing their jobs. Thus they lashed out against those who seemed most threatening and whose numbers the abolitionists sought to increase a millionfold—the free black people in their midst.

A. Collective ("Mob") Violence in the United States, 1812–1849

1812–1819	7 incidents reported
1820–1829	21
1830–1839	115
1840–1849	64

SOURCE: From *Gentlemen of Property and Standing: Anti-Abolitionist Mobs in Jacksonian America* by Leonard L. Richards. Copyright © 1970 by Oxford University Press, Inc. Reprinted by permission.

B. Antiabolitionist and "Other" Mobs in the United States, 1834–1838

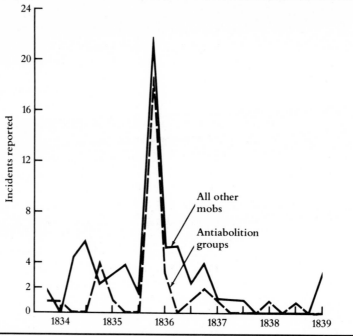

SOURCE: From *Gentlemen of Property and Standing: Anti-Abolitionist Mobs in Jacksonian America* by Leonard L. Richards. Copyright © 1970 by Oxford University Press, Inc. Reprinted by permission.

C. Mobs and the Founding of Antislavery Societies in Fifteen New York Counties, 1833–1838

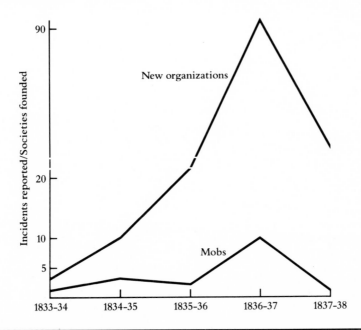

SOURCE: From *Gentlemen of Property and Standing: Anti-Abolitionist Mobs in Jacksonian America* by Leonard L. Richards. Copyright © 1970 by Oxford University Press, Inc. Reprinted by permission.

D. Characteristics of Mobs and Abolitionist Groups, Utica, New York, 1835

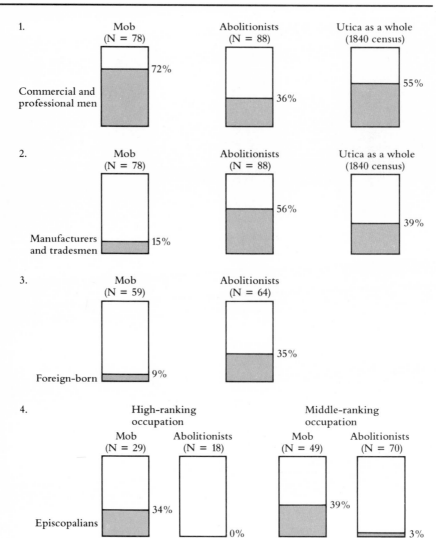

1. Mob (N = 78) — Commercial and professional men: 72%; Abolitionists (N = 88): 36%; Utica as a whole (1840 census): 55%

2. Mob (N = 78) — Manufacturers and tradesmen: 15%; Abolitionists (N = 88): 56%; Utica as a whole (1840 census): 39%

3. Mob (N = 59) — Foreign-born: 9%; Abolitionists (N = 64): 35%

4. Episcopalians — High-ranking occupation: Mob (N = 29): 34%; Abolitionists (N = 18): 0%; Middle-ranking occupation: Mob (N = 49): 39%; Abolitionists (N = 70): 3%

E. Occupations of Men Arrested in Riot Against Blacks, New York City, 1834

Professional and commercial men	17% of sample
Skilled laborers and tradesmen	45
Men	(36)
Sons	(9)
Semiskilled and unskilled	24
Paupers and criminals	4
Unknowns	10

SOURCE: From *Gentlemen of Property and Standing: Anti-Abolitionist Mobs in Jacksonian America* by Leonard L. Richards. Copyright © 1970 by Oxford University Press, Inc. Reprinted by permission.

F. Wards with High Percentages of Antiblack Rioters and Location of Targets, Lower Manhattan, 1834

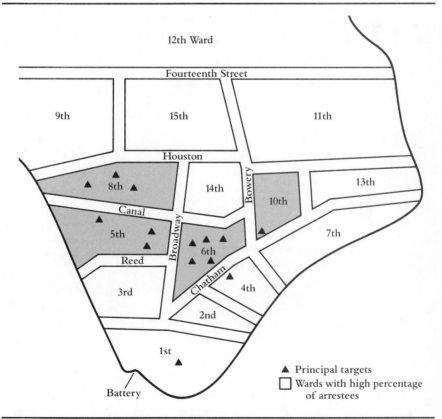

SOURCE: From *Gentlemen of Property and Standing: Anti-Abolitionist Mobs in Jacksonian America* by Leonard L. Richards. Copyright © 1970 by Oxford University Press, Inc. Reprinted by permission.

The United States Army of the Potomac, Virginia, 1865. (National Archives)

CHAPTER FIVE

Rebels, Yankees, and Freedmen

34.

FLIGHT FROM UNION

The election of 1860 centered on slavery and the Union. The Republicans ran Abraham Lincoln for president on a platform opposing the further extension of slavery. The Democrats split over the issue. The Northern Democrats ran Illinois Senator Stephen A. Douglas on a platform calling for "popular sovereignty," that is, the right of people in the federal territories to decide for themselves whether they wanted slavery. The Southern Democrats ran Kentucky's John C. Breckenridge on a frankly proslavery platform demanding federal protection of slavery in the territories. A fourth party, the Constitutional Union party, which ran John Bell of Tennessee, tried to play down the slavery issue by emphasizing the preservation of the Union. This division of Lincoln's opponents made his victory an almost foregone conclusion. Though Lincoln did not win the majority of popular votes cast in the election, he won more popular votes than any of his three opponents and he also took the majority of electoral votes. But he received not one electoral vote in the South.

Even before Lincoln's election, Mississippi had contemplated withdrawing from the Union if the Republicans won. When Lincoln did win, Governor John J. Pettus issued a proclamation denouncing the "Black Republicans," held a conference with the state's congressional delegation, including Jefferson Davis, and recommended a state convention to take action on secession. Late in November 1860, the Mississippi legislature met in Jackson, received the governor's recommendation, and passed a bill providing for elections the following month for a convention to meet on January 7 "to consider the then existing relations between the government of the United States and the government and people of the State of Mississippi." It also passed a series of resolutions outlining the reasons for adopting secession as "the proper remedy" for the state's grievances.

On December 20, South Carolina seceded from the Union. Shortly afterward ten other states followed its lead: Mississippi, Florida, Alabama, Georgia, Louisiana, Texas, Virginia, Arkansas, Tennessee, and North Carolina. In February 1861, delegates from the seceding states met in Montgomery, Alabama, to adopt a constitution for the Confederate States of America. They chose Mississippi's Jefferson Davis as president. On April 12, the Civil War began.

Questions to consider. The Mississippi resolutions contained a succinct summary of the outlook of Southern secessionists. To what extent did they depend on John C. Calhoun's "compact" theory of the Union (Document 21)? Were the resolutions correct in stating that the Northern states had "assumed a revolutionary position" toward the Southern states? Was the charge that the Northern states had violated the Constitution in their behavior toward the South valid? Was it accurate to say that Northerners sought an abolitionist amendment to the Constitution? To what "incendiary publications" do the resolutions refer? What "hostile invasion of a Southern State" did the drafters of the resolutions have in mind? The resolutions concluded by stating that the election of Lincoln meant that the North intended to use the powers of the federal government for the "overthrow of the Southern Section of this great Confederacy." How much truth was there in this belief? Do you see any similarities between the arguments advanced here and those appearing in the Declaration of Independence (Document 12)?

Mississippi Resolutions on Secession (1860)

Whereas, The Constitutional Union was formed by the several States in their separate sovereign capacity for the purpose of mutual advantage and protection;

That the several States are distinct sovereignties, whose supremacy is limited so far only as the same has been delegated by voluntary compact to a Federal Government, and when it fails to accomplish the ends for which it was established, the parties to the compact have the right to resume, each State for itself, such delegated powers;

That the institution of slavery existed prior to the formation of the Federal Constitution, and is recognized by its letter, and all efforts to impair its value or lessen its duration by Congress, or any of the free States, is a violation of the compact of Union and is destructive of the ends for which it was ordained, but in defiance of the principles of the Union thus established, the people of the Northern States have assumed a revolutionary position towards the Southern States;

That they have set at defiance that provision of the Constitution which was intended to secure domestic tranquillity among the States and promote their general welfare, namely: "No person held to service or labor in one State, under the laws thereof, escaping into another, shall, in consequence of any law or regulation therein, be discharged from such service or labor, but

Reprinted by permission of Louisiana State University Press from **Mississippi in the Confederacy,** edited by John K. Bettersworth, copyright © 1961, pp. 22–24.

Lincoln campaign poster. The election of 1860, the most fateful ever held in this country, was a four-cornered race. The Republicans ran Abraham Lincoln of Illinois and Hannibal Hamlin of Maine on a platform calling for the containment of slavery within the states where it already existed. The Republican campaign was a lively one, replete with songs, slogans, posters, torchlight parades, barbecues, picnics, and pole-raisings. The Republicans scoffed at warnings by Southerners that the South would leave the Union if Lincoln won. But Lincoln's victory in November was followed by secession and Civil War. (Library of Congress)

shall be delivered up on claim of the party to whom such service or labor may be due;"

That they have by voluntary associations, individual agencies and State legislation interfered with slavery as it prevails in the slave-holding States;

That they have enticed our slaves from us, and by State intervention obstructed and prevented their rendition under the fugitive slave law;

That they continue their system of agitation obviously for the purpose of encouraging other slaves to escape from service, to weaken the institution in the slave-holding States by rendering the holding of such property insecure, and as a consequence its ultimate abolition certain;

That they claim the right and demand its execution by Congress to exclude slavery from the Territories, but claim the right of protection for every species of property owned by themselves;

That they declare in every manner in which public opinion is expressed their unalterable determination to exclude from admittance into the Union any new State that tolerates slavery in its Constitution, and thereby force Congress to a condemnation of that species of property;

That they thus seek by an increase of abolition States "to acquire two-thirds of both houses" for the purpose of preparing an amendment to the Constitution of the United States, abolishing slavery in the States, and so continue the agitation that the proposed amendment shall be ratified by the Legislatures of three-fourths of the States;

That they have in violation of the comity of all civilized nations, and in violation of the comity established by the Constitution of the United States, insulted and outraged our citizens when travelling among them for pleasure, health or business, by taking their servants and liberating the same, under the forms of State laws, and subjecting their owners to degrading and ignominious punishment;

That to encourage the stealing of our property they have put at defiance that provision of the Constitution which declares that fugitives from justice (escaping) into another State, on demand of the Executive authority of that State from which he fled, shall be delivered up;

That they have sought to create domestic discord in the Southern States by incendiary publications;

That they encouraged a hostile invasion of a Southern State to excite insurrection, murder and rapine;

That they have deprived Southern citizens of their property and continue an unfriendly agitation of their domestic institutions, claiming for themselves perfect immunity from external interference with their domestic policy. . . .

That they have elected a majority of Electors for President and Vice-President on the ground that there exists an irreconcilable conflict between the two sections of the Confederacy in reference to their respective systems of labor and in pursuance of their hostility to us and our institutions, thus declaring to the civilized world that the powers of this Government are to be used for the dishonor and overthrow of the Southern Section of this great Confederacy. Therefore,

Be it resolved by the Legislature of the State of Mississippi, That in the opinion of those who now constitute the said Legislature, the secession of each aggrieved State is the proper remedy for these injuries.

35.

A DECLARATION OF FREEDOM

From the outset, the abolitionists urged Abraham Lincoln to make freeing the slaves the major objective of the war. But Lincoln declared: "My paramount object in this struggle is to save the Union." The Republican platform had promised to check the extension of slavery, but it also pledged not to interfere with slavery where it legally existed. Four border slave states—Maryland, Kentucky, Missouri, and Delaware—had remained in the Union, and Lincoln was afraid that an abolitionist policy would drive them into the Confederacy, with disastrous results for the Union cause. He was not convinced at first, moreover, that the majority of Northerners favored abolition.

As the Civil War progressed, Northern public opinion moved slowly in the direction of emancipation. At the same time it was becoming clear that a Union victory would mean the end of slavery. Whenever Union troops occupied any part of the Confederacy, the slaves promptly left the plantations and became camp followers of the Northern armies. Union generals began asking what policy to adopt toward slavery in the occupied parts of the South. In addition, the European public was becoming critical of the North for its failure to emancipate the blacks. Lincoln finally decided that the time had come to take action.

At a secret cabinet meeting on July 22, 1862, Lincoln presented a proclamation abolishing slavery, on which he had been working nearly a month. Secretary of State William H. Seward urged him not to issue it until after a Union victory. Then, on September 17, came the battle of Antietam, at which the Union armies of General George M. McClellan halted the advance of General Robert E. Lee's troops. On September 22, Lincoln officially proclaimed emancipation. In his capacity as commander in chief he announced that, "on the 1st day of January, A.D. 1863, all persons held as slaves within any State or designated part of a State the people whereof shall then be in rebellion against the United States shall be then, thenceforward, and forever free."

The Emancipation Proclamation did not immediately end slavery. It did not apply to the border states because they were not in rebellion. Nor did it apply to those parts of the Confederacy then held by Union troops. Nevertheless, in all Confederate territories subsequently occupied by Northern troops, the slaves became free by the terms of Lincoln's proclamation. Furthermore, the proclamation led to the voluntary freeing of slaves in many places where it did not apply; Missouri and Maryland freed their slaves in 1863 and 1864. But it was the Thirteenth Amendment that ended slavery everywhere in the United States for all time. Introduced in Congress in December 1863 and adopted with Lincoln's energetic support in January 1865, it became part of the Constitution the following December when the necessary three-fourths of the states had ratified it.

Born to a frontier farming family in Kentucky in 1809, Abraham Lincoln grew up in Indiana and Illinois. As a young man he worked as a farmer, rail-splitter, boatsman, and storekeeper before turning to law and politics. He became enormously successful as a lawyer and served several years in the Illinois legislature and one term in the House of Representatives. Lincoln was largely self-educated; he read and reread such books as the Bible, Aesop's fables, the works of Shakespeare, and the poems of Robert Burns and developed great skill as a writer. In 1858 his debates with Stephen Douglas over slavery brought him national prominence and helped win him the Republican nomination for president in 1860. During the Civil War he made restoration of the Union his primary objective, but he also made it clear it must be a Union without slavery. On April 14, while attending a performance at Ford's Theatre in Washington, he was shot by actor John Wilkes Booth, a Confederate sympathizer. He died the next morning.

Questions to consider. The Emancipation Proclamation has been called as prosaic as a bill of lading. Do you think this is a fair appraisal? Do you think a statement more like the preamble to the Declaration of Independence would have been better? Why do you think Lincoln, a great prose master, avoided exalted language in writing the proclamation? On what constitutional powers as president did he depend in announcing his policy? In what ways does the proclamation demonstrate that Lincoln was a practical man? Reactions to the proclamation were varied. The London **Spectator** made fun of it. "The principle," sneered the editor, "is not that a human being cannot justly own another, but that he cannot own him unless he is loyal to the United States." Was the editor's comment justified? Not everyone agreed with the **Spectator.** Many abolitionists and most Southern blacks hailed the proclamation as a giant step on the road to freedom. To what extent were they correct? ·

The Emancipation Proclamation (1863)
Abraham Lincoln

Whereas on the 22d day of September, A.D. 1862, a proclamation was issued by the President of the United States, containing among other things, the following, to wit:

"That on the 1st day of January, A.D. 1863, all persons held as slaves within any State or designated part of a State the people whereof shall then be in rebellion against the United States shall be then, thenceforward, and forever free; and the executive government of the United States, including the military and naval authority thereof, will recognize and maintain the freedom of such persons and will do no act or acts to repress such persons, or any of them, in any efforts they may make for their actual freedom.

"That the executive will on the 1st day of January aforesaid, by proclamation, designate the States and parts of States, if any, in which the people thereof, respectively, shall then be in rebellion against the United States; and the fact that any State or the people thereof shall on that day be in good faith represented in the Congress of the United States by members chosen thereto at elections wherein a majority of the qualified voters of such States shall have participated shall, in the absence of strong countervailing testimony, be deemed conclusive evidence that such State and the people thereof are not then in rebellion against the United States."

Now, therefore, I, Abraham Lincoln, President of the United States, by virtue of the power in me vested as Commander-in-Chief of the Army and Navy of the United States in time of actual armed rebellion against the authority and government of the United States, and as a fit and necessary war measure for suppressing said rebellion, do, on this 1st day of January, A.D. 1863, and in accordance with my purpose so to do, publicly proclaimed for the full period of one hundred days from the first day above mentioned, order and designate as the States and parts of States wherein the people thereof, respectively, are this day in rebellion against the United States the following, to wit:

Arkansas, Texas, Louisiana (except the parishes of St. Bernard, Plaquemines, Jefferson, St. John, St. Charles, St. James, Ascension, Assumption, Terrebonne, Lafourche, St. Mary, St. Martin, and Orleans, including the city of New Orleans), Mississippi, Alabama, Florida, Georgia, South Carolina, North Carolina, and Virginia (except the forty-eight counties designated as West Virginia, and also the counties of Berkeley, Accomac, Northhampton, Elizabeth City, York, Princess Anne, and Norfolk, including the cities of Norfolk and Portsmouth), and which excepted parts are for the present left precisely as if this proclamation were not issued.

From John Nicolay and John Hay, eds., **Complete Works of Abraham Lincoln** (12 v., Lincoln Memorial University, n.p., 1894), VIII: 161–164.

Black Union soldier. Free blacks in the North were abolitionism's staunchest supporters throughout the prewar decades, and when war came they staunchly supported that too, by volunteering, like the young man in this daguerreotype, by the tens of thousands for service in the Union army. Mindful of opinion in the loyal slave states of Kentucky and Maryland, however, and infected by their own racism, federal leaders at first refused to permit black enlistments, then permitted them only for work behind the lines, and finally allowed them to carry arms but only under white officers and for half-pay. Once in the field, black troops were ardent soldiers; their commanders, observing this, sometimes gave them the toughest objectives, producing horrendous casualty rates. Lincoln issued the Emancipation Proclamation when he did in part to guarantee blacks' continued ardor for the Union cause. (Chicago Historical Society)

And by virtue of the power and for the purpose aforesaid, I do order and declare that all persons held as slaves within said designated States and parts of States are, and henceforward shall be, free; and that the Executive Government of the United States, including the military and naval authorities thereof, will recognize and maintain the freedom of said persons.

And I hereby enjoin upon the people so declared to be free to abstain from all violence, unless in necessary self-defense; and I recommend to them that, in all cases when allowed, they labor faithfully for reasonable wages.

And I further declare and make known that such persons of suitable condition will be received into the armed service of the United States to garrison forts, positions, stations, and other places, and to man vessels of all sorts in said service.

And upon this act, sincerely believed to be an act of justice, warranted by the Constitution upon military necessity, I invoke the considerate judgment of mankind and the gracious favor of Almighty God.

36.

PEOPLE'S GOVERNMENT

Late in June 1863, General Robert E. Lee crossed the Potomac River and moved his Confederate army rapidly through Maryland into Pennsylvania. On July 1 his troops met the Union army, commanded by General George G. Meade, at Gettysburg, Pennsylvania. After three days of fierce fighting, with thousands of casualties, Lee's greatly weakened army began to retreat. Lincoln was disappointed that Lee's army was able to escape, but he realized that the Confederates had suffered a decisive defeat. "I am very grateful to Meade," he said, "for the great service he did at Gettysburg." The Gettysburg battle marked the peak of the Confederate effort. Never again were the Confederates able to invade the North, and they never came close to winning the war after that time.

Four months after the bloody encounter—on November 19, 1863—when a national cemetery was dedicated on the Gettysburg battlefield, Lincoln delivered perhaps his most famous address. Edward Everett, famed for his oratory, spoke first, talking for almost two hours. Lincoln's address lasted only a couple of minutes. Afterward, it is said, Everett took Lincoln's hand and told him, "My speech will soon be forgotten; yours never will be. How gladly I would exchange my hundred pages for your twenty lines!" Everett was right. His own speech was soon forgotten, whereas Lincoln's brief address came to be regarded as one of the most powerful statements of the democratic outlook ever made.

Questions to consider. Why was Everett so impressed with Lincoln's address? Lincoln once said that his basic political ideas came from the Declaration of Independence. Do you think this influence appears in the Gettysburg Address? What in Lincoln's opinion was the basic meaning of the Civil War? To what extent was style, as well as substance, important in the address Lincoln wrote for the Gettysburg dedication?

Lincoln's inauguration. More than 10,000 people gathered to hear Abraham Lincoln's inaugural address on March 4, 1861, and many of them clapped and cheered when he took his place on the platform in front of the Capitol building. Lincoln put his cane in a corner of the platform but did not seem to know what to do with his hat. Illinois Senator Stephen A. Douglas, his old political foe, reached out his hand, took it, and held it during the half-hour inaugural ceremony. (National Archives)

The Gettysburg Address (1863)
Abraham Lincoln

Fourscore and seven years ago our fathers brought forth on this continent a new nation, conceived in liberty, and dedicated to the proposition that all men are created equal.

Now we are engaged in a great civil war, testing whether that nation, or any nation so conceived and so dedicated, can long endure. We are met on a great battle-field of that war. We have come to dedicate a portion of that field as a final resting-place for those who here gave their lives that that nation might live. It is altogether fitting and proper that we should do this.

But, in a larger sense, we cannot dedicate—we cannot consecrate—we cannot hallow—this ground. The brave men, living and dead, who struggled here, have consecrated it far above our poor power to add or detract. The world will little note nor long remember what we say here, but it can never forget what they did here. It is for us, the living, rather, to be dedicated here to the unfinished work which they who fought here have thus far so nobly advanced. It is rather for us to be here dedicated to the great task remaining before us—that from these honored dead we take increased devotion to that cause for which they gave the last full measure of devotion; that we here highly resolve that these dead shall not have died in vain; that this nation, under God, shall have a new birth of freedom; and that government of the people, by the people, for the people, shall not perish from the earth.

From John Nicolay and John Hay, eds., **Complete Works of Abraham Lincoln** (12 v., Lincoln Memorial University, n.p., 1894), IX: 209–210.

37.

BINDING WOUNDS

In June 1864, when the Republicans nominated Abraham Lincoln for a second term, the end of the war seemed as far away as ever. Northerners were shocked at the heavy casualties reported from battlefields in Virginia, and criticism of the administration had become so harsh that in mid-August Lincoln was convinced he would not be re-elected. The Radical Republicans, who spoke for the antislavery faction of the party, condemned him as "politically, militarily, and financially a failure" and for a time backed John C. Frémont for the presidency. The Northern Democrats nominated General George. B. McClellan, a former federal commander, and adopted a platform calling for the immediate cessation of hostilities and the restoration of the Union by a negotiated peace. Lincoln was so sure McClellan would defeat him that he wrote a secret memorandum explaining how he would cooperate with the new president after the election in order to save the Union.

But a series of federal victories—the closing of Mobile Bay, the capture of Atlanta, and the routing of Southern forces in the Shenandoah Valley—led public opinion to swing back rapidly to Lincoln. Republican newspapers began ridiculing the "war-is-a-failure" platform of the Democrats, and Frémont decided to drop out of the campaign. Lincoln's prediction that he would not be re-elected proved wrong. On election day he won a plurality of nearly half a million votes and carried every state in the Union except Kentucky, Delaware, and New Jersey.

In his second inaugural address on March 4, 1865, Lincoln singled out slavery as the cause of the Civil War and stated that its eradication was inevitable. He expressed hope for a speedy end to the conflict, called for "malice toward none" and "charity for all," and looked forward to the day when Americans would achieve a "just and lasting peace" among themselves and with all nations. On April 9, Lee surrendered to Grant at Appomattox; two days later Lincoln made his last public address, outlining his reconstruction policy. He had never considered the South to be outside of the Union and hoped for a speedy reconciliation. On April 14, at his last cabinet meeting, he urged the cabinet members to put aside all thoughts of hatred and revenge. That evening he was shot.

Questions to consider. Lincoln's second inaugural address is commonly regarded as one of the greatest addresses ever made by an American president. Why do you think this is so? What did he regard as the basic issue of the Civil War? What irony did he see in the attitude of the contestants? What use of the Bible did he make? Do you think this was likely to appeal to Americans in 1865?

═══════

Second Inaugural Address (1865)
Abraham Lincoln

FELLOW-COUNTRYMEN:—At this second appearing to take the oath of the presidential office there is less occasion for an extended address than there was at the first. Then a statement somewhat in detail of a course to be pursued seemed fitting and proper. Now, at the expiration of four years, during which public declarations have been constantly called forth on every point and phase of the great contest which still absorbs the attention and engrosses the energies of the nation, little that is new could be presented. The progress of our arms, upon which all else chiefly depends, is as well known to the public as to myself, and it is, I trust, reasonably satisfactory and encouraging to all. With high hope for the future, no prediction in regard to it is ventured.

On the occasion corresponding to this four years ago all thoughts were anxiously directed to an impending civil war. All dreaded it, all sought to avert it. While the inaugural address was being delivered from this place, devoted altogether to *saving* the Union without war, insurgent agents were in the city seeking to *destroy* it without war—seeking to dissolve the Union and divide effects by negotiation. Both parties deprecated war, but one of them would *make* war rather than let the nation survive, and the other would *accept* war rather than let it perish, and the war came.

One eighth of the whole population was colored slaves, not distributed generally over the Union, but localized in the southern part of it. These slaves constituted a peculiar and powerful interest. All knew that this interest was somehow the cause of the war. To strengthen, perpetuate, and extend this interest was the object for which the insurgents would rend the Union even by war, while the Government claimed no right to do more than to restrict the territorial enlargement of it. Neither party expected for the war the magnitude nor the duration which it has already attained. Neither anticipated that the *cause* of the conflict might cease with or even before the conflict itself should cease. Each looked for an easier triumph, and a result less fundamental and astounding. Both read the same Bible and pray to the same God, and each invokes His aid against the other. It may seem strange that any men should

From James D. Richardson, ed., **A Compilation of the Messages and Papers of the Presidents** (Government Printing Office, Washington, D.C., 1897–1907), VIII: 3477–3478.

dare to ask a just God's assistance in wringing their bread from the sweat of other men's faces, but let us judge not, that we be not judged. The prayers of both could not be answered. That of neither has been answered fully. The Almighty has His own purposes. "Woe unto the world because of offenses; for it must needs be that offenses come, but woe to that man by whom the offense cometh." If we shall suppose that American slavery is one of those offenses which, in the providence of God, must needs come, but which, having continued through His appointed time, He now wills to remove, and that He gives to both North and South this terrible war as the woe due to those by whom the offense came, shall we discern therein any departure from those divine attributes which the believers in a living God always ascribe to Him? Fondly do we hope, fervently do we pray, that this mighty scourge of war may speedily pass away. Yet, if God wills that it continue until all the wealth piled by the bondsman's two hundred and fifty years of unrequited toil shall be sunk, and until every drop of blood drawn with the lash shall be paid by another drawn with the sword, as was said three thousand years ago, so still it must be said, "The judgments of the Lord are true and righteous altogether."

With malice toward none, with charity for all, with firmness in the right as God gives us to see the right, let us strive on to finish the work we are in, to bind up the nation's wounds, to care for him who shall have borne the battle and for his widow and his orphan, to do all which may achieve and cherish a just and lasting peace among ourselves and with all nations.

38.

A HELPING HAND

The Thirteenth Amendment, which became part of the Constitution in 1865, freed about four million slaves in the South. But with freedom came uncertainty, insecurity, and perplexity. Unlike the peasants of France and Russia, who stayed on the land on which they had been working when they were freed from serfdom, the former American slaves were cast adrift at the end of the Civil War with no means of livelihood. They found themselves without property, legal rights, education, training, and any experience as independent farmers or laborers. Thousands began roaming the countryside looking for work and ways to survive. The first year of freedom brought hunger, disease, suffering, and death.

The freedmen did receive some assistance from the federal government after the war. In March 1865, Congress established the Bureau of Refugees, Freedmen, and Abandoned Lands (commonly called the Freedmen's Bureau) to provide them with food, clothing, shelter, and medical aid. Under the direction of General Oliver O. Howard (the "Christian General"), the Freedmen's Bureau also established schools and colleges for young blacks, founded savings banks, set up courts to protect their civil rights, and tried to get them jobs and fair contracts of employment. During its seven years of existence (1865–1872), the bureau spent more than fifteen million dollars for food and other aid and over six million dollars on schools and educational work, and gave medical attention to nearly half a million patients. Bureau agents also registered black voters and encouraged political participation. The hostility of Southern whites and the growing indifference of whites in the North, however, negated much of the bureau's work.

The report excerpted below was written by Colonel Eliphalet Whittlesey, assistant bureau commissioner for North Carolina, in October 1865. Whittlesey later became a general and moved to Washington, where he served as a trustee of the national Freedman's Savings Bank. In North Carolina where blacks made up only a third of the population and therefore only a third of the potential voters, the Republican party and the national government soon began to lose political control. By 1871 the white Democratic party once again controlled the state, ending Reconstruction there.

Questions to consider. Southern whites argued repeatedly that the fundamental objective of the Freedmen's Bureau was not to help the needy but to punish its foes by transforming Southern racial and economic relations. Does Whittlesey's report support this contention? Who received federal assistance in 1865? On what grounds was assistance given? Who made the decisions? What staff was available to the bureau? In what ways did Whittlesey sound like the commander of an occupying army? Of the bureau's four goals, which did he seem to feel were most urgent? Do you agree with his priorities? Was he genuinely committed to them? Was he optimistic? Which of its goals was the bureau most likely to achieve in the short run? In the long run?

Report on the Freedmen's Bureau (1865)

On the 22d of June I arrived at Raleigh with instructions from you to take the control of all subjects relating to "refugees, freedmen, and the abandoned lands" within this State. I found these subjects in much confusion. Hundreds of white refugees and thousands of blacks were collected about this and other towns, occupying every hovel and shanty, living upon government rations, without employment and without comfort, many dying for want of proper food and medical supplies. A much larger number, both white and black, were crowding into the towns, and literally swarming about every depot of supplies to receive their rations. My first effort was to reduce this class of suffering and idle humanity to order, and to discover how large a proportion of these applicants were really deserving of help. The whites, excepting "loyal refugees," were referred to the military authorities. To investigate the condition of refugees and freedmen and minister to the wants of the destitute, I saw at once would require the services of a large number of efficient officers. As fast as suitable persons could be selected, application was made to the department and district commanders for their detail, in accordance with General Order No. 102, War Department, May 31, 1865. In many cases these applications were unsuccessful because the officers asked for could not be spared. The difficulties and delays experienced in obtaining the help needed for a proper organization of my work will be seen from the fact that upon thirty-four written requests, in due form, only eleven officers have been detailed by the department and district commanders. . . .

With this brief history of my efforts to organize the bureau, I proceed to state

From **Report of the Joint Committee on Reconstruction,** 1st Session, 39th Congress (Government Printing Office, Washington, D.C., 1866), II: 186–192.

The Design and Work Proposed

In my circulars Nos. 1 and 2 (copies of which are herewith enclosed) the objects to be attained are fully stated. All officers of the bureau are instructed—

1. To aid the destitutes, yet in such a way as not to encourage dependence.
2. To protect freedmen from injustice.
3. To assist freedmen in obtaining employment and fair wages for their labor.
4. To encourage education, intellectual and moral.

Under these four divisions the operations of the bureau can best be presented.

Relief Afforded

It was evident at the outset that large numbers were drawing rations who might support themselves. The street in front of the post commissary's office was blocked up with vehicles of all the descriptions peculiar to North Carolina, and with people who had come from the country around, in some instances from a distance of sixty miles, for government rations. These were destitute whites, and were supplied by order of the department commander. Our own headquarters, and every office of the bureau, was besieged from morning till night by freedmen, some coming many miles on foot, others in wagons and carts. The rations issued would scarcely last till they reached home, and in many instances they were sold before leaving the town, in exchange for luxuries. To correct these evils, orders were issued that no able-bodied man or woman should receive supplies, except such as were known to be industrious, and to be entirely destitute. Great care was needed to protect the bureau from imposition, and at the same time to relieve the really deserving. By constant inquiry and effort the throng of beggars was gradually removed. The homeless and helpless were gathered in camps, where shelter and food could be furnished, and the sick collected in hospitals, where they could receive proper care. . . .

Protection

Regarding this bureau as the appointed instrument for redeeming the solemn pledge of the nation, through its Chief Magistrate, to secure the rights of freedmen, I have made every effort to protect them from wrong. Suddenly set free, they were at first exhilarated by the air of liberty, and committed some excesses. To be sure of their freedom, many thought they must leave the old scenes of oppression and seek new homes. Others regarded the property accumulated by their labor as in part their own, and demanded a share of it. On the other hand, the former masters, suddenly stripped of their wealth, at first looked upon the freedmen with a mixture of hate and fear. In these circumstances some collisions were inevitable. The negroes were complained of as idle, insolent, and dishonest; while they complained that they were treated with more cruelty than when they were slaves. Some were tied up and whipped without trial; some were driven from their homes without pay for their labor, without clothing or means of support; others were forbidden to leave on pain of death, and a few were shot or otherwise murdered. All officers of the bureau were directed, in accordance with your circular No. 5, to investigate these difficulties between the two classes, to settle them by counsel and arbitration as far as possible, to punish light offences by fines or otherwise, and to report more serious cases of crime to the military authorities for trial. The exact number of cases heard and decided cannot be given; they have been so numerous that no complete record could be kept; one officer reported that he had heard and disposed of as many as 180 complaints in a single day. The method pursued may be best presented by citing a few cases and the action thereon. From the report of Captain James, for August, I quote the following:

"I forward to you, in his own language, a report of a case which occurred in Gates county, on the northern border of the State, far away from any influence of troops, and where the military power of the government had been little felt. No doubt it illustrates others in similar localities far from garrisons and northern influences. The report will repay perusal, and appears to have been managed with admirable tact on the part of Captain Hill. Reports had reached me of the way in which David Parker, of Gates county, treated his colored people, and I determined to ascertain for myself their truth. Accordingly, last Monday, August 20, accompanied by a guard of six men from this post, (Elizabeth City,) I proceeded to his residence, about forty miles distant. He is very wealthy. I ascertained, after due investigation, and after convincing his colored people that I was really their friend, that the worst reports in regard to him were true. He had twenty-three negroes on his farm, large and small. Of these, fourteen were fieldhands; they all bore unmistakable evidence of the way they had been worked; very much undersized, rarely exceeding, man or women, 4 feet 6 inches—men and women of thirty and forty years of age looking like boys and girls. It has been his habit for years to work them from sunrise to sunset, and often long after, only stopping one hour for dinner—food always cooked for them to save time. He had, and has had for many years, an old colored man, one-eyed and worn out in the service, for an overseer or 'over-looker,' as he called himself. In addition, he has two sons at home, one of whom has made it a point to be with them all summer long—not so much to superintend as to drive. The old colored overseer always went behind the gang with a cane or whip, and woe betide the unlucky wretch who did not continually do his part; he had been brought up to work, and had not the least pity for any one who could not work as well as he.

"Mr. Parker told me that he had hired his people for the season: that directly after the surrender of General Lee he called them up and told them they were free; that he was better used to them than to others, and would prefer hiring them; that he would give them board and two suits of clothing to stay with him till the 1st day of January, 1866, and one Sunday suit at the end of that time; that they consented willingly—in fact, preferred to remain with him, &c. But from his people I learned that though he did call them up, as stated, yet when one of them demurred at the offer his son James flew at him and cuffed and kicked him; that after that they were all 'perfectly willing to stay'; they were watched night and day; that Bob, one of the men, had been kept chained nights; that they were actually afraid to try to get away. There was no complaint of the food nor much of the clothing, but they were in constant terror of the whip. Only three days before my arrival, Bob had been stripped in the field and given fifty lashes for hitting Adam, the colored over-looker, while James Parker stood by with a gun, and told him to run if he wanted to, he had a gun there. About four weeks before, four of them who went to church and returned before sunset were treated to twenty-five lashes each. Some were beaten or whipped almost every day. Having ascertained these and other similar facts, I directed him to call them up and pay them for the first of May last up to the present time. I investigated each case, taking into consideration age, family, physical condition, &c., estimating their work from $8 down, and saw him pay them off then and there, allowing for clothing and medical bill. I then arrested him and his two sons, and brought them here, except Dr. Joseph Parker, whose sister is very sick, with all the colored people I thought necessary as witnesses, intending to send them to Newbern for trial. But on account of the want of immediate transportation I concluded to release them on their giving a bond in the sum of $2,000 to Colonel E. Whittlesey, assistant commissioner for the State of North Carolina, and to his successors in office, conditioned as follows:

"That whereas David Parker and James Parker have heretofore maltreated their colored people, and have enforced the compulsory system instead of the free labor system: Now, therefore, if they, each of them, shall hereafter well and kindly treat, and cause to be treated, the hired laborers under their or his charge, and shall adopt the free labor system in lieu of the compulsory system, then this bond to be void and of no effect; otherwise to remain in full force and effect, with good security."

Lieutenant Colonel Clapp, superintendent central district, reports three cases of cruel beating, which have been investigated, and the offenders turned over to the military authorities for trial; besides very many instances of defrauding freedmen of their wages.

From the reports of Major Wickersham, superintendent of southern district, I quote the following:

"August 25.—A. S. Miller, Bladen county, states that Henry Miller (colored) neglects to support his family. Action: required Henry Miller to use his wages for the support of his wife and children, who have no claims on their former master, and can look to no one else than the husband and father for support.

"27th.—Betsy Powell (colored) states that Mrs. Frank Powell, Columbus county, has driven her away without pay for her labor. Gave letter to Mrs. Powell directing her to pay Betsy for her labor since April 27, 1865.

"29th.—Len Shiner (colored) states that he made an agreement with Mr. David Russell, of Robeson county, to work and gather his crop, for which he was to receive subsistence and one-third of the crop, when gathered. Mr. Russell has driven him off and refuses to pay. Wrote to Mr. Russell directing him to comply with terms of agreement, or furnish satisfactory reasons for not doing so. These are but examples of hundreds of complaints heard and acted upon by Major Wickersham and other officers in the southern district."

The following cases are taken from the report of Captain Barritt, assistant commissioner, at Charlotte:

"Morrison Miller charged with whipping a girl Hannah (colored.) Found guilty. Action: ordered to pay said Hannah fifty bushels of corn towards supporting herself and children, two of said children being the offspring of Miller.

"Wm. Wallace charged with whipping Martha (colored.) Plead guilty. Action: fined said Wallace $15, with assurance that if the above offence was repeated, the fine would be doubled.

"Council Best attempts to defraud six families of their summer labor, by offering to sell at auction the crop on his leased plantation. Action: sent military force and stopped the sale until contract with laborers was complied with."

A hundred pages of similar reports might be copied, showing, on the one side, that many freedmen need the presence of some authority to enforce upon them their new duties; and on the other, that so far from being true that "there is no county in which a freedman can be imposed upon," there is no county in which he is not oftener wronged; and these wrongs increase just in proportion to their distance from United States authorities. There has been great improvement, during the quarter, in this respect. The efforts of the bureau to protect the freedmen have done much to restrain violence and injustice. Such efforts must be continued until civil government is fully restored, just laws enacted, or great suffering and serious disturbance will be the result.

Industry

Contrary to the fears and predictions of many, the great mass of colored people have remained quietly at work upon the plantations of their former masters during the entire summer. The crowds seen about the towns in the early part of the season had followed in the wake of the Union army, to escape from slavery. After hostilities ceased these refugees returned to their homes, so that but few vagrants can now be found. In truth, a much larger amount of vagrancy exists among the whites than among the blacks. It is the almost uniform report of officers of the bureau that freedmen are industrious.

The report is confirmed by the fact that out of a colored population of nearly 350,000 in the State, only about 5,000 are now receiving support from the government. Probably some others are receiving aid from kind-hearted men who have enjoyed the benefit of their services from childhood. To the general quiet and industry of this people there can be no doubt that the efforts of the bureau have contributed greatly. I have visited some of the larger towns, as Wilmington, Newbern, Goldsborough, and both by public addresses and private instructions counselled the freedmen to secure employment and maintain themselves. Captain James has made an extensive tour through the eastern district for the same purpose, and has exerted a most happy influence. Lieutenant Colonel Clapp has spent much of his time in visiting the county seats of the central district, and everywhere been listened to by all classes with deep interest. Other officers have done much good in this way. They have visited plantations, explained the difference between slave and free labor, the nature and the solemn obligation of contracts. The chief difficulty met with has been a want of confidence between the two parties. The employer, accustomed only to the system of compulsory labor, is slow to believe that he can secure fruitful services by the stimulus of wages. The laborer is unwilling to trust the promises of those for whom he had toiled all his days without pay; hence but few contracts for long periods have been effected. The bargains for the present year are generally vague, and their settlement as the crops are gathered in requires much labor. In a great majority of cases the landowners seem disposed to do justly, and even generously; and when this year's work is done, and the proceeds divided, it is hoped that a large number of freedmen will enter into contracts for the coming year. They will, however, labor much more cheerfully for money, with prompt and frequent payments, than for a share of the crop, for which they must wait twelve months. A large farmer in Pitt county hires hands by the job, and states that he never saw negroes work so well. Another in Lenoir county pays monthly, and is satisfied so far with the experiment of free labor. Another obstacle to long contracts was found in the impression which had become prevalent to some degree, *i.e.,* that lands were to be given to freedmen by the government. To correct this false impression I published a circular, No. 3, and directed all officers of the bureau to make it as widely known as possible. From the statistical reports enclosed, it will be seen that during the quarter 257 written contracts for labor have been prepared and witnessed; that the average rate of wages, when paid in money, is from $8 to $10 per month; that 128 farms are under the control of the bureau and cultivated for the benefit of freedmen; that 8,540 acres are under cultivation, and 6,102 are employed. Many of the farms were rented by agents of the treasury as abandoned lands, previous to the establishing of this bureau, and were transferred to us with the leases upon them. Nearly all have been restored to their owners, under the President's proclamation of amnesty, and our tenure of the few that remain is so uncertain that I have not deemed it prudent to set apart any for use of refugees and freedmen, in accordance with the act of Congress approved March 3, 1865. But many freedmen are taking this matter into their own hands, and renting lands from the owners for one or more years. . . .

I am also endeavoring to purchase or rent, for a long period, the lands upon which houses have been erected by freedmen, so that they may not lose

Former slave children at a Freedmen's Bureau school.   The Freedmen's Bureau, created by Congress in March 1865 to help the former slaves adjust to freedom, provided emergency food and shelter at first. Later on it helped the freedmen obtain work, conducted military courts to hear complaints, established schools at both the elementary and college levels, and registered black voters. By 1872, when the bureau was abolished, it had spent more than $15 million in aiding the freedmen and had established many schools and colleges for educating blacks. (Valentine Museum, Cook Collection)

what has been expended. The most important local interest of this kind is the Trent river settlement. The village was carefully laid out by Captain James, and now contains a population of nearly 3,000, all but about 300 self-supporting. "Although," says Captain James, "in interest a part of the city of Newbern, it lies outside of the corporate limits, and therefore came under no municipal regulations." I therefore issued an order erecting it into a separate municipality. I imposed a small tax upon the trades and occupations of the people, and a very moderate ground rent upon the lots, to raise a fund for meeting the necessary expenses of maintaining the settlement. They pay these sums with pleasure, deeming them an evidence of citizenship. From the fund thus raised the superintendent, assistant superintendent, a clerk, six nurses in hospital, and some fifteen mechanics and laborers employed about the settlement, are paid. A good market is now nearly completed, the stalls of which have been taken up beforehand at high rates. It needs only the power to sell these people their lots of land to induce them to put more permanent improvements on them. The settlement, as such, is by all confessed to be well ordered, quiet, healthy, and better regulated than the city proper.

Education

The quarter has been one of vacation rather than active work in this department. Still some progress has been made, and much done to prepare for the coming autumn and winter. Rev. F. A. Fiske, a Massachusetts teacher, has been appointed superintendent of education, and has devoted himself with energy to his duties. From his report it will be seen that the whole number of schools, during the whole or any part of the quarter, is 63, the number of teachers 85, and the number of scholars 5,624. A few of the schools are self-supporting, and taught by colored teachers, but the majority are sustained by northern societies and northern teachers. The officers of the bureau have, as far as practicable, assigned buildings for their use, and assisted in making them suitable; but the time is nearly past when such facilities can be given. The societies will be obliged hereafter to pay rent for school-rooms and for teachers' homes. The teachers are engaged in a noble and self-denying work. They report a surprising thirst for knowledge among the colored people—children giving earnest attention and learning rapidly, and adults, after the day's work is done, devoting the evening to study. In this connexion it may be mentioned, as a result of moral instruction, that 512 marriages have been reported and registered, and 42 orphans provided with good homes.

39.

KLANSMEN OF THE CAROLINAS

Reconstruction developed in a series of moves and countermoves. In a white Southern backlash to Union victory and emancipation came the "black codes" for coercing black laborers and President Andrew Johnson's pardon of Confederate landowners. Then in a Northern backlash to these codes and pardons came the Civil Rights bills, the sweeping Reconstruction Acts of 1867, and the Fourteenth and Fifteenth Amendments, all designed to guarantee black political rights. White Southerners reacted to these impositions in turn with secret night-time terrorist or "night rider" organizations designed to shatter Republican political power. Congress tried to protect Republican voters and the freedmen with the Force Acts of 1870 allowing the use of the army to prevent physical assaults, but Northern willingness to commit troops and resources to the struggle was waning. By the mid-1870s only three states remained in Republican hands, and within three years racist Democrats controlled these, too. The night riders had turned the tide.

Although numerous secret societies for whites appeared in the Reconstruction South—including the Order of the White Camelia (Louisiana), the Pale Faces (Tennessee), the White Brotherhood (North Carolina), and the Invisible Circle (South Carolina)—the largest and most influential society, and the one that spawned these imitators, was the Ku Klux Klan, the so-called Invisible Empire. The Klan began in Tennessee in 1866 as a young men's social club with secret costumes and rituals similar to those of the Masons, the Odd-Fellows, and other popular societies. In 1867, however, following passage of the Reconstruction Acts, anti-Republican racists began to see the usefulness of such a spookily secret order, and the Klan was reorganized to provide for "dens," "provinces" (counties), and "realms" (states), all under the authority of a "Grand Wizard," who in 1867 was believed to have been Nathan B. Forrest, a former slave trader and Confederate general.

The Klan structure was probably never fully established because of the disorganized conditions of the postwar South. Other societies with different names emerged, and the Reconstruction-era "Ku-Klux" may have disbanded as a formal entity in the early 1870s. But it clearly survived in spirit and in loosely formed groups, continuing to terrorize Republicans and their allies among the newly enfranchised freedmen into the 1870s and sowing fear among the black families who composed, after all, the labor force on which the white planters still depended. The excerpt reprinted below includes congressional testimony by David

Schenck, a member of the North Carolina Klan seeking to portray it in the best possible light, followed by testimony from Elias Hill, a South Carolina black man victimized by a local "den" of the Klan. Schenck and Hill were testifying before a joint Senate-House committee concerned with anti-black terrorism.

Questions to consider. The oath taken by David Schenck emphasizes the Klan's religious, constitutional, and benevolent qualities, whereas Elias Hill's story reveals its terrorist features. Are there elements in the Klan oath that seem to hint at or justify the use of violence? Why does the oath contain the phrases "original purity," "pecuniary embarrassments," and "traitor's doom"? What "secrets of this order" could deserve death? Klansmen later claimed that because they could terrorize the superstitious freedmen simply by using masks, odd voices, and ghostly sheets, no real violence was necessary. Opponents have claimed, on the other hand, that Klansmen were basically sadists acting out sexual phobias and deep paranoia. What light does Elias Hill's testimony shed on these conflicting claims? What position did Hill seem to hold in the black community? Did the Klansmen seem to be assaulting him because of his condition or because of his position in the black community? Why did they ask Hill to pray for them? Would it be fair or accurate to call the Ku Klux Klan an example of a political terrorist organization that succeeded?

———

Report of the Joint Committee on Reconstruction (1872)

A select committee of the Senate, upon the 10th of March, 1871, made a report of the result of their investigation into the security of person and property in the State of North Carolina. . . . A sub-committee of their number proceeded to the State of South Carolina, and examined witnesses in that State until July 29. . . .

David Schenck, esq., a member of the bar of Lincoln County, North Carolina . . . was initiated in October, 1868, as a member of the Invisible Empire. . . . In his own words: "We were in favor of constitutional liberty as handed down to us by our forefathers. I think the idea incorporated was that we were opposed to the [fourteenth and fifteenth] amendments to the

From **Report of the Joint Select Committee to Inquire into the Condition of Affairs in the Late Insurrectionary States** (Government Printing Office, Washington, D.C., 1872), 25–27, 44–47.

Constitution. I desire to explain in regard to that that it was not to be—at least, I did not intend by that that it should be—forcible resistance, but a political principle."

The oath itself is as follows:

> I, (name,) before the great immaculate Judge of heaven and earth, and upon the Holy Evangelist of Almighty God, do, of my own free will and accord, subscribe to the following sacred, binding obligation:
>
> I. I am on the side of justice and humanity and constitutional liberty, as bequeathed to us by our forefathers in its original purity.
>
> II. I reject and oppose the principles of the radical [Republican] party.
>
> III. I pledge aid to a brother of the Ku-Klux Klan in sickness, distress, or pecuniary embarrassments. Females, friends, widows, and their households shall be the special objects of my care and protection.
>
> IV. Should I ever divulge, or cause to be divulged, any of the secrets of this order, or any of the foregoing obligations, I must meet with the fearful punishment of death and traitor's doom, which is death, death, death, at the hands of the brethren. . . .

Elias Hill of York County, South Carolina, is a remarkable character. He is crippled in both legs and arms, which are shriveled by rheumatism; he cannot walk, cannot help himself . . .; was in early life a slave, whose freedom was purchased by his father. . . . He learned his letters and to read by calling the school children into the cabin as they passed, and also learned to write. He became a Baptist preacher, and after the war engaged in teaching colored children, and conducted the business correspondence of many of his colored neighbors. . . . We put the story of his wrongs in his own language:

"On the night of the 5th of May, after I had heard a great deal of what they had done in that neighborhood, they came . . . to my brother's door, which is in the same yard, and broke open the door and attacked his wife, and I heard her screaming and mourning. I could not understand what they said, for they were talking in an outlandish and unnatural tone, which I had heard they generally used at a negro's house. They said, 'Where's Elias?' She said, 'He doesn't stay here; yon is his house.' I had heard them strike her five or six licks. Someone then hit my door. . . .

"They carried me into the yard between the houses, my brother's and mine, and put me on the ground. . . . 'Who did that burning? Who burned our houses?' I told them it was not me. I could not burn houses. Then they hit me with their fists, and said I did it, I ordered it. They went on asking me didn't I tell the black men to ravish all the white women. No, I answered them. They struck me again. . . . 'Haven't you been preaching and praying about the Ku-Klux? Haven't you been preaching political sermons? Doesn't a [Republican Party newspaper] come to your house? Haven't you written letters?' Generally one asked me all the questions, but the rest were squatting over me—some six men I counted as I lay there. . . . I told them if they would

A visit of the Ku Klux Klan.   This popular drawing from the early 1870s renders its black subjects with exaggerated, stereotyped features. But the one-room cabin—small, sparsely furnished, with food dangling from the ceiling—rings true to life. The illustrator effectively captured the aura of invasion without warning and the startled terror that accompanied Ku Klux Klan raids. These succeeded so well partly because they reached directly into black homes in this way. Faced with assaults on their children as well as themselves and lacking weaponry and military or police protection, the freedmen eventually buckled to Klan terror, although total segregation and disfranchisement did not take place until the 1890s. (Library of Congress)

take me back into the house, and lay me in the bed, which was close adjoining my books and papers, I would try and get it. They said I would never go back to that bed, for they were going to kill me. . . . They caught my leg and pulled me over the yard, and then left me there, knowing I could not walk nor crawl. . . .

"After they had stayed in the house for a considerable time, they came back to where I lay and asked if I wasn't afraid at all. They pointed pistols at me all around my head once or twice, as if they were going to shoot me. . . . One caught me by the leg and hurt me, for my leg for forty years has been drawn each year, more and more, and I made moan when it hurt so. One said, 'G-d d—n it, hush!' He had a horsewhip, [and] I reckon he struck me eight cuts right on the hip bone; it was almost the only place he could hit my body, my legs are so short. They all had disguises. . . . One of them then took a strap, and buckled it around my neck and said, 'Let's take him to the river and drown him.' . . .

"Then they said, 'Look here! Will you put a card in the paper to renounce all republicanism? Will you quit preaching?' I told them I did not know. I said that to save my life. . . . They said if I did not they would come back the next week and kill me. [After more licks with the strap] one of them went into the house where my brother and sister-in-law lived, and brought her to pick me up. As she stooped down to pick me up one of them struck her, and as she was carrying me into the house another struck her with a strap. . . . They said, 'Don't you pray against Ku-Klux, but pray that God may forgive Ku-Klux. Pray that God may bless and save us.' I was so chilled with cold lying out of doors so long and in such pain I could not speak to pray, but I tried to, and they said that would do very well, and all went out of the house. . . ."

Satisfied that he could no longer live in that community, Hill wrote to make inquiry about the means of going to Liberia. Hearing this, many of his neighbors desired to go also. . . . Others are still hoping for relief, through the means of this sub-committee.

40.

THE GREAT RETREAT

During the election of 1876 both parties resorted to fraud. Two sets of electoral returns came in from Southern states still occupied by federal troops, and it was necessary for Congress to set up an electoral commission to decide whether Rutherford B. Hayes, the Republican candidate, or Samuel J. Tilden, the Democratic standard-bearer, had won. Seven commission members were Republicans and seven were Democrats. The fifteenth member was to have been an independent, but as it turned out, he voted with the Republicans. By a strict party vote of 8 to 7, the commission awarded all 20 of the disputed electoral votes to the Republicans, and Hayes became president with 185 votes to Tilden's 184. Most Democrats felt they had been cheated out of victory; some of them even talked of rejecting the commission's decision and trying to block Hayes's inauguration. Had they done so, the quarrel over the election would have continued far beyond Inauguration Day, with grave consequences for the nation.

In the end, Southern Democrats reached a compromise with Northern Republicans. At a series of secret meetings between party leaders the Southern Democrats agreed to accept the electoral commission's decision. In return, the Republicans promised that Hayes would withdraw the remaining federal troops from the South, appoint at least one Southerner to his cabinet, and see to it that the South received federal aid to promote industrialization. The Compromise of 1877 brought the crisis to an end, and Hayes became the new president. After his inauguration in March 1877, Hayes took prompt action to fulfill the promises made to the Southern Democrats: he appointed a Tennessee Democrat to his cabinet, he withdrew the last of the federal soldiers from the South, and he began supporting federal-aid bills to benefit the South. The withdrawal of federal troops from Louisiana and South Carolina in April 1877 led to the demise of Republican governments in the South and the end of Reconstruction.

In his first annual message to Congress in December 1877, Hayes recalled the 1876 crisis and expressed satisfaction that it had been peacefully resolved. He also reminded Congress of the plea he had made at his inauguration that love of country would mute the racial and sectional tensions agitating the nation. He went on to mention his efforts to reduce antagonisms between North and South and ventured the opinion that they had had "beneficent results." He was especially pleased with the consequences of ending military reconstruction. Returning the

Southern states to local self-government had ended political turmoil and lawlessness there, he declared, and had produced a general restoration of order and "the orderly administration of justice." He did not mention the freedmen.

Hayes was born in Delaware, Ohio, in 1822. After he was graduated from Kenyon College, he studied law at Harvard and later established a successful law practice in Cincinnati. When the Civil War came, he joined a volunteer unit, rising to the rank of brevet major-general. He was wounded several times in action. After the war he served two terms in Congress, supporting Radical Reconstruction measures over President Johnson's veto and voting for Johnson's impeachment. He went on to serve as governor of Ohio and was elected to that office three times. In the Republican convention of 1876 he was a dark horse; he did not receive the presidential nomination until the seventh ballot. Though his presidency was generally undistinguished, he did please bankers by his sound money policies, and civil service reformers by his efforts to combat the spoils system. After leaving the White House he quickly dropped into obscurity. He died in 1893.

Questions to consider. Some Northern Democrats bitterly resented the electoral commission's decision for Hayes. They called him His Fraudulency, the Usurper, and Ruther-fraud B. Hayes. Was Hayes's first annual message to Congress, reproduced here, likely to win them over? To what "recent amendments" to the Constitution was he referring? What actions to restore national harmony did he emphasize? What policies did he fail to mention?

═══════

First Annual Message to Congress (1877)
Rutherford B. Hayes

To complete and make permanent the pacification of the country continues to be, and until it is fully accomplished must remain, the most important of all our national interests. The earnest purpose of good citizens generally to unite their efforts in this endeavor is evident. It found decided expression in the resolutions announced in 1876 by the national conventions of the leading political parties of the country. There was a widespread apprehension that the

From James D. Richardson, ed., *A Compilation of the Messages and Papers of the Presidents* (Government Printing Office, Washington, D.C., 1897–1907), IX: 4394–4397.

"Great Acrobatic Feat of Rutherford B. Hayes."   Hayes had a difficult acrobatic act to perform if he was to succeed as president. It had taken an Electoral Commission set up by Congress to declare him a winner by one electoral vote over Samuel J. Tilden, even though he won fewer popular votes than Tilden. Even after his inauguration on March 4, 1877, some people continued to jeer at him as "His Fraudulency" and "Ruther-fraud B. Hayes." As president, Hayes had to show people he was determined to end the graft and corruption that had discredited the Grant administration. He did reasonably well: he appointed reformers to his cabinet, launched a cleanup of the civil service, and removed several notorious spoilsmen from office. But while he was president, the Republican party for all practical purposes abandoned the cause of civil rights for blacks. (Library of Congress)

momentous results in our progress as a nation marked by the recent amendments to the Constitution were in imminent jeopardy; that the good understanding which prompted their adoption, in the interest of a loyal devotion to the general welfare, might prove a barren truce, and that the two sections of the country, once engaged in civil strife, might be again almost as widely severed and disunited as they were when arrayed in arms against each other.

The course to be pursued, which, in my judgment, seemed wisest in the presence of this emergency, was plainly indicated in my inaugural address. It pointed to the time, which all our people desire to see, when a genuine love of our whole country and of all that concerns its true welfare shall supplant the destructive forces of the mutual animosity of races and of sectional hostility. Opinions have differed widely as to the measures best calculated to secure this great end. This was to be expected. The measures adopted by the Administration have been subjected to severe and varied criticism. Any course whatever which might have been entered upon would certainly have encountered distrust and opposition. These measures were, in my judgment, such as were most in harmony with the Constitution and with the genius of our people, and best adapted, under all the circumstances, to attain the end in view. Beneficent results, already apparent, prove that these endeavors are not to be regarded as a mere experiment, and should sustain and encourage us in our efforts. Already, in the brief period which has elapsed, the immediate effectiveness, no less than the justice, of the course pursued is demonstrated, and I have an abiding faith that time will furnish its ample vindication in the minds of the great majority of my fellow-citizens. The discontinuance of the use of the Army for the purpose of upholding local governments in two States of the Union was no less a constitutional duty and requirement, under the circumstances existing at the time, than it was a much-needed measure for the restoration of local self-government and the promotion of national harmony. The withdrawal of the troops from such employment was effected deliberately, and with solicitous care for the peace and good order of society and the protection of the property and persons and every right of all classes of citizens.

The results that have followed are indeed significant and encouraging. All apprehension of danger from remitting those States to local self-government is dispelled, and a most salutary change in the minds of the people has begun and is in progress in every part of that section of the country once the theater of unhappy civil strife, substituting for suspicion, distrust, and aversion, concord, friendship, and patriotic attachment to the Union. No unprejudiced mind will deny that the terrible and often fatal collisions which for several years have been of frequent occurrence and have agitated and alarmed the public mind have almost entirely ceased, and that a spirit of mutual forbearance and hearty national interest has succeeded. There has been a general reestablishment of order and of the orderly administration of justice. Instances of remaining lawlessness have become of rare occurrence; political turmoil and turbulence have disappeared; useful industries have been resumed; public credit in the Southern States has been greatly strengthened, and the encouraging benefits of a revival of commerce between the sections of the country lately embroiled in civil war are fully enjoyed. Such are some of the results already attained, upon which the country is to be congratulated. They are of such importance that we may with confidence patiently await the desired consummation that will surely come with the natural progress of events. . . .

41.

AFTERMATH

Frederick Douglass regarded the Declaration of Independence as a "watchword of freedom." But he was tempted to turn it to the wall, he said, because its human rights principles were so shamelessly violated. A former slave himself, Douglass knew what he was talking about. Douglass thought that enslaving blacks fettered whites as well and that the United States would never be truly free until it ended chattel slavery. During the Civil War, he had several conversations with Lincoln, urging him to make emancipation his major aim. He also put unremitting pressure on the Union army to accept black volunteers, and after resistance to admitting blacks into the army gave way, he toured the country encouraging blacks to enlist and imploring the government to treat black and white solders equally in matters of pay and promotion.

Douglass had great hopes for his fellow blacks after the Civil War. He demanded they be given full rights—political, legal, educational, and economic—as citizens. He also wanted to see the wall of separation between the races crumble and see "the colored people of this country, enjoying the same freedom [as whites], voting at the same ballot-box, using the same cartridge-box, going to the same schools, attending the same churches, travelling in the same street cars, in the same railroad cars, on the same steam-boats, proud of the same country, fighting the same war, and enjoying the same peace and all its advantages." He regarded the Republican party as the "party of progress, justice and freedom" and at election time took to the stump and rallied black votes for the party. He was rewarded for these services by appointment as marshal of the District of Columbia in 1877, as recorder of deeds for the District in 1881, and as minister to Haiti in 1889. But he was also asked by Republican leaders to keep a low profile, was omitted from White House guest lists, and was excluded from presidential receptions even though one duty of the District marshal was to introduce the guests at White House state occasions.

Douglass was puzzled and then upset by the increasing indifference of Republican leaders to conditions among blacks after the Civil War. In 1883 he attended a convention of blacks in Louisville, Kentucky, which met to discuss their plight and reaffirm their demand for full civil rights. In his keynote address, which is reprinted here, Douglass vividly portrayed the discrimination and persecution his people encountered, but he continued to believe that "prejudice, with all its malign accomplishments, may yet be removed by peaceful means."

Born into slavery in Maryland in 1817, Frederick Augustus Washington Bailey learned to read and write despite efforts to keep him illiterate. In 1838 he managed to escape to freedom and adopted the name Frederick Douglass. Shortly afterward he became associated with William Lloyd Garrison and developed into such an articulate spokesman for the antislavery cause that people doubted he had ever been a slave. In 1845 he published his **Narrative of the Life of Frederick Douglass, an American Slave,** naming names, places, dates, and precise events to convince people he had been born in bondage. Douglass continued to be an articulate spokesman for the black cause throughout his life. Shortly before his death in 1895 a college student asked him what a young black could do to help the cause. "Agitate! Agitate! Agitate!" Douglass is supposed to have told him.

Questions to consider. In the following address Douglass was speaking to a convention of blacks in Louisville, but his appeal was primarily to American whites. How did he try to convince them that blacks deserved the same rights and opportunities as all Americans? How powerful did he think the color line was? What outrages against his people did he report? What was his attitude toward the Republican party, which he had so faithfully served? Were the grievances he cited largely economic or were they social and political in nature?

=====

Address to the Louisville Convention (1883)
Frederick Douglass

Born on American soil in common with yourselves, deriving our bodies and our minds from its dust, centuries having passed away since our ancestors were torn from the shores of Africa, we, like yourselves, hold ourselves to be in every sense Americans, and that we may, therefore, venture to speak to you in a tone not lower than that which becomes earnest men and American citizens. Having watered your soil with our tears, enriched it with our blood, performed its roughest labor in time of peace, defended it against enemies in time of war, and at all times been loyal and true to its best interests, we deem it no arrogance or presumption to manifest now a common concern with you for its welfare, prosperity, honor and glory. . . .

From Philip Foner, ed., **The Life and Writings of Frederick Douglass** (4 v., International Publishers, New York, 1955), IV: 373–392. Reprinted by permission.

It is our lot to live among a people whose laws, traditions, and prejudices have been against us for centuries, and from these they are not yet free. To assume that they are free from these evils simply because they have changed their laws is to assume what is utterly unreasonable and contrary to facts. Large bodies move slowly. Individuals may be converted on the instant and change their whole course of life. Nations never. Time and events are required for the conversion of nations. Not even the character of a great political organization can be changed by a new platform. It will be the same old snake though in a new skin. Though we have had war, reconstruction and abolition as a nation, we still linger in the shadow and blight of an extinct institution. Though the colored man is no longer subject to be bought and sold, he is still surrounded by an adverse sentiment which fetters all his movements. In his downward course he meets with no resistance, but his course upward is resented and resisted at every step of his progress. If he comes in ignorance, rags, and wretchedness, he conforms to the popular belief of his character, and in that character he is welcome. But if he shall come as a gentleman, a scholar, and a statesman, he is hailed as a contradiction to the national faith concerning his race, and his coming is resented as impudence. In the one case he may provoke contempt and derision, but in the other he is an affront to pride, and provokes malice. Let him do what he will, there is at present, therefore, no escape for him. The color line meets him everywhere, and in a measure shuts him out from all respectable and profitable trades and callings. In spite of all your religion and laws he is a rejected man.

He is rejected by trade unions, of every trade, and refused work while he lives, and burial when he dies, and yet he is asked to forget his color, and forget that which everybody else remembers. If he offers himself to a builder as a mechanic, to a client as a lawyer, to a patient as a physician, to a college as a professor, to a firm as a clerk, to a Government Department as an agent, or an officer, he is sternly met on the color line, and his claim to consideration in some way is disputed on the ground of color.

Not even our churches, whose members profess to follow the despised Nazarene, whose home, when on earth, was among the lowly and despised, have yet conquered this feeling of color madness, and what is true of our churches is also true of our courts of law. Neither is free from this all-pervading atmosphere of color hate. The one describes the Deity as impartial, no respecter of persons, and the other the Goddess of Justice as blindfolded, with sword by her side and scales in her hand held evenly between high and low, rich and low, white and black, but both are the images of American imagination, rather than American practices.

Taking advantage of the general disposition in this country to impute crime to color, white men *color* their faces to commit crime and wash off the hated color to escape punishment. In many places where the commission of crime is alleged against one of our color, the ordinary processes of law are set aside as too slow for the impetuous justice of the infuriated populace. They take the law into their own bloody hands and proceed to whip, stab, shoot, hang, or burn the alleged culprit, without the intervention of courts, counsel, judges, juries, or witnesses. In such cases it is not the business of the accusers to prove guilt, but it is for the accused to prove his innocence, a thing hard for him to do in these infernal Lynch courts. A man accused, surprised, frightened and captured by a motley crowd, dragged with a rope about his neck in midnight-darkness to the nearest tree, and told in the coarsest terms of profanity to prepare for death, would be more than human if he did not, in his terror-stricken appearance, more confirm suspicion of guilt than the contrary. Worse still, in the presence of such hell-black outrages, the pulpit is usually dumb, and the press in the neighborhood is silent or openly takes side with the mob. There are occasional cases in which white men are lynched, but one sparrow does not make a summer. Every one knows that what is called Lynch law is peculiarly the law for colored people and for nobody else. If there were no other grievance than this horrible and barbarous Lynch law custom, we should be justified in assembling, as we have now done, to expose and denounce it. But this is not all. Even now, after twenty years of so-called emancipation, we are subject to lawless raids of midnight riders, who, with blackened faces, invade our homes and perpetrate the foulest of crimes upon us and our families. This condition of things is too flagrant and notorious to require specifications or proof. Thus in all the relations of life and death we are met by the color line. We cannot ignore it if we would, and ought not if we could. It hunts us at midnight, it denies us accommodation in hotels and justice in the courts; excludes our children from schools, refuses our sons the chance to learn trades, and compels us to pursue only such labor as will bring the least reward. While we recognize the color line as a hurtful force, a mountain barrier to our progress, wounding our bleeding feet with its flinty rocks at every step, we do not despair. We are a hopeful people. This convention is a proof of our faith in you, in reason, in truth and justice—our belief that prejudice, with all its malign accomplishments, may yet be removed by peaceful means; that, assisted by time and events and the growing enlightenment of both races, the color line will ultimately become harmless. When this shall come it will then only be used, as it should be, to distinguish one variety of the human family from another. It will cease to have any civil, political, or moral significance, and colored conventions will then be dispensed with as anachronisms, wholly out of place, but not till then. Do not marvel that we are discouraged. The faith within us has a rational basis, and is confirmed by facts. When we consider how deep-seated this feeling against us is; the long centuries it has been forming; the forces of avarice which have been marshaled to sustain it; how the language and literature of the country have been pervaded with it; how the church, the press, the play-house, and other influences of the country have been arrayed in its support, the progress toward its extinction must be considered vast and wonderful. . . .

We do not believe, as we are often told, that the Negro is the ugly child of the national family, and the more he is kept out of sight the better it will

Frederick Douglass.   Douglass's greatest work came before and during the Civil War. One of the most eloquent and magnetic of all the abolitionist leaders, he contributed enormously to the antislavery cause. During the Civil War he pressed hard for the enlistment of blacks to fight in the Union armies on an equal footing with whites. After the war he continued his efforts for civil rights, including black suffrage. For his services to the Republican party he received appointments as secretary to the Santo Domingo commission, marshal and recorder of deeds for the District of Columbia, and U.S. minister to Haiti. (National Portrait Gallery, Smithsonian Institution, Washington, D.C.)

be for him. You know that liberty given is never so precious as liberty sought for and fought for. The man outraged is the man to make the outcry. Depend upon it, men will not care much for a people who do not care for themselves. Our meeting here was opposed by some of our members, because it would disturb the peace of the Republican party. The suggestion came from coward lips and misapprehended the character of that party. If the Republican party cannot stand a demand for justice and fair play, it ought to go down. We were men before that party was born, and our manhood is more sacred than any party can be. Parties were made for men, not men for parties.

The colored people of the South are the laboring people of the South. The labor of a country is the source of its wealth; without the colored laborer to-day the South would be a howling wilderness, given up to bats, owls, wolves, and bears. He was the source of its wealth before the war, and has been the source of its prosperity since the war. He almost alone is visible in her fields, with implements of toil in his hands, and laboriously using them to-day.

Let us look candidly at the matter. While we see and hear that the South is more prosperous than it ever was before and rapidly recovering from the waste of war, while we read that it raises more cotton, sugar, rice, tobacco, corn, and other valuable products than it ever produced before, how happens it, we sternly ask, that the houses of its laborers are miserable huts, that their clothes are rags, and their food the coarsest and scantiest? How happens it that the land-owner is becoming richer and the laborer poorer?

The implication is irresistible—that where the landlord is prosperous the laborer ought to share his prosperity, and whenever and wherever we find this is not the case there is manifestly wrong somewhere. . . .

Flagrant as have been the outrages committed upon colored citizens in respect to their civil rights, more flagrant, shocking, and scandalous still have been the outrages committed upon our political rights by means of bull-dozing and Kukluxing, Mississippi plans, fraudulent courts, tissue ballots, and the like devices. Three States in which the colored people outnumber the white population are without colored representation and their political voice suppressed. The colored citizens in those States are virtually disfranchised, the Constitution held in utter contempt and its provisions nullified. This has been done in the face of the Republican party and successive Republican administrations. . . .

This is no question of party. It is a question of law and government. It is a question whether men shall be protected by law, or be left to the mercy of cyclones of anarchy and bloodshed. It is whether the Government or the mob shall rule this land; whether the promises solemnly made to us in the constitution be manfully kept or meanly and flagrantly broken. Upon this vital point we ask the whole people of the United States to take notice that whatever of political power we have shall be exerted for no man of any party who will not, in advance of election, promise to use every power given him by the Government, State or National, to make the black man's path to the ballot-box as straight, smooth and safe as that of any other American citizen. . . .

We hold it to be self-evident that no class or color should be the exclusive rulers of this country. If there is such a ruling class, there must of course be a subject class, and when this condition is once established this Government of the people, by the people, and for the people, will have perished from the earth.

COUNTERPOINT V

Slavery, Secession, and War

Mississippi's secession resolutions of 1860 (Document 34) addressed the same constitutional issues that John C. Calhoun (Document 21) had considered for South Carolina in 1828: federal power versus states' rights. But the documents were very different. Calhoun worried that high tariffs on imported manufactured goods would damage Southern agricultural trade by making it harder for foreigners to buy cotton and other cash crops; he mentioned slavery only once, and then only to argue that the existence of this kind of labor force virtually compelled the South to remain agricultural. The Mississippians, by contrast, referred to "their servants" and "that species of property" several times and to "slavery," "slaves," or "slave-holding" ten times. They also denounced the "revolutionary position" of Northerners toward Southern states and the evident intention to destroy "domestic tranquillity" among the states and to excite "insurrection, murder and rapine." Far more than Calhoun in 1828, the Mississippians of 1860 were "fire-eaters"—militants demanding immediate secession, and if necessary war, to preserve the institution of slavery.

Who were these Mississippians, and how typical were they of political leaders in other states? Ralph Wooster has provided a partial answer by comparing the property and slave ownership of Southern secessionists and antisecessionists. Mississippi secessionists, it turns out, were typical of fire-eaters throughout the South in two respects. First, they were quite wealthy; only the secessionists of South Carolina, Louisiana, and Alabama were wealthier (table A). Second, they were richer than the nonsecessionists; only in Kentucky were the secessionists less wealthy than their opponents (table A.2).

But Wooster goes on to show that significant differences in total wealth did not always mean significant differences in slave holdings. In Mississippi and Louisiana, two major slave states, secessionists actually owned fewer slaves than their opponents (table A.3); in Kentucky, it was the same (table A.4). Thus, although most secessionists were large property owners, they sometimes owned fewer slaves than their opponents but probably more land. These men, in other words, were apparently defending slavery as a system of labor as well as a system of property. Certainly emancipation would have damaged them economically. But it might have damaged them as much by "disrupting" their labor force, their ability to grow cotton and sugar, as by "confiscating" their property. Whereas Calhoun had worried about markets, the Mississippians worried about production—perhaps not so great a difference after all. Areas with large slave populations, however, were also areas where blacks often outnumbered whites—hence the Southern concern not only with economics but with "insurrection, murder and rapine."

Ronald Takaki makes a similar point in his examination of two key votes in the South Carolina legislature. The first vote came on a motion for Southern independence in 1856 (figure B.1). Representatives from interior "up-country" districts with small farms and small slave populations generally opposed the motion; whereas those from coastal and "low-country" districts with large plantations and slave populations—districts where emancipation would mean the confiscation of enormous slave wealth—generally favored it—except for Charleston, which had a large nonslaveholding population. The same low-country districts also supported an 1858 motion to reopen the African slave trade (figure B.2), presumably because even though importing more slaves into South Carolina would lower the value of the slaves already there, more slaves would also lower the price of slave labor and therefore the cost of agricultural production. South Carolina secessionists, like their Mississippi counterparts, feared emancipation as a danger to cheap labor as well as to expensive slave property. And in South Carolina, too, no doubt, large slave populations begat large worries about "insurrection, murder and rapine."

But talking and voting are one thing, fighting another. Did the Southern elites back up their political militancy by joining the Confederate army? According to information provided by James McPherson, the answer is apparently yes, or at least maybe (table C). A disproportionate number of planters, farmers, and farm laborers served in the Confederate army: about 4 percentage points more than the census figure for the same category. Fewer skilled and unskilled laborers served: about 6 percent less than the total of the census figures. But the first category is too inclusive to reveal much; poor farmers and landless laborers appear in the same category as wealthy landowners. And the total of the next two groups when compared with the first category reveals mainly that the war was waged more by farmers than by townsmen. More revealing, probably, is the information about the white-collar and commercial category and the professional category, which together compose almost as large a share of the army as of the population. But most soldiers were young, and most members of these prestigious occupations were not. Therefore, an army share of over 12 percent is actually very substantial—evidence, probably, that the region's "young gentlemen," many of them scions of slave wealth, did flock to the Stars and Bars. The men who led the secession movement may not themselves have placed their bodies in the line. But their sons probably did.

A. Property and Slaveholding in Secession Conventions and Legislatures, 1860–1861

1. Median Property Holdings of Factions in Conventions of the Lower South

State	Conditional Unionists[a]	Cooperationists	Immediate Secessionists
South Carolina	$	$	$68,875
Mississippi	47,000	48,409	57,765
Alabama		16,400	57,913
Florida		13,012	30,300
Georgia		23,840	25,000
Louisiana	19,500	59,900	60,250
Texas	13,000		16,000

2. Median Property Holdings of Factions in Conventions and Legislatures of Upper and Border South

State	Antisecessionists	Secessionists
Virginia	$28,536	$33,700
Arkansas	5,000	23,170
Tennessee	9,175	15,300
North Carolina	26,700	33,185
Kentucky	9,250	7,725
Missouri	13,000	27,454

3. Median Number of Slaves Held by Delegates to Conventions in the Lower South

State	Conditional Unionists	Cooperationists	Immediate Secessionists
South Carolina			37
Mississippi	12	21	16
Alabama		12	19
Florida		5	13
Georgia		14	14
Louisiana	9	17	12
Texas	4.5		5

4. Median Number of Slaves Held by Delegates to Conventions and Legislatures in the Upper and Border South

State	Antisecessionists	Secessionists
Virginia	4	9
Arkansas		10
Tennessee	2	6.5
North Carolina	12.5	25
Kentucky	3	2
Missouri	1	1

[a]Conditional unionists were those who would remain in the Union only if Congress resolved to protect slavery in the Territories as well as in the South.

SOURCE: Ralph A. Wooster, *The Secession Conventions of the South*. Copyright © 1962 by Princeton University Press. Tables 65, 66, 67, 68 reprinted with permission of Princeton University Press.

B. Votes on Key Motions in the South Carolina Legislature, Late 1850s, by District

1. Motion for Southern Independence, 1856

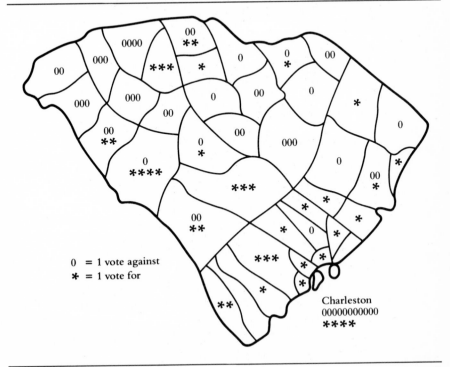

0 = 1 vote against
✱ = 1 vote for

Charleston
00000000000
✱✱✱✱

(continued)

B continued

2. Motion for Reopening African Slave Trade, 1858

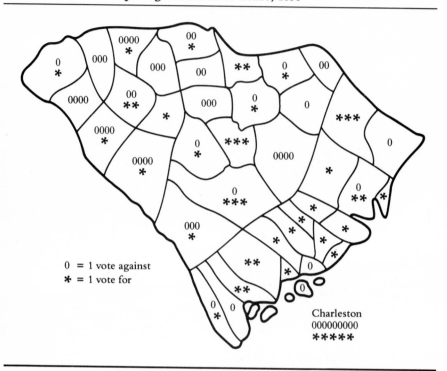

0 = 1 vote against
✱ = 1 vote for

Charleston
000000000
✱✱✱✱✱

SOURCE: Reprinted with permission of The Free Press, a Division of Macmillan Inc. from *A Pro-Slavery Crusade* by Ronald Takaki. Copyright © 1971 by The Free Press.

C. Previous Occupations of Confederate Soldiers from Alabama, Arkansas, Georgia, Louisiana, Mississippi, North Carolina, and Virginia Compared with 1860 Occupations of White Males in These States

Occupational Categories	Confederate Soldiers	White Males (from 1860 Census)
Planters, farmers, and farm laborers	61.5%	57.5%
Skilled laborers	14.1	15.7
Unskilled laborers	8.5	12.7
White-collar and commercial	7.0	8.3
Professional	5.2	5.0
Miscellaneous and Unknown	3.7	0.8

SOURCE: From *Ordeal by Fire: The Civil War and Reconstruction* by James M. McPherson. Copyright © 1982 by Alfred A. Knopf, Inc. Reprinted by permission of the publisher.

A STATISTICAL APPENDIX

List of Appendix Tables

All the information in the appendix tables comes from **U.S. Historical Statistics from Colonial Times to 1970,** published by the U.S. Government Printing Office, Washington, D.C., 1975; and **Statistical Abstract of the United States, 1982–83,** also published by the U.S. Government Printing Office, 1984. In the tables a dash (—) means zero; the small letters na mean that figures are not available.

i

Table A.1   U.S. Population and Selected State Populations, 1790–1980

The population of the United States has grown steadily since the nation's founding, just as observers like Gottlieb Mittelberger (Vol. 1, Document 10) and James Madison (Vol. 1, Document 14) thought it would. It has grown faster in some periods than in others, however, and faster in some regions than in others, as shown by the figures for the six states below. Stemming chiefly from economics, immigration, and climate, this regional divergence has had profound political and social consequences—the early prominence of Massachusetts and Virginia statesmen, for example, and the election of two Californians and a Texan to the presidency since 1960.

Year	Mass.	N.Y.	Va.	Ill.	Tex.	Cal.	U.S. Total
			Population (in Millions)				
1790	.4	.3	.7	—	—	—	3.9
1810	.5	1.0	.9	.01	—	—	7.2
1830	.6	1.9	1.0	.2	—	—	12.9
1850	1.0	3.1	1.1	.9	.2	.1	23.2
1870	1.5	4.4	1.2	2.5	.8	.6	39.8
1890	2.2	6.0	1.7	3.8	2.2	1.2	62.9
1910	3.4	9.1	2.1	5.6	3.9	2.4	91.9
1930	4.3	12.6	2.4	7.6	5.8	5.7	122.8
1950	4.7	14.8	3.3	8.7	7.7	10.6	150.7
1970	5.7	18.2	4.6	11.1	11.2	19.9	203.2
1980	5.7	17.6	5.3	11.4	14.2	23.7	226.5

Table A.2 U.S. Population and Breakdown by Urban Population Sizes, 1790–1980

The population of the United States grew rapidly from the start. But as the following figures show, towns and cities grew faster than rural areas even in the early decades of agricultural and frontier expansion. America seems to have been destined to be an urbanized society, which of course it largely was by the twentieth century.

Recently, almost all growth has been urban. But rapid urbanization has not always meant that big cities set the pace. For instance, the population in cities from 25,000 to 250,000 more than doubled from 27.2 million in 1950 to 60.3 million in 1980, while that in cities over 250,000 only went from 34.8 million to 40.6 million, and in the last decade actually lost over a million and a half people. (These figures do not indicate, however, how many cities are in each category nor give how the number of cities increased over the decades.) During the 1950–1980 period, towns of 2,500 and over grew from 96.5 million to 167.1 million in population. Cities of 250,000 and over grew most rapidly in population during 1850–1910, a period of great industrial growth.

	Population (in Millions)				
Year	2,500 and over	2,500– 25,000	25,000– 250,000	250,000 and Over	Total
1790	.2	.14	.06	—	3.9
1810	.5	.3	.2	—	7.2
1830	1.1	.6	.5	—	12.9
1850	3.5	1.3	1.6	.6	23.2
1870	9.9	4.2	2.6	3.1	39.8
1890	22.1	8.1	7.1	6.9	62.9
1910	42.0	13.6	13.0	15.4	91.9
1930	68.9	20.7	20.4	27.8	122.8
1950	96.5	34.5	27.2	34.8	150.7
1970	149.3	58.3	48.8	42.2	203.2
1980	167.1	52.3	60.3	40.6	226.5[a]

[a]Includes 13.9 million in "urbanized areas" that are unincorporated and therefore not distributed in specific city sizes.

Table A.3   U.S. Immigrant Population by Origin, Occupation, Sex, and Age, 1820–1980

The United States has been called a nation of immigrants, and surely few nations were so influenced by newcomers as this one. Immigration, clearly a force behind the great surge in national population, also contributed to the development of cities, social classes, and ethnic and cultural diversity. The make-up of the immigrants themselves changed over time as well, not only in numbers but in nationality, occupational status, and even family structure (as suggested by the shifting proportions of males and of children). For example, in 1910 during industrial expansion, about 70 percent of the immigrants came from eastern and southern European countries, and about 60 percent were laborers or servants. In 1980, the same area provided less than 10 percent of the immigrants, while over 40 percent came from the Americas and 40 percent from Asia; the occupational skills had also shifted, with only 10 percent in the laborer and servant categories, and 20 percent being professionals or skilled workers.

Thus, not only do the totals below ebb and flow according to the coming of war or peace, prosperity or depression, tolerance or persecution, in both the country of origin and the United States, but later immigrants seldom possessed the same characteristics as their counterparts who came one, two, or three generations earlier. Here one may find, among other things, a context for James T. Farrell's portrait in the excerpt from **Young Lonigan** (Vol. 2, Document 11), the Chinese Exclusion Act (Vol. 2, Document 7), and the current debate over further immigration restriction.

	1820	1850	1880	1910	1940	1970	1980
Total[a]	10,311	324,098	457,257	1,041,570	70,756	373,326	460,000
Northern Europe[b]	7,467	307,044	310,213	202,198	37,520	35,375	24,700
Eastern and southern Europe	224	1,279	38,478	724,083	11,976	75,278	34,800
Asia	5	7	5,839	23,533	2,050	90,215	183,000
The Americas	387	15,768	101,692	89,534	17,822	161,727	198,000
Professional-commercial	1,038	7,318	9,699	36,639	18,578	68,497	63,400
Skilled workers and farmers	1,964	69,242	97,133	133,640	6,557	50,461	21,100
Laborers	334	46,640	105,012	505,654	2,372	18,480	39,700
Servants	139	3,203	18,580	105,735	3,940	19,751	8,600
None	6,836	188,931	217,446	260,002	39,409	216,137	275,400
Males	7,197	196,138	287,623	736,038	33,460	176,990	219,500
Under age 15	1,313	62,543	87,154	120,509	9,602	104,880	110,900

[a]Includes immigrants from Africa, Australasia, France, and the Low Countries as well as areas of origin listed below.
[b]Great Britain, Ireland, Scandinavia, and Germany.

Table A.4 U.S. Workers by Economic Sectors (Agriculture, Manufacturing, Construction, and Trade), 1810–1980

This table sorts American workers into four basic sectors of the economy. Here we see evidence of (among other things) the decline in the number of farmers after 1919 (though agricultural production has risen—see Table A.6), the growth of manufacturing before 1900 and its pre-eminence by 1950, the strong showing of construction for a hundred years and its subsequent slower growth (close to the low level of agriculture), and the steady advance of the trade and finance sector to have more than 5 million more workers than in the manufacturing sector. We thus pass from the "farmer's age" to the "workshop of the world" to, at last, the "service economy." Observe how the rise of manufacturing and trade parallels the growth of cities (Table A.2) and how decline in agriculture and slow growth in construction show up in the occupations of the immigrants (Table A.3).

Year	Workers (in Millions)				
	Agriculture	*Manufacturing*	*Construction*	*Trade/Finance*	*Total*
1810	1.9	.08	na	na	2.3
1830	2.9	na	na	na	4.2
1850	4.5	1.2	.4	.5	8.3
1870	6.8	2.5	.8	1.3	12.9
1890	10.0	4.4	1.5	2.9	23.3
1910	11.8	8.3	1.9	5.3	37.5
1930	10.6	9.9	2.0	8.1	48.8
1950	7.9	15.7	3.0	12.2	65.5
1970	3.7	19.4	3.4	18.6	85.9
1980	3.5	20.3	4.2	25.4	109.0

Table A.5 Growth of U.S. Transportation (Ship, Railroad, Airplane, and Automobile), 1790–1980

The following figures illustrate the evolution of transportation in the United States. Each new type of transportation has represented a technological advance— steam power, the internal combustion engine, heavier-than-air flight—and thus mirrors the progress of the Industrial Revolution. Each type has also coincided with a phase of national development: post-Revolutionary foreign trade, the winning of the West, suburbanization, and the modern aerospace era. The hugeness of the transportation system as a whole suggests both the size of the country and the frequency and speed with which Americans have tended to move themselves and their commodities. The individual columns show when each part of the system really took off—or, as in ship tonnage in the age of the supertanker, when it took off anew.

Year	Ship Tonnage into U.S. Ports (in Millions)	Railroad Track Miles (in Thousands)	Motor-Vehicle Registration (in Millions)	Scheduled Commercial Air Routes (in Thousands of Miles)
1790	.6	—	—	—
1810	1.0	—	—	—
1830	1.1	—	—	—
1850	3.7	9	—	—
1870	9.2	53	—	—
1890	18.1	200	—	—
1910	40.2	352	.5	—
1930	81.3	430	22.1	30
1950	86.6	396	49.2	77
1970	254.2	350	108.4	172
1980	492.0	320	155.9	317

Table A.6 U.S. Production of Selected Commodities, 1870–1980

Whether industrialization advanced in a spurt after the Civil War, as Terence Powderly (Vol. 2, Document 13) and Upton Sinclair (Vol. 2, Document 16) believed, or steadily throughout the nineteenth century, as the occupational and transportation data in Tables A.4 and A.5 hint, there is no doubt that the process was very far along by the early twentieth century. The figures below show American gains in the production of a number of important commodities. All of them have gone up sharply over the past century. Yet the listing of the items in pairs highlights divergent growth rates of some interest. Production of sugar in 1970 was twenty times the amount produced in 1870, while that of flour was only three times what was produced a century earlier. The rates of growth of rayon and cigarettes are extraordinarily high when compared with those for cotton and cigars. The number of pairs of shoes produced for women was less than that for men in 1910, but in 1980, women's shoes were 40 percent higher than the number made for men. In most cases the difference in growth rates comes at a particular point in time rather than steadily. What causes the various differences? What does it say about American society that industry begins to produce typewriters and light bulbs? Does the speeding up or slowing down of production growth rates have to do more with technological change or with shifts in consumption habits?

Commodity	Production (in Millions)						
	1870	*1890*	*1910*	*1930*	*1950*	*1970*	*1980*
Flour (barrels)	48	83	107	120	115	129	na
Sugar (lbs.)	1.2	3.2	7.3	12	14.7	20.8	20.1
Bricks[a]	2.8	8	9.9	5.1	6.3	6.7	na
Steel (tons)	.08	4.8	28.3	44.6	96.8	131.5	111.8
Beer (barrels)	7	28	59.5	3.7	88.8	134.7	193
Liquor (gals.)	72	111	164	—	194	355	236
Cotton (bales)	3	8.6	11.6	13.9	10	10.2	11.1
Rayon (lbs.)	—	—	2	118	957	851	438
Cigars	1	4.2	6.8	5.9	5.5	8.0	4.9
Cigarettes	.02	2.5	9.8	124.2	392	562	702
Men's shoes (pairs)	na	na	98	77	103	100	102
Women's shoes (pairs)	na	na	87	112	195	230	143
Typewriters	—	na	.2	.9	1.4	1.4	1.5
Light bulbs	—	na	70	350	1,200	1,582	1,780

[a]Billions.

Table A.7 Growth of U.S. Commercial Banks and U.S. Bank Assets, 1790–1980

The increase in the number of banks and in bank assets provides one measure of American economic growth, especially of growth as related to credit and money transactions—exactly the sort of thing that concerned Benjamin Franklin (Vol. 1, Document 11) and Andrew Jackson (Vol. 1, Document 22). Comparison of the two columns in the table below shows, too, that while bank assets grew steadily from 1790 to 1980, the number of banks shot up all through the era of territorial expansion (1830–1890) and early urbanization (1850–1910), then fell off after 1910 and especially after 1930. This, of course, reflects the ravages of the Great Depression, when so many banks failed that President Franklin Roosevelt declared a bank holiday. But the decline after 1930 reflects a trend that this table does not fully encompass: a pattern of consolidation, takeover, and merger whereby fewer firms dominate **many** important sectors of the American economy.

Year	Number of Commercial Banks	Bank Assets (in Millions of Dollars)
1790	na	na
1810	80	na
1830	330	350
1850	824	532
1870	1,937	1,781
1890	8,201	6,358
1910	25,151	22,922
1930	24,273	74,290
1950	14,676	179,165
1970	14,187	611,305
1980	14,870	1,543,500

Table A.8 U.S. Consumer Price Index and Average Daily Wages of Construction, Manufacturing, and Unskilled Laborers, 1790–1980

The figures here provide a rough view of how ordinary laboring people fared under capitalism from 1790 to 1980. Although wages did not rise quickly for any group until well into the twentieth century, prices also remained fairly steady before that time, and therefore workers may have done better than first appears. The table shows the comparative advantage enjoyed by construction workers over other workers, and the smaller advantage of those in manufacturing over the unskilled. Observe that periods of steady or falling wages usually coincided with periods of heavy immigration (see Table A.3). Table A.8 does not reveal how the work day grew gradually shorter, particularly after 1890. But shown very clearly is the sharp wage increase after 1930, in part the handiwork of labor organizers such as John L. Lewis (Vol. 2, Document 28), whose successes were all the more important because of the tremendous recent growth of the manufacturing sector of the economy.

All the money figures, of course, must be viewed in light of changes in the cost of living over the decades. The consumer price index, which is based on the arbitrary assignment of the value 100 to 1967 prices, provides a rough measure of this cost-of-living change. Construction wages fell in the years from 1830 to 1850, for example. But the cost of living fell even more. Construction workers, therefore, fared better than might appear at first glance. Manufacturing workers made twice as much in 1930 as in 1910. But prices almost doubled, too, so that workers' gains were actually slight.

		Daily Wage (in Current Dollars)[a]		
Year	Price Index[b]	Construction	Manufacturing	Unskilled Labor
1790	na	1.00	na	.50
1810	47	1.70	na	1.00
1830	32	1.75	na	1.00
1850	25	1.50	na	.90
1870	38	2.50	na	1.75
1890	27	3.00	2.00	1.50
1910	28	4.00	2.40	2.00
1930	50	5.00	5.50	na
1950	72	16.00	12.00	na
1970	116	42.00	27.00	na
1980	247	79.00	58.00	38.00

[a]Wages for 1790–1830 are from the Philadelphia area, for 1850–1870 from the Erie Canal area, and for 1890–1980 from the entire nation. "Current dollars" means the actual wage, *not* adjusted for cost-of-living changes over the years.
[b]A price index assigns a base year (in this case 1967) a value of 100 to represent the price of important commodities (rent, food, clothing, and so forth), then assigns values to other years that relate to 100 as the prices of the same commodities in those years relate to prices in the base year. A glance at the index tells us instantly, therefore, that it cost approximately half as much to live in 1850 as it had in 1810, but about five times as much in 1980 as in 1930.

Table A.9   Selected Religious Affiliations of the U.S. Population
(Methodist, Presbyterian, Southern Baptist,
Episcopalian, and Roman Catholic), 1790–1980

Religious diversity became a hallmark of American society, just as Roger Williams
(Vol. 1, Document 5) hoped it would. But the United States has remained a
broadly Christian land despite its diversity, and a heavily Protestant one despite
its broad Christianity. The figures here show the growth of four important Protestant denominations and also of the Roman Catholic Church.

Methodism and Presbyterianism, both intimately intertwined with the great
reform movements of the nineteenth century, have grown steadily over the decades. Methodism tripled from 1850 to 1890 and tripled again from 1890 to 1980;
the Presbyterians in this latter period quadrupled their numbers. The Southern
Baptists, born partly in reaction to Northern antislavery agitation before the Civil
War, almost quadrupled their membership from 1930 to 1980. Episcopalianism,
initially prominent in the South and later attractive to wealthy industrialists, in
contrast had a much smaller increase after 1930 and a decline after 1970.

Membership in the Roman Catholic Church increased two and a half times
from 1890 to 1930, but it took a longer time period, from 1930 to 1980, for the
same increase to take place again. The great Catholic tide thus coincided with
the great tide of immigration. Within a quarter-century, Catholics, though still a
minority in the United States, outnumbered the combined membership of all the
four large Protestant denominations listed in Table A.9. Comparison with the
totals for the United States population in Table A.1 will reveal, however, that all
but one of these Protestant denominations grew at a pace faster than the population for the period from 1930 to 1980—perhaps a surprising development in
what has often been called an age of materialism.

		Number of Members (in Thousands)			
Year	Methodist[a]	Presbyterian	Southern Baptist	Episcopalian	Roman Catholic
1790	58	na	—	na	na
1810	175	na	—	na	na
1830	478	173	—	na	na
1850	1,186	207	400[b]	na	na
1870	1,822	445	na	na	na
1890	3,442	761	1,236	na	8,000[b]
1910	5,073	1,315	2,332	na	14,347
1930	7,319	1,937	3,850	1,939	20,204
1950	8,936	2,364	7,080	2,541	27,766
1970	10,672	3,096	11,629	3,475	47,872
1980	10,372	3,353	13,600	2,786	50,450

[a]Beginning with 1890 figures, the table lists United Methodist Church membership only.
[b]Estimate.

Table A.10 U.S. School Enrollments of School-Age Populations by Race and Sex, 1850–1980

Americans have always prized education, the Puritans, for example, to encourage Bible reading, Franklin and Jefferson to make good citizens. But modern public schools really began only after 1830 when reformers sought to use free schools to reduce social dislocations and foster unity. Enrollments grew rapidly, although mostly for Northern white males at that time. By 1890, however, about the same percentage of girls as boys went to school and a third of the country's black children were in school, which suggests that the Southern educational system was growing. This expansion of Southern schools and black education was one positive result of the Reconstruction effort. The expansion of education generally is testimony to the strength of American local government.

Year	Whites Only	Blacks Only	Males Only	Females Only	Total[a]
1850	56%	2%	50%	45%	47%
1870	54	10	50	47	48
1890	58	33	55	54	54
1910	61	45	59	59	59
1930	71	60	70	70	70
1950	79	75	79	78	79
1970	88	85	89	87	88
1980	86	84	83	86	85

[a]School-age has varied according to time and place over this period, but may generally be understood to mean from about six years old to the mid-teens.

Table A.11   U.S. Federal Civilian Employees (Total) and
Numbers Employed by the U.S. Postal Service
and the Department of Defense, 1816–1980

The growth of the federal government has been of great interest and concern to Americans recently. In the early nineteenth century, the central government employed only 0.5 percent of the nation's work force; in the early twentieth century, a full 1 percent; and by 1970, more than 3 percent. The table shows the main sources of this rising federal percentage: the post office, which loomed large from the start and then grew with the country; and nonuniformed military personnel, who have been the dominant federal presence for several decades. The decline in the number of employees after 1970 stems mainly from the use of automation equipment in the postal service and the reduction in defense personnel after the end of the Vietnam War.

Year	Post Office	Defense	Total Government Civilian Employees
1816	3,341	190	4,837
1831	8,764	377	11,491
1851	21,391	403	26,274
1871	36,696	1,183	51,020
1891	95,449	20,561	157,442
1910	209,005	58,320	388,708
1930	297,895	103,462	601,319
1950	484,679	753,149	1,960,708
1970	741,216	1,219,125	2,981,574
1980	667,000	973,100	2,883,000

Table A.12   U.S. Federal Expenditures (Total) and Selected
           Expenditure Categories (National Defense, Interest
           on the Public Debt, U.S. Postal Service, Veterans'
           Benefits, and Income Security Including General
           Retirement—Social Security and Medicare—and
           Public Assistance), 1791–1980

The federal government was an insignificant force in the economy of the nine-teenth century, except perhaps directly after the Civil War, when interest on the war debt, veterans' pensions, postal spending, and outlays for military reconstruc-tion and the Indian wars all drove the budget higher. Although the budget grew at a good clip between 1890 and 1930, the real leap came only after World War II.

Interest on the national debt was a key component of federal spending in the time of George Washington and remains so today: it is the third largest category, far ahead of veterans' benefits and the post office combined, and is growing faster than any other part of the budget. Defense spending grew from 25 percent of the total in 1930 to 33 percent in 1950 to 40 percent in 1970, before falling to 25 percent again after the Vietnam War. If one includes interest and veterans' benefits, both up mainly because of wars, the total military component of the budget suddenly rises to one-half. Even so, defense has multiplied less rapidly than social security, now grown far beyond the expectations (if not the hopes) of Frances Perkins (Vol. 2, Document 27).

Remember that these figures must be modified for population growth and inflation. Even so, the federal government is clearly an important part of the nation's economy—far greater than ever before—because of the unprecedented mix of welfare and warfare.

	Expenditures (in Millions of Current Dollars)					
Year	Defense	Interest	Post Office	Veterans' Benefits	Social Security	Total Expenditures
1791	.6	2.3	.04	.2	—	4.3
1810	3.9	2.8	.6	.8	—	8.1
1830	8	1.9	1.9	1.4	—	15
1850	17	3.8	5.2	1.9	—	40
1870	79	129	24	28	—	310
1890	67	36	66	107	—	318
1910	313	21	230	161	—	694
1930	839	659	804	221	—	3,320
1950	13,440	5,750	2,223	2,223	784	39,544
1970	78,360	18,340	7,867	8,307	36,835	196,588
1980	135,900	64,500	19,400	21,200	117,100	576,700